# ON
# REINCARNATION

## THE GOSPEL ACCORDING TO PAUL

An Interpretive Matrix Explaining Romans

## BY MARILYN GRACE GRAHAM

Quest Publishing
Miami

ISBN  0-9665824-0-3

Library of Congress Catalog Card Number  98-67232


Quest Publishing
7614 SW 106th Avenue
Miami, FL 33173

Edited by Lisa E. Graham
Cover design by Gil Roschuni
Illustration by Alexander Hunter
This book is typeset in 12 point Bembo

Printed in the United States of America on acid-free paper

To Truth

# Acknowledgements

Special thanks to the following individuals, without whom this book would not have been published.

Blanche Corsie
John Farina
Lee J. Graham
Lisa E. Graham
Michael H. Graham
Edith Jacobson
Brian Mitchell
Antionette Nelson
Larry Witham

# Dedication

The Graham family, Michael and the three children of Michael and Marilyn, Laura, Lisa and Lee, dedicate the publishing and distribution of this book in memory of the author, Marilyn Grace Fusco Graham, beloved wife and mother, who died of breast cancer in June of 1998 at the age of fifty-five.

The following quotations demonstrate scholarly acknowledgment of a "missing link," so to speak, without which Paul's letter to the Romans cannot be completely understood. This book provides that link.

> Paul's Gospel did not originate in a vacuum, it has a pre-history. Unless the pre-history is known, the gospel cannot be understood.
>
> William S. Campbell
> *The Romans Debate*

> Only when we can take for granted what Paul and his readers took for granted with regard to the law and its function will we be able to hear the allusions he was making and understand the argument he was offering.
>
> James D.G. Dunn
> *The Romans Debate*

> Until I have proof to the contrary I proceed on the assumption that the text (Romans) has a central concern and a remarkable inner logic that may no longer be entirely comprehensible to us.
>
> Ernst Kasemann
> *Commentary on Romans*

> The confusion and disagreement still remaining with regard to the role of the law in first-century Judaism strongly suggest that the role of the law within the Judaism against which Paul was reacting has not as yet been perceived.
>
> James D.G. Dunn
> *The Romans Debate*

# TABLE OF CONTENTS

# PREFACE

M ine is a voice crying in the wilderness. Is anyone there? Eminent Pauline scholars such as William S. Campbell, James D.G. Dunn, Ernst Kasemann and explicitly, Robert J. Karris, have called for an interpretive matrix for explaining Paul's letter to the Romans. This book answers that call. But who will heed a voice unknown—a voice not of one's own?

This work was spiritually inspired, sustained and written. It exemplifies the life of the Spirit and intellectual endeavor working in tandem—separate, yet inseparable from each other, over the course of a lifetime.

Since childhood I had an inordinate interest in philosophy, metaphysics, parapsychology and, subsequently, religion, which culminated in the writing of this book. I am not religious, nor am I a professor of religion. I did not have colleagues with whom I could collaborate and to whom I could turn for camaraderie and support as I worked. Compelled by a deep sense of obligation, I worked in agonizing isolation while at the same time "being there" for my husband and three children, who are now adults. I was sustained by a blind faith that I was writing for a purpose. I didn't know what that purpose was until, during the course of my research, I read *The Romans Debate*, a collection of essays that are a standard for those studying Romans, and Ernst Kasemann's *Commentary on Romans*, both of which explain the need for an interpretive matrix for explaining Romans. I was writing to answer that call!

My formal education in the field of religion consists of a bachelor of arts in religious studies, conferred in 1984 from the University of Illinois. Being thus limited, I was obliged to use secondary, albeit highly respected, sources for my research.

Despite the definitive tenor of this work, it is not meant to be an end, but a beginning. It is my hope that others in the field more technically qualified than I will take up the torch, correct and expand my work and run with it.

This book, like the Spirit in which it was written, is being published in faith.

Faith that this book is meant to be.

Faith that this book has profound implications for the scholarly interpretation of Paul's letter to the Romans, the other Pauline epistles (authentic or not) and indeed the New Testament as a whole.

Faith that this book has profound implications for ecumenism, East and West.

Faith that my voice crying in the wilderness will waft and wend through the rarefied atmosphere of academe to the ears of those in the ivory towers above—and be heard.

# INTRODUCTION

Paul's letter to the Romans is the first of his letters in the canonical order of the New Testament. It is also the most theological and the most difficult to understand. This is because the existence and nature of the cultural matrix to which Romans is a logical response—and within which it makes sense—has been obscured through the centuries. Scholarly books on Romans, such as *The Romans Debate*, edited by Karl P. Donfried, and Ernst Kasemann's *Commentary on Romans*, acknowledge that this "missing link" has been sought to no avail. This book purports to have found IT.

The premise of this work is that Paul's letter to the Romans, and his theology with respect to the Jewish (Pharisaic) law and the significance of the Christ event, was a response to a pre- and first-century cross-cultural belief in reincarnation—a worldview consistent with the caste system of social organization then in existence. If this interpretive matrix is presumed when reading Romans, most if not all of the much-debated issues posed in books such as *The Romans Debate*, *Commentary on Romans* and other works and articles on the subject are resolved.

This book is a synthesis of the life of the Spirit and intellectual endeavor working in tandem over the course of my lifetime. Virtually all books about spirituality and religion that lay claim to the spiritual dimension lack the research component necessary to afford them credibility. Conversely, virtually all books about spirituality and religion that lay claim to academic credibility lack the spiritual dimension necessary to afford them singular authority. This work has both.

This book is divided into three parts. Part I, Chapter One sets forth the spiritual component of this work. It presents those events of my personal history—events that took place over the course of my lifetime—which, taken together, make up the spiritual odyssey through which this work was inspired, sustained, and written.

Part II establishes the cultural context of Paul's audience, and is divided into Chapters Two through Five. Chapter Two presents the ancient cross-cultural worldview of belief in reincarnation according to the Hindu, Hebrew, Greek and Platonic models. Chapter Three presents the pre- and first-century Pharisaic worldview of belief in reincarnation. This data has been obtained from the Jewish *Tannaitic* literature, the writings of Josephus, a first-century Pharisee and historian who was a contemporary of Saul of Tarsus (St. Paul), and finally from the New Testament. Chapter Four presents Pharisaic and Pagan Voices of Despair that indicate the presence of a cross-cultural subcultural negative attitude toward the then culturally dominant positive attitude toward the process of reincarnation. These hopeless voices appear in the Hebrew book of *Koheleth* (Ecclesiastes) and in both rare and not so rare Gnostic literature. Chapter Five presents the socioeconomic and philosophical structure of the Roman Empire in existence prior to and throughout the first century, the relationship of the Jews to the Roman social order, and the complex nature of the Apostle Paul.

Part III, Chapter Six presents an introduction to Paul's letter to the Romans. It offers a scenario with respect to the constitution of the Roman church(es), the reason for the careful construction of Paul's letter to the Romans and the unmistakable rhetorical and apologetic tone of the letter, as well as an explanation of those instances in which Paul's text appears to be fragmented and inconsistent. This scenario is a reconstruction offered on the basis of the cultural ideas and realities explained in Part II, Chapters Two through Five. Finally, Chapter Six sets forth two versions of Romans, one the standard text and the other an illuminated version. The illuminated version presents how Paul might have written Romans had he known that the cultural matrix to which Romans is a response would become obfuscated to future generations. The texts are both from the *Revised Standard Version* (RSV) of the New Testament. The illuminated Romans is substantially unchanged from the RSV text, but it is heavily footnoted.

Paul's letter to the Romans then, is to be read, understood and interpreted within the logical parameters of a pre- and first-century cross-cultural belief in reincarnation—a worldview consistent with the caste system of social organization then in existence—as set forth in Part II, Chapters Two through Five.

The validity of the premise that the interpretive matrix for explaining Romans is a pre- and first-century cross-cultural belief in reincarnation—a worldview consistent with the then existing caste system—should be apparent from the interdependence of biblical and extra-biblical texts explained in this work—an interdependence that is unexplainable apart from that premise. No doubt then remains that the premise is correct.

# PART I

# CHAPTER ONE

# THE SPIRITUAL ODYSSEY

Before presenting the academic component of this book, I will set forth the spiritual odyssey through which it was inspired, sustained and written. To this end I will present data and events of my personal history that are separate, yet inseparable from the academic component.

Hindsight is 20/20. Time must pass before one can look back and see a pattern.

I am an only child of Italian descent.

I heard bits and pieces of my family history over the years during family arguments. At those times my parents would accuse each other of having crazy people in their respective families, followed by a description of this or that eccentricity. Every aspect of the subject matter was scorned, laughed at and generally disbelieved.

My mother and maternal grandmother were born in Navarons, in the Province of Udine in Northern Italy. The family name was Pielli. My maternal grandfather was born in a neighboring town, Meduno. His family name was DeStefano. My grandfather's mother healed people with folk remedies.

My paternal ancestors were from Bari and Naples. Their family name was DeNino. My great-grandfather was a Catholic monk for twenty years before he married. There is a church in Binetto, Bari, which contains two statues of saints that my great-grandfather made. Somehow he ceased to be a monk. How this came about was never made clear to me—something about papers never being finalized. What is clear is that he remained in good standing with the Church, as his job after being a monk was overseer of the town cemetery. He married and had six children, one of whom was Grace, my grandmother. His sister, Filomena, was purported to see "writing on the wall." I do not know the subject matter of these writings. One of his daughters, Rose, intended to become a nun, but to do so she would have had to have moved to a different town, and this was unacceptable to the family.

I didn't think much about my family background one way or another until many years after hearing about it.

Looking back, I realize that some people in my family were spiritually and/or psychically gifted.

My father's mother, Grace, immigrated to the United States. She married Joe Fusco and had three sons. Eventually Joe left, leaving Grace to raise their sons alone.

My mother and her three siblings were born in Italy. Her father, Peter DeStefano, was finally able to bring his family to America in 1928—smack into the stock-market crash and the Depression. They settled in New York City.

Times were really tough. No one in the family spoke English. No work, no hot water, little heat in the tenements, secondhand clothes, little food. Although they initially attended a Roman Catholic church, during one cold winter in the Depression my parents and all their siblings were given coal to warm their homes by, and otherwise were taken under the wing of the Episcopal church (The Church of England)—via The Chapel of the Incarnation on East 31st Street (now The Church of the Good Shepherd). Under the tough but loving care of English headmaster-like Father Nicholas Feringer (a legend in his time) and his assistant, Father Charles Geerts (and I am sure, many unnamed others), the church acted as a surrogate parent for many children who would otherwise have been left to their own devices. My father often said that if it weren't for Father Feringer, Father Geerts and the church, he might have become a gangster. No doubt the same was true for others as well. The church ran sports programs for the boys and provided hot showers, holiday parties and free medical and dental checkups and services. There was even the occasional dinner out with the good fathers. All this came at a price, of course. My father and undoubtedly some of his cronies were pressed into service as acolytes as well as choir boys.

Most wonderful of all, the church provided camp for a month in the summer for boys and girls free of charge. The camp was located in Ivoryton, Connecticut, on about five hundred and fifty of the most beautiful acreage imaginable. There was a mile-long lake set in a deep valley, with a lily pond at one end and a dam at the other. There were also plenty of rocks across the lake to climb. The sleeping quarters were near the lake, consisting of covered tents mounted on wooden platforms. My father told me that "Feringer" would sneak around after lights out to make sure the boys were asleep. One night the boys, knowing "Feringer" was there, parted the tent flaps and spat in unison into the night. At this, Feringer jumped up, calling them asinine (his favorite word). Everyone had a good laugh—everyone except "Feringer."

Father Feringer's given names were Nicholas Matthew. Coincidentally, my father's name was Nicholas. My father took the name Matthew for his confirmation in honor of the man who was like a father to him. My father's brother Rudy changed his last name from Fusco to Kent, saying that his "father" was English, not Italian. (At the time my uncle did not know Father Feringer was of Dutch descent.)

My parents met and married at The Chapel of the Incarnation, and that is how I, a full-blooded Italian whose great-grandfather was a Catholic monk, became an Episcopalian.

I was born on November 20, 1942. Because of his love for my father, Father Feringer scheduled a special baptism for me at The Chapel of the Incarnation. The rite was held on a Sunday evening at 8 P.M. Father Feringer played the organ and Father Geerts performed the baptism. My mother told me that as a rule, night baptisms were not performed in those days. She also told me that Father Feringer had asked her if I was going to be named Grace after his wife (they were childless). My mother told him my middle name would be Grace, but that it was after my father's mother.

Years later Father Feringer served as headmaster at the prestigious St. Paul's Episcopal School in Garden City, Long Island, New York. In his declining years, he said that the years spent caring for the children at The Chapel of the Incarnation were the best and most rewarding years of his life.

Looking back, I think the baptism was the beginning.

I went to church as a child and attended Incarnation Camp, as had my parents before me, every year from age eight to twelve (for a nominal fee). The only differences were the counselors and the sleeping quarters, which then consisted of seven wall-less but railed cabins that were cantilevered at the bottom of a steep hill and lined up along the lake front.

Now, you might think that going to church camp every year and my family background in the church would make me religious or obedient or—something. On the contrary, I was not impressed. I remember looking around the church when I was six or seven and wondering how "grown-ups" could really believe that a man could be raised from the dead. Still, they appeared to take the whole thing quite seriously. I knew they were wrong.

Looking back I see that my early irreverence was necessary. I had to have a mind empty of fixed beliefs in order to be willing to seriously consider the beliefs of others.

At church camp I was always in some sort of trouble. I wore

hair rollers to church. Got reprimanded for that. Once, during "free time," I took a rowboat out and went to the lily pond, which was at the far end of the lake. Because of its distance and the fact that the lake was elliptical in shape, the lily pond was not visible from the campsite—so it was off limits (It figured.) The counselors never took us there, and I wanted to see it. So I went. Got reprimanded for that. It was worth it!

Another time, I took a canoe out on the lake alone without permission. A very big no-no. The canoes were new, and we had not been instructed on how to use them. I thought, how hard can it be? I didn't know that it was necessary to sit in the middle of a canoe when canoeing solo, and I sat in the back. It was a windy day and there was a strong current. The canoe began to spin uncontrollably while at the same time moving downstream toward the dam. I had to be rescued. (I would have abandoned the canoe before it reached the dam.) Got reprimanded for that.

One summer (I think I was ten) I brought cigarettes to camp and encouraged others to smoke with me in the woods. When I ran out of cigarettes, I stole a pack from a counselor. I hid them in a flashlight. The counselor reported the cigarettes missing. The entire camp was gathered on the top of the hill next to the mess hall overlooking the cabins below, watching as the counselors conducted a cabin-wide search. I was found out!

I was brought before the priests, who made a circle around me by joining hands. They prayed for me big time! I thought they were ridiculous.

There was a game we played once at camp called Hare and Hound, which I later realized was a metaphor for the Christian salvation process. The counselors would drop torn newspapers to create pathways throughout the campgrounds. Some paths were true and some were false. The true paths led to a changing house near the lake where everyone who arrived awaited the rest. The false paths were dead ends. I followed a lot of false paths. At last, out of breath and panting, I stepped from the bright sunlight into the dark changing house. I squinted. Initially, the only thing I saw was a priest's white collar. That stuck in my mind. Why?

Looking back, I realize that "something" would not let me go.

In grade school in New York City (PS 116), my third-grade teacher told my parents that I did not respect authority and was as incorrigible as a sixteen-year-old boy. That was true. Actually, I didn't give authority much thought one way or another except to notice that whenever I wanted to have fun, there was Authority breathing down my neck.

Looking back, I see that my defiance of authority gave me the strength to resist intimidation when those in authority denigrated my interests and by so doing might have deterred me from writing this book.

In 1951, when I was eight years old, my family moved to Levittown, Long Island. It was rural. Churches were few and far between so I didn't go to services much. I was glad. At my father's insistence, I went to a Pentecostal church for a short while because a Pentecostal neighbor was willing to drive me. I attended long enough to observe that the Pentecostals administered to the sick by the laying on of hands. Interesting.

Though I didn't go to church much as a teenager, I did do the fun stuff. I went to confraternity dances with my Roman Catholic friends. I also went to teen programs at the synagogue with my Jewish friends. It was at a synagogue program that I first observed a hypnotist. Interesting.

Looking back, I see that my unconscious ecumenism gave me the open-mindedness toward other religions that would be needed for the synthesis of this work.

I was about thirteen when I began to wonder why there were so many religions. How did one know which religion was the true one? After school I often stood on a corner with my friends (my future husband, who was Jewish, was among them) and argued against the existence of God. Eventually I convinced myself.

My grades in junior and senior high school directly corresponded to whether the subject interested me. I concentrated on commercial courses as I had no intention of going to college (though I was advised to by the school counselor). Yet I would check out books such as Dante's *Inferno* and *The Canterbury Tales* from the public library. I also liked reading philosophy—Plato, Aristotle, etc. What drew a person like me with a working-class background who was not college bound to read books of that sort?

At the age of eighteen, I was a convinced atheist.

One bright sunny day sometime during my eighteenth year as I was driving east on a Long Island parkway, I had what I later came to understand was a spiritual experience. A shape appeared about four inches outside and to the right of the windshield. Simultaneously, the sunlight grew brighter. I squinted. The shape filled the windshield vertically. It was formed by two slightly curved parallel lines about nine inches apart. The top and bottom of the shape were flat. There were "prickles" along the outside of the lines, and shadowy movement between them. The following sketch illustrates how the shape appeared from the inside of the car:

At the same time, I experienced a feeling of "One," "Good,"

"Harmony." Paradoxically, the One, Good and Harmony were one, yet separate. The One was somehow dominant. I "knew" the words "All is well." I use the word "knew" because the words were not seen or heard. The "voice" was neither male nor female. I grasped the steering wheel for balance so that I could lean to the right and investigate. I remember saying, "What's happening?" But "it" was gone.

Now here's the strange thing: I never mentioned the incident to friends or family because I was not sure it had happened. I later learned that I wasn't sure the experience had happened because it was timeless. The experience of timelessness cannot be explained. The closest I can come to describing it is that in timelessness there is nothing against which to bounce thought—no points of reference. Thus, in timelessness, thought cannot differentiate itself. It is consciousness, so to speak, which is boundless, eternal.

About twenty years later, while I was reading William James' *The Varieties of Religious Experience*, it struck me that one of the individuals in the book appeared to be describing the internal structure of plants. At once I recalled the incident of twenty years past with clarity. The shape outside of my windshield was an ordinary blade of grass common on the side of Long Island parkways. Somehow it was magnified, and the sunlight shining through it was magnified along with it and made me squint. I cannot explain the source of the words "All is well," (not seen or heard, not male or female) except to say that at that time in my life, I never spoke in such a formal manner. I would have said "Everything's OK," or "It's all right." The One was not a number. The Good was known without a contingent value.

Let me explain what I mean when I say that the Good was known without a contingent value through a little mental exercise. Try to think of good without reference to a particular value. In other words, try to think of good without also thinking of why something is good or not good. Take your time.

You see, it is impossible. Yet the Good without a particular value was known to me. Thinking about this phenomenon, I wondered if the imposition of a particular structure of cultural values on the individual is what is impressed on the conscience and thus constitutes the "good." Opposition to the imposed value system would necessarily constitute the "bad," or sin. For instance: Our culture is disgusted by the notion of cannibalism. For a cannibal, however, eating people is the cultural norm. But if the cultural prescription for a cannibal is to eat, let's say for argument's sake, one individual every three months, but for some reason the cannibal eats two individuals every three months, he is transgressing the cultural norm, and would probably have feelings of guilt.

Ultimately this experience of the Good, and the subsequent thoughts I had regarding it and the Jewish law, were essential to my understanding of Pauline theology with respect to Paul's words about people whose "conscience . . . bears witness and [whose] . . . conflicting thoughts . . . accuse or perhaps excuse them" (Rom. 2:15).

Harmony was simply Harmony, but it was not related to music. Now here's another thing: The One, Good, and Harmony (a Trinity?) were paradoxically One, yet separate. The logical faculty cannot experience paradox. Another reason why the experience cannot be accurately described is because language that belongs to the logical faculty is sequential and, therefore, inadequate for the task. For the same reason, the experience cannot be imagined or created.

Looking back I see that the experience (this particular experience happened only once) gave me authoritative insight into the concept of *gnosis*, derived from the Greek word meaning "to know," which I would later come to write about in the context of Paul's letter to the Romans.

One of the problems I had with accepting religious truth was religion's claims regarding prophecy. I simply did not believe foreknowledge to be possible. Through my Aunt Blanche and later through my own experience, I found out that I was wrong.

When I was twenty, my Aunt Blanche told me she had read about a psychic, Jeanne Dixon, who had predicted that President John F. Kennedy would be assassinated. I told her that was the most ridiculous thing I had ever heard. I knew it was impossible to foresee the future. But my aunt wasn't crazy. So I made a mental note to recall the prediction should the event occur.

In 1963, I was working as a secretary in the now defunct Grumman Aircraft Corporation on Long Island when an announcement came over the loudspeaker. President Kennedy had been shot. I froze in my tracks. My aunt was right! She suggested I visit a psychic who she said was "very good." I decided to investigate and made an appointment. I wrote down the psychic's predictions and, over time, kept track of them to see whether or not they manifested. As it turned out, this particular psychic proved to be remarkably accurate and detailed with respect to predicting future events. I visited many psychics after that for the purpose of observing the phenomenon.

Looking back, I see that my aunt was an instrument through which I learned that there are people who can predict future events. This led to my reconsideration of religious claims about prophecy. I decided to pay more attention.

In 1964 I married Michael Graham. While living in New York, we had two children, Laura, born in 1967, and Lisa, born in 1972. In 1974 we moved from Long Island to Champaign-Urbana, Illinois, where Michael began his first teaching job at the University of Illinois School of Law. Our son, Lee, was born in 1976. I had taken some courses at Nassau Community College when we lived on Long Island and continued at Parkland Junior College in Champaign, Illinois. I didn't have a particular goal in mind. I simply liked to learn.

Eventually, a guidance counselor from Parkland contacted me and said that I had the credits and grades to transfer to the University of Illinois. I decided to major in religious studies. It was at the University of Illinois that I became familiar with the technical aspects of the Bible, which, as it happened, was necessary for the creation of this book. Some of the required course books proved invaluable as well. Once I told a professor, William Schoedel, that I felt I had to write something, but I didn't know what. The feeling was one of obligation.

While attending the University of Illinois, I joined a private group that investigated the paranormal and the occult. We sponsored people in the field from all over the country to come and share their knowledge. Information about reincarnation, *karma* and related matters was channeled from the "other side" through trance mediums. I discovered that it seemed that virtually all people who dabble in these matters believe in reincarnation.

I developed an interest in St. Paul at an adult Sunday school class at Temple Baptist Church in Champaign. Inexplicably, some of the ambiguous passages in Paul's letter to the Romans began to bother me. Why are there so many passages in Romans that don't make sense? Paul's letter was directed towards a largely "uneducated" audience. How is it possible that such an audience understood him, yet we don't?

I had read books about the renowned trance medium Edgar Cayce. He was a good man who helped heal the sick with information received while in trances. Once, in answer to questions posed to him by Arthur Lammers, a wealthy Jewish printer from Dayton, Ohio whose hobbies were philosophy and metaphysics, Cayce spewed forth information about internal morality, karmic debt and reincarnation. When Cayce came out of the trance he was disturbed to learn what he had said. As a Christian he knew that Christianity did not accept belief in reincarnation. He never resolved the dilemma. I wondered:

What does it all mean? Does reincarnation exist? If not, why do virtually all the trance mediums speak of it? If so, why does Christianity deny it? Is there a relationship between reincarnation, Judaism and Christianity? If so, what is it? My mind flitted from one incongruity to another. I remembered the fact that many people who investigated the occult and the paranormal believed in reincarnation. I thought of Edgar Cayce. I thought of the enigmatic nature of Romans. I thought, and I thought, and I thought. Bingo!

Paul's letter to the Romans and his theology with respect to the Jewish (Pharisaic) law and the significance of the Christ event was a response to a pre- and first-century cross-cultural worldview of belief in reincarnation, a worldview consistent with the caste system of social organization then in existence. If this pre-Christian cross-cultural worldview were assumed when reading Romans, virtually all of the heretofore enigmatic passages would be immediately understandable.

That is what I had to write about!

But where to begin?

The information, experiences, and people I needed to come in contact with in order to write this book "came to me" over time and in ways that can only be described as miraculous. Some events happened long before the thought of writing a book entered my mind. The process continued until this work was completed. I will share the most remarkable of those events.

Some of the books I needed for research came to me during the time I lived in Illinois (1974-1984), long before I had the feeling that I had to write something. A book would catch my eye in a shop or bookstand. I would buy it, read it and take notes for no apparent reason. Once when I was taking notes, a friend, Barbara Robinson, asked me why I was doing it. I said I didn't know. Another time I accompanied a friend to a secondhand bookstore on the University of Illinois' campus called Acres and Acres of Books. They weren't kidding. Books were strewn all over the place. I noticed a lone book on its side on a shelf. It was titled *Man and Time*. It felt like something I would need so I bought it. As it happened, the book was an indispensable source of information about the Greeks and the cyclical worldview of ancient man. (I later learned that the book was part of a six-volume series of collected papers from the Jungian *Eranos Yearbook*, and I sent for the set.) I lived in Champaign-Urbana for ten years, but that was the first and last time I went into that bookstore.

I earned a bachelor of arts degree in religious studies from the University of Illinois in 1984. Just in time! That year my husband accepted a professorship at the University of Miami School of Law. We headed for sunny Florida.

After we had been in Miami for about a year, I wrote a thirty-page article interpreting Paul's letter to the Romans within the context of belief in reincarnation. I sent it off to some religious journal (I don't recall which one) and received a reply saying that the article had been sent to a committee of four for review. Three voted against publication and one voted for. The three were right. I knew before sending it off that justice could not be done to the subject without an immense amount of work. I really didn't want to do what I knew I had to do—write a book. Who knew how anyway? Basically I was trying to get away with something. Now my hand was forced—literally.

Reluctantly, I began to write in earnest. I wrote sporadically amidst long intervals of thinking, questioning and "waiting" for answers. It took a long time because I didn't know how to go about it. Instead of constructing an outline and making a beeline for what I wanted to say, I circled in on it.

Looking back, I see that even my inefficiency worked to my advantage. As it turned out, I read much about what I needed to know while circling in.

I was isolated in Miami. I longed for contact with others

whose interests were philosophy and religion. I was coming to the point in my writing where I needed information about the Pharisees. Where was I going to get it? (God forbid I would have to do research in a library!) One day on the front page of the Neighbors section of the *Miami Herald* there was a full-page picture of a woman and a related article. Edith Jacobson, a Jewish woman, had established a lecture series on Jewish-Christian dialogue at Barry University, a Roman Catholic institution. It was meant to be a bridge between the Jewish and Christian communities. About a year or so before reading the article about Edith, I had been told by a psychic that "a man—no, a woman" would help me with my book. I wondered about this prediction as it was imprecise, the sort of statement that gives skeptics a field day. I called Edith at Barry. We became great friends. She was quite a powerful woman inside and out. In her youth she taught medical and surgical nursing techniques to new nurses. She later obtained a master's degree in theology and philosophy at Barry University. No wonder the psychic got mixed vibes! Over time, Edith recommended, or supplied to me, books on the Pharisees.

I ordered several books for research from publishing-house catalogs that were delivered to my home. A few more sources came with the help of the University of Miami library via my husband.

As I was getting close to actually working on annotating Romans itself, I wondered where I would get scholarly input on it. Lo and behold! A publisher's catalog showed up at my home advertising *The Romans Debate*, a new, expanded edition of a collection of essays that was originally published fourteen years earlier! It was the standard for studying the purpose and occasion of Romans. I ordered it. Upon reading *The Romans Debate* and later reading Ernst Kasemann's *Commentary on Romans*, I realized that I had been writing about what Pauline scholars had long been searching for—an interpretive matrix for explaining Romans. Amazing grace!

I didn't know much about publishers. Through Edith I learned that the Paulist Press published religious books. About eight years before Edith told me about Paulist Press (in 1988 or 1989), I went to a psychic and asked if the book I was working on would ever be published. (I needed all the encouragement I could get.) She said "yes" and that she saw the letters RAM "around the publisher." About two years after that psychic reading (in 1990 or 1991), I attended a Spiritual Frontiers Fellowship International retreat on metaphysics. Spiritual Frontiers Fellowship International, headquartered in Philadelphia, was incorporated in 1956 by about seventy-five religious leaders and writers from all over the United States to interpret to and to receive interpretation from the churches concerning the rising tide of interest in mystical, psychical and paranormal experience. While meandering in the bookstore that had been set up temporarily for the retreat, I opened a book. The publisher was Paulist Press. On the bottom of the back jacket were the words "New York, RAMsey, Montreal." Hmmmmm.

In 1992, I was diagnosed with breast cancer. I had chemotherapy, a double mastectomy and a stem cell replacement. I was very sick for more than a year. I was unable to write, nor did I want to. I felt that if it was God's will that I write, I would not have gotten sick. After a while I felt better. I was still alive, so I resumed writing. In 1993 my daughter Lisa entered New York University School of Law. That same year, a psychic told me that a young man would help me with my book. Right.

I got to the point where the book was nearly ready to be presented to someone who knew something about publishing. But who? Every day before writing, I lit a candle that I had bought in Assisi, Italy. It had an image of St. Francis on it. I held crystal rosary beads that I had bought in Rome. (Episcopalians don't use rosary beads.) They had been blessed by a

Vatican cardinal (sometimes when writing I wore them around my neck). I crossed myself with the beads. I prayed in the name of the Father, the Son and the Holy Spirit. I asked God to please send whoever the man is who is supposed to help me. I said that I had done what I thought was required of me; I had done all that I could. I said that it was up to God to do the rest. Finally, I said that His help was necessary, for without Him I am nothing and can do nothing. (I often used this phrase in prayer before writing, and I meant it.)

In 1995, Lisa was home from law school for a visit. She was standing near me in the kitchen when I happened to open a package that had just been delivered. It was a book I had ordered about the Christian mystic Emanuel Swedenborg and was a part of *The Classics of Western Spirituality* series published by Paulist Press. Lisa took the book from my hand and flipped through the pages. She was surprised to see the name John Farina, editor-in-chief of the Editorial Board, on the inside of the front jacket cover. Lisa showed me a picture in the new student magazine of a John Farina in her class at NYU law whom she knew had been previously involved somehow in religious studies. It turned out that he had worked at Paulist Press for nearly ten years and had a deep interest in, and knowledge of, religion. He had left the publishing field to attend law school.

I remembered the psychic prediction, and I asked Lisa to contact John when she returned to NYU and tell him exactly what had happened. I subsequently went to New York to visit my daughter and to meet John. We got acquainted over dinner. After I returned to Florida, I invited John to Miami to peruse and discuss my work. He was very enthusiastic about it and agreed to help me.

God could not have sent an individual more suited to His purpose than John Farina. Academically he knows his stuff. A Phi Beta Kappa honors graduate from Vassar, he went on to get a master of divinity degree from Yale and a doctorate in comparative religion from Columbia. Practically, John spent nearly ten years with the Paulist Press, most recently serving as editor-in-chief of *The Classics of Western Spirituality*. In addition he has written extensively about religion in the *New Catholic World* (a magazine published by Paulist Press) and for the National Conference of Catholic Bishops. He has taught at George Mason University in Virginia and Iliff School of Theology in Denver. He has published four books, the first when he was twenty-three. But of at least equal importance was that he is a believer.

A year passed. I didn't work on the book because I thought I had plenty of time. In December 1996, I was told that the breast cancer had spread to my lungs. So much for taking life and time for granted! I contacted John shortly after receiving the news. Under the circumstances, John asked me to mail him my current material as soon as possible.

I spent most of February 1997 rewriting and correcting my work. While I was working, a strange thing happened. I hesitate to include it, as it is even hard for me to believe. Yet I feel an obligation to tell all of the truth as it is.

I was working on the section on *Koheleth* (Ecclesiastes) on the computer and began the printout process. The printer stopped. I removed the printout and placed it on my desk. The last sheet was sticking out a bit from the rest, so I went to fix it before picking it up and rereading the text. For some nonreason I pulled it out instead. I was astounded at what I saw— a quotation from Arthur Schopenhauer, the nineteenth century German philosopher. Recall that I said that now and then I would come across a book I thought I would need or take notes on something without knowing the reason why. About seven years earlier, I had come across a quote by Schopenhauer, which I felt I should keep. I was so impressed with this quotation that I filed it on my computer hard-drive on its own file, even though it was only a paragraph long.

The quotation is as follows:

> The theory which sets forth the unifying principle on
> which Christianity and the religions of the East meet
> should find the warranty of its truth in the unity estab-
> lished between Biblical and extra-Biblical texts—a unity
> which is not apparent apart from that theory. No doubt
> then remains that the theory is correct.
>
> — Schopenhauer

Looking at the quotation, I realized this: The interpretive
matrix that was needed to explain Romans, that was called for
in *The Romans Debate* and Kasemann's *Commentary on Romans,*
and that Schopenhauer pointed to when he wrote of a unify-
ing principle on which Christianity and the religions of the
East could meet, were one and the same!

Looking back, I think it is fair to say that I was unconsciously
preparing to write this book for most of my life, and though I
was writing consciously for about twelve years, I didn't really
appreciate the profound implications to biblical scholarship of
what I was writing until I read *The Romans Debate* and Ernst
Kasemann's *Commentary on Romans,* and then experienced the
Schopenhauer event.

Last but not least, I focused on the fact that something very
strange had just occurred with the computer. I scrolled through
the *Koheleth* file to make sure that the paragraph was not somehow (though I didn't know how) in the file. Nothing. I called
my husband at his office in the law school and told him what
had happened. He suggested that I reprint *Koheleth.* I did. Nothing. I checked the computer's file index with the thought that
the *Koheleth* file and the Schopenhauer file might have been
adjacent to each other, thus forming a synapse of some sort
that would allow the electrical impulses to pass from one file to
the other. Chapter Four (the file that contained *Koheleth*) was

on the left side of the index, fourth from the top. The Schopenhauer file was the very last one on the right side. My daughter Laura, who lives next door, happened to come in while I was trying to figure out what was going on. She suggested that perhaps the quotation had been on my desk all along and had gotten mixed up with my printout. No way. I'm very orderly. When I work there are no superfluous papers anywhere—they make me nervous. Besides, I had not printed the Schopenhauer file for at least a year. I called my daughter Lisa at the firm where she works as a lawyer in New York City. She said she thought that if I included the incident in the book, people might think that I was crazy. Finally, I called my son, Lee, "the computer expert" (I suppose there's one in every family) at Duke University, where he was an undergraduate. I told him what had happened. He said I "must have done something" to cause the file to print—he didn't know what—but it must have been something. Well, I hadn't. The fact is (and my son is aware of this) that I have mastered only the rudimentary functions with respect to the computer that are necessary to do my work. These do not include learning how to move a document from one file to another. (For that once necessary task I waited for my son to come home from college.) Yet he insisted that I must have done something.

Concerned that the extraordinary way in which the Schopenhauer event had manifested would be rejected by intelligent, educated people, I considered leaving it out. But I knew doing so would be wrong. It happened, and it should be known even at the risk of my being considered a crackpot. God knows—I have been a fool for lesser things. Nevertheless, the lack of support from my family in this matter had me concerned. They knew me. They knew I wasn't crazy. They knew I didn't lie. And they knew I have occasional paranormal experiences. Yet they were skeptical.

Undecided and agonizing over whether to include the

Schopenhauer event in this chapter, I called Rhea A. White, director of the Exceptional Human Experience Network, headquartered in New Bern, North Carolina. Not only did Rhea advise me to include it, but she implied that it is obligatory for those who have had exceptional human experiences to make them known. I knew that she was right.

This should be a sad time for me. I am undergoing a third round of chemotherapy. I'm bald and generally have aches and pains. I have been informed that the cancer I have is terminal. Yet I am joyful. The way the writing of this book came about—that it came about at all—the manner in which the right people and information appeared at the right time, as well as the occurrence of the Schopenhauer event, confirm what I now know has always been.

Looking back, I know there has always been an invisible Presence guiding me throughout my life in matters great and small. A Presence that "knew" before I knew. A Presence that went before and made straight the Way.

Surely I will not be forsaken in the Valley of Death.

# PART II

# CHAPTER TWO

# THE ANCIENT WORLDVIEW: BELIEF IN REINCARNATION

The Christian era initiated a series of episodes of vast historical moment that changed the world for the better in a profound way. The beginnings of Christianity emerged during the first century. However, the worldview to which Christian theology (exemplified in Paul's letter to the Romans) was a direct response, a cross-cultural belief in reincarnation, originated in prehistory and was the worldview of many ancient peoples. Indeed, we will see in Chapters Five and Six that Romans contains references to such a belief in reincarnation.

In the introduction to *Reincarnation and World Thought*, W. Macneile Dixon informs us that the doctrine of rebirth, which carries with it the idea of pre-existence, is by far the most ancient and most widely held worldview.[1] W.R. Alger concurs and further states:

"No other doctrine has exerted so extensive, controlling, and permanent an influence upon mankind as that of metempsychosis—the notion that when the soul leaves the body, its rank, character, circumstances, and experience in each successive existence depend on its qualities, deeds, and attainments in its preceding lives."[2] [The] "(karmic-like) dependence which has been virtually always conjoined with metempsychosis is probably due to the fact that the hypothesis explains the chaos of evil, injustice, and moral inequality intrinsic to human existence."[3]

To appreciate Paul's view of the positive impact of Christianity on individual dignity and freedom, it is necessary to have an understanding of the ancient belief in reincarnation as well as the human conditions that prevailed as the logical consequence of this worldview.

To this end I will present an overview of the ancient worldview obtained from the Hindu, Hebrew and Greek (pagan and Platonic) models, respectively. These models all share a belief in reincarnation, but view differently the mechanisms and purposes of the process.

## A. THE HINDU MODEL

Hinduism is perhaps the oldest and most complex of all the religions of the world. It traces some of its religious forms and themes to the third millennium B.C.E. The word Hindu generally applies to the religion of the people of India.[4] We are concerned with Hinduism chiefly because its concept of *karma*, described below, is reflected in the cross-cultural worldview of Paul's Roman audience, an audience that believed in reincarnation. In fact, it is important to keep in mind that Jewish religious customs originated in the Orient.[5]

Our overview of Hinduism begins with the early Aryans, a nomadic tribal people who came in migratory waves into India during the period between 1750 and 1200 B.C.E.[6] The Aryans spoke an Indo-European language. They were polytheistic, worshipping deities similar to those of other Indo-European peoples. Animal sacrifice was the primary manner of worship of the Aryan gods—the purpose of which was to atone for sin.[7] As the Aryans settled in India, the Aryan religion mingled with the religion of the native people, and the resultant religious culture became classical Hinduism.[8]

In about the sixth century B.C.E., the Aryans began to settle in cities in the Indus Valley. Early sources indicate that initially Aryan society developed into three basic classes. Class divisions were maintained for centuries in Indian society and eventually became subdivided into the multiple classes that became the basis of the Hindu caste system.[9]

The sacred scripture of Hinduism is the *Vedic* literature, and in it the Hindu view of the universe is grounded. These books are the source of Hindu understanding of the universe. All later Hindu material refers to them and is viewed as commentary in light of them. There is no way of knowing the exact time of the writing and development of the *Vedas*. Scholarly projections range from some time prior to 2000 B.C.E., with further development as late as the sixth century C.E. Some believe that the bulk of the *Vedic* material was written between 1500 and 400 B.C.E.[10]

There are four *Vedic* books. Each book contains four parts. The fourth section of each book, together called the *Upanishads,* comprise the Hindu worldview.[11] Unlike the earlier *Vedic* literature, the *Upanishads* probably originated in the ninth century B.C.E. It is noteworthy that the *Upanishads* contain a collection of material similar to that found in the Jewish *Talmud*.[12] As we shall see in Chapter Three, the Jews, like Hindus, believed in reincarnation and the worldly incurrence of negative *karma*, or sin.

The *Upanishads* assume only one reality, Brahman. Brahman is infinite, eternal, sexless, unknowable, without past, present or future, and totally impersonal.[13] All living beings of the world are only expressions of Brahman. They are souls (*atman*) that make up part of the myriad souls that constitute Brahman. What is not Brahman is not real. Thus, phenomenal existence is illusion (*maya*). Each experience of individuality, the world and what one sees, hears, touches and feels is an illusion—a dream. The individual is enmeshed in this world of ignorance and illusion, thinking that it is real, unaware of its true identification with Brahman. It is the task of religion to reveal each individual's divine spark and to show us how to live on the new plane of Brahman.

Indian philosophers introduced the concept of *samsara*. The term means "to wander across." Indian philosophy holds that when an individual dies, the life force "wanders across"—moves on to another time and body.[14] Some Hindu sects include plant life in this process, and thus believe it possible for rebirth to reach into the vegetable kingdom.[15] In Western thought this process is referred to both as reincarnation and the transmigration of souls.[16]

The *Upanishads* discuss the concept of *karma*, a Sanskrit word, the root of which means "to do or act." Indian thought, unlike that of the West, attributes individual differences such as kindness, intelligence, talent, etc. to choices (*karma*) made in previous lives. The effects of choices made in a particular lifetime manifest in either the current life or in a succeeding one.[17] It follows logically then that in Indian thought, *karma* was viewed as either negative or positive. To act in accordance with the norms of the established Indian caste system incurred positive *karma*. Conversely, to act in ways in conflict with such norms incurred negative *karma*. Positive *karma* led to reincarnation into a higher state than one's previous incarnation(s). Negative *karma* led to reincarnation into a lower state than one's previous incarnation(s). The word for negative *karma* in Indian thought was "sin." (Note again that the Aryans atoned for sin in religious rite.)

I submit *a priori*, if you will, that "sin" was the operative cross-cultural term for negative *karma* within the Roman Empire prior to and during the first century. I further submit that the concept of reincarnation and/or the transmigration of souls was understood as a form of resurrection within the Roman Empire prior to and during the first-century. These ideas will be more fully developed in Parts II and III, Chapters Three and Six.

The inevitability of continual birth (resurrection) and death, a sort of immortality, may be viewed by some as a blessing. However, in Indian thought, *samsara*—incessant birth, suffering and dying over and over again through countless generations—is a curse. Thus, the goal of most Indian religions is to break the hold of sin/negative *karma* that drives the cyclical process of rebirth, thereby releasing the soul unto true eternal life in Brahman. This breaking free from the necessity of renewed mortal existence (resurrection) is called *moksha*. According to the *Upanishads*, the cycle is broken when true knowledge of the illusion of life is realized.[18] "By knowing God man is freed from all bonds."[19] This breaking-away process is difficult, and comes only after much study with a guru, if at all.

Traditional Indian literature also contains the ethical *Code of Manu*, a statement of the moral and ethical ideals of the Indian classical era. Probably written sometime between 300 B.C.E. and 300 C.E., it is of value to us because of what it tells us about Indian life during the period. Within the *Code of Manu* one finds the roots of many of the social and religious traditions that ultimately characterized Hinduism into modern times.

The *Code of Manu* assumes the *Varna* system, which apparently developed from the early Aryan divisions of society. The societal divisions are viewed as divinely ordained. They are hierarchically arranged as follows:

For the growth of the worlds, (Brahman), created Brahmanas (Brahmins), Kshatriyas (warriors), Vaishyas (traders) and Shudras (manual workers) from his face, arms, thighs, and feet respectively. (The Code of Manu, 1:31)[20]

The first three are "twice born" and the fourth, the Shudras, are "once born." Members of each group have specified caste opportunities and requirements (*dharma*) they must obey.

It is apparent that people were thought to begin as Shudras, and should serve willingly, obediently and without envy of the above three castes. The Shudras hoped to move by gradual ascent from reincarnation to reincarnation through the system until they attained the exalted rank of Brahmin. Thus, under the caste system, Indian society was stratified into fixed classes with membership determined by birth. The only means of inter-class mobility was through the process of death and reincarnation.[21]

The *Code of Manu* also indicates that the Indians conceived divine time as endless. Generally, Indian philosophy viewed time as moving perpetually through various cycles. At the beginning of each cycle, Brahman creates the world. Initially, there is peace, abundance, and morality. But then decay sets in. The god Vishnu intervenes on humanity's behalf; but over time the world continues to decay. Famines, wars and general immorality reign. Ultimately the world is destroyed by the god Shiva. Upon the completion of the cycle, the world dissolves and all souls depart into suspended being. After a period of inaction, the world begins again and the souls assume new bodies.[22]

As we continue, it is important to keep the following concepts in mind with respect to Indian philosophy:

1. Indian philosophy assumes only one reality, Brahman. All living things are only expressions of Brahman. Thus the world and all that is in it are illusion.

2. In the ethical *Code of Manu*, Brahman is expressed anthropologically.

3. Indian philosophy holds that the individual is en-

meshed in a world of ignorance and illusion. Thinking that the world is real and unaware of its true identification with Brahman, the soul is fated to perpetual reincarnation. The task of Indian religion is to reveal our divine spark and to show us how to live on the new plane of Brahman.

4. Indian philosophy conjoins the concepts of reincarnation and *karma*. *Karma* is a Sanskrit word meaning "to do or act." *Karma* places the origin of individual differences like kindness, intelligence, talent, etc. as the result of choices made in a previous life. The effects of the choices made in a lifetime will manifest either in such lifetime or in a succeeding one. Thus, individuals are affected by and indebted to unknown positive or negative actions (*karma*/sin) from past existence(s). "*Samsara*" is a Sanskrit word meaning "to wander across." Indian philosophy holds that when an individual dies, the life force "wanders across"—moves on to another time and body. Some Indian sects believe that it is possible for rebirth to reach into the vegetable kingdom.

5. In Indian thought the process of continual birth and death (*samsara*) is a curse. Thus, the goal of Indian religion is to break the karmic/sin cycle and release the soul unto eternal life in Brahman.

6. According to the *Upanishads*, the cycle of rebirth is broken when true knowledge of the illusion of life is realized. This process is difficult and comes only after much study with a guru, if at all.

7. The Indian social order was hierarchical and arranged

in descending order as follows:

> Brahmins
> Warriors
> Traders
> Manual workers

Caste was determined by birth. The only means of inter-class mobility was for a member of each caste to fulfill his particular caste requirements before death. The individual hoped to gradually ascend through the caste hierarchy via the process of reincarnation until ultimately reaching the exalted rank of Brahmin.

8. The Indians conceived divine time as endless. Generally time is viewed as moving perpetually through various cycles. Brahman creates the world at the beginning of each cycle.

The human realm of time, nature and change represented a fall from an ideal, timeless and primitive state into a world of generation and death.

This final concept regarding the fall of man into the human realm is recognizable in the Hebrew myth of the fall of man (Adam). We will now turn to the Hebrew model.

## B. THE HEBREW MODEL

The biblical book of Genesis relates the Hebrew model of the cyclical mortal nature of the soul's existence. Genesis tells us that God put Adam into the garden of Eden and later created Eve from Adam's rib. Adam and Eve were given the freedom to eat the fruit of any tree in the garden except the tree that was in the center—the tree of the knowledge of good and evil. Nor were they to touch it, lest they die (Gen. 2:15-17;

3:2,3). Tempted by a serpent and seeing that the tree was good for food, a delight to the eyes, and was desired to make one wise (Gen. 3:4-6), Eve ate the forbidden fruit and gave some to Adam (Gen. 3:6). Then the eyes of both were opened, and they knew that they were naked, and they sewed fig leaves together and made themselves aprons (Gen. 3:7). God found them out. He knew that Adam and Eve had eaten of the tree of the knowledge of good and evil. They were guilty and ashamed (Gen. 3:11). God cursed them with expulsion from the garden, condemning them to the misery associated with mortal existence. Among the resulting difficulties were enmity between the sexes, pain in childbearing, the necessity of hard work for minimum sustenance (Gen. 3:15-19), fratricide, exemplified in Cain and Abel (Gen. 4:8), and the inevitability of death (Gen. 2:15-17; 3:2).

Thus, the story of Adam and Eve is a metaphor for man's previous idyllic existence in God/the One/Unity and man's subsequent fall into the world. The garden of Eden is a timeless realm where there is no death. The forbidden fruit of the tree of the knowledge of good and evil (the knowledge of opposites/duality/plurality) is the temptation of the knowledge, good and bad, of the world. In body, man has eyes (sense organs) that can open and discriminate. When man, separated from God/the One perceives duality—epitomized in male and female genitalia, he incurs guilt. When he incurs guilt, he is caught in the cycle of guilt/generation (through sex and birth)/guilt (Gen. 4:1, 2, 17-26). In the Hebrew model, the cycle of generation begins with the sons of Adam and Eve—Cain and Abel (Gen. 4:1-32).

Thus we see that like the Hindu model, the Hebrew model incorporates a belief in the fall of man from God into a cycle of reincarnation. We will now turn to the Greek pagan model for further insight into the ancient worldview. Understanding Greek or pagan culture is important for our inquiry because Greco-Roman culture was the immediate socioeconomic and philosophical milieu to which Paul's letter to the Romans was a direct response. We will see references to aspects of the Greek model in Paul's letter to the Romans in Chapters Five and Six, and learn in Chapter Three that the Pharisees whom Paul addressed shared many of the Greek ideas. Greco-Roman culture was also the cultural matrix from which Christianity evolved into a universal (catholic) religion.

## C. THE GREEK MODEL

According to ancient Greek philosophy, reality includes two distinct yet interrelated aspects, the realm of timelessness and the realm of time.

> Dominated by an ideal of intelligibility . . . which is in itself identical with itself, in the eternal and immutable, . . . the Greeks regarded movement and change as inferior degrees of reality, in which, at best, identity can be apprehended in the form of permanence and perpetuity, hence of recurrence. The circular movement which assures the survival of the same things by repeating them, . . . by bringing about their continuous return, is the perfect and most immediate expression of the absolute immobility at the summit of the hierarchy.[23]

The pagan Greeks speculated as to the mode of existence in timeless eternity. However, they focused on the "Immutable Law of Nature," or cyclical time, with which they considered the cosmos, the world and man to be inextricably bound:

> . . . The Greek world conceived of time as above all cyclical or circular, returning perpetually upon itself, self-enclosed, under the influence of astronomical movements which command and regulate its course with necessity.[24]

Though the Greeks believed that death is an inevitable part of being within time, they held that nothing, not the cosmos, the world, nor man will pass away in the ultimate sense:

> . . . Both the entire cosmic process and the time of our world of generation and decay develop in a circle or according to an indefinite succession of cycles, in the course of which the same reality is made, unmade, and remade, in conformity with an *immutable law* and determinate alternations. The same sum of being is preserved; nothing is created and nothing lost.[25] (Italics mine.)

Some held that all of creation, i.e., the cosmos, the world and all that it contains, or the cycle of time, will disappear at once, only to return again along with all of its past inhabitants, and that:

> . . . within each of these cycles of time, of these *aiones*, these *aeva*, . . . the same individuals have appeared, appear, and will appear at every turn of the circle.[26]

In addition, though the idea of continual renewal was in a sense reassuring, the whole process of life, rebirth and death appeared to the Greek to be an exercise in futility:

> . . . the core of the Greek's feeling about time [is that] it was experienced as a degenerance. . . . The resultant laws were laws of "decadence" rather than of development . . . they represent change as a fall from an ideal primitive state . . .[27]

It is important to keep the following concepts in mind with respect to Greek philosophy as they, in particular, are necessary to understanding Paul's letter to the Romans:

1. The Greek philosophers assumed two distinct yet interrelated aspects of reality, the realm of timelessness and the realm of time. The realm of timelessness was the ideal. The realm of time, in which there was movement and change, was regarded as the inferior degree of reality in which identity can be observed in the forms of permanence and perpetuity.

2. The Greek philosophers conceived cyclical time to be under the influence of astronomical movements that necessarily commanded and regulated its course.

3. The Greek philosophers held that the entire cosmic process and the process of time in our world of generation and decay develops according to an indefinite succession of cycles in conformity with an "Immutable Law." Thus, nothing will pass away in the ultimate sense.

4. Some Greek philosophers held that the cosmos and all that it contains will disappear at once, only to return again along with those very individuals who inhabited it in the past.

It has been illustrated that the ancient Indian, Hebrew and Greek worldviews were similar in that they included belief in the existence of an idyllic and timeless reality apart from tangible reality. Some comparisons to keep in mind are the following:

1. Indian and Hebrew thought conceived of the timeless realm (Brahman/God) anthropologically.

2. Indian philosophy did not consider phenomenal re-

ality to be truly real, but rather illusion. Man is enmeshed in the illusory world and is ignorant of that fact.

3. Greek philosophers viewed the realm of time to be inferior to the timeless, but thought it to reflect the absolute immobility of timelessness.

4. Greek philosophers viewed cyclical regeneration in a quasi-scientific sense to be an Immutable Law under the influence of astronomical movements that necessarily command and regulate its course.

5. Hebrew philosophy relates in Genesis that man's expulsion from the timeless garden of Eden was God's punishment for not obeying his commands (Gen. 3:11).

6. Indian, Hebrew and Greek philosophy each held that man has fallen from an ideal primitive state.

We now will turn to the Greek worldview depicted in the Platonic model, which held a more positive view of the cyclical path of the soul.

## D. The Platonic Model

The Greek philosopher and seer Plato (427?-347? B.C.E.), relating the myth of the charioteer and winged steeds, provides insight into the ancient Greek view of the makeup of the soul of man and its cyclical regeneration within the realm of the intelligible, as well as within the realm of nature or natural law. According to Plato:

All soul is immortal, for she is the source of all motion

both in herself and in others. Her form may be described in a figure as a composite nature made up of a charioteer and a pair of winged steeds. The steeds of the gods are immortal, but ours are one mortal and the other immortal. The immortal soul soars upward into the heavens, but the mortal drops her plumes and settles upon the earth.[28]

Thus, for the ancient Platonic Greek, the soul is immortal and is the source of all motion, including its own. Plato also informs us of the Greek belief that the soul of man consists of a mortal inclination, which is earthbound, and an immortal inclination, which is heaven-bound. Further, the mortal tendency of the soul resists the upward force of the immortal tendency. But man is equipped with a "wing," the purpose of which:

. . . is to rise and carry the downward element into the upper world. . . [29]

This Platonic model of the soul of man suggests that the Greek believed that man has within himself two tendencies (1) earthbound, downward and (2) heaven-bound, upward. Moreover, these two tendencies are in a constant state of tension. The very makeup of the human soul, its balance, if you will, creates a situation in which it has little hope of glimpsing its everlasting essence within the intelligible realm. The human soul:

. . . tries to reach the same heights, but hardly succeeds; and sometimes the head of the charioteer rises above, and sometimes sinks below, the fair vision, and he is at last obliged, after much contention, to turn away and leave the plain of truth.[30]

Notice Plato tells us that the human soul "hardly succeeds"

in reaching the upper regions, though now and then the prize is won—albeit temporarily. This blessed state is reserved for the gods alone to enjoy in permanence:

> This is the life of the gods; . . . The divine mind in her revolution enjoys this fair prospect, and beholds justice, temperance, and knowledge of their everlasting essence.[31]

But if the soul has followed in the train of her god and once beheld the truth, she is preserved from harm and is carried round in the next revolution of the spheres; and if always following and always seeing the truth, is then for ever unharmed.[32]

We can see that at least some Greeks of Plato's day viewed in a positive sense the condition of man's soul within the natural law of cyclical regeneration. Indeed, if the human soul followed the "train of her god" and has seen truth, she goes unharmed and is enabled to return in the next revolution of the spheres. To be "unharmed," then, is to be able to resurrect in the next revolution of the spheres. In other words, at this time in Greek philosophical thought, some Greeks viewed reincarnation or bodily resurrection in a positive light and believed it to be the highest good man could hope for, considering the dual character of his nature, which precluded him from permanently dwelling within the intelligible realm enjoyed by the gods.

As in the Hindu model, the Platonic idea of reincarnation was progressive. Plato further informs us of the Greek belief that the mode of resurrection of the soul on earth depends on the degree of truth it glimpsed while in immobile eternity:

> . . . then she (the soul) takes the form of man, and the soul which has seen most of the truth passes into a philosopher or lover; that which has seen truth in the sec-

ond degree, into a king or warrior; . . . householder or money-maker; . . . gymnast; . . . prophet or mystic; poet or imitator; . . . husbandman or craftsman; . . . sophist or demagogue; . . . tyrant. All these are states of probation, wherein he who lives righteously is improved, and he who lives unrighteously deteriorates. After death comes judgment; the bad depart to houses of correction under the earth, the good to places of joy in heaven. When a thousand years have elapsed the souls meet together and choose the lives which they will lead for another period of existence. The soul which three times in succession has chosen the life of a philosopher or of a lover who is not without philosophy receives her wings at the close of the third millennium; the remainder have to complete a cycle of ten thousand years before their wings are restored to them. Each time there is full liberty of choice. The soul of a man may descend into a beast, and return again into the form of a man.[33]

The following points in Plato's teachings should be kept in mind throughout our later discussion of the beliefs and modifications imposed upon the Greek worldview by Pharisaic Judaism:

1. Plato conceived ideal existence to be within the intelligible realm (timeless state).

2. Ancient Greek society was hierarchically ordered as follows:

> Philosopher or lover
> King and warrior
> Householder or money-maker

THE ANCIENT WORLDVIEW / 43

Gymnast
Prophet or mystic
Poet or imitator
Husbandman or craftsman

Note that in Platonic Greek thought all castes were considered to be states of probation, and the philosopher or lover, king and warrior constitute the first and second-highest castes. The righteous (those who fulfill their caste requirements) improve. The unrighteous (those who do not fulfill their caste requirements) deteriorate.

3. Plato said the human soul has two tendencies. The immortal tendency is to soar upward into the heavens. The mortal tendency is to drop and settle upon the earth.

4. The gods (the divine mind) behold justice, temperance and knowledge of their everlasting essence. The human soul rarely succeeds to glimpse this fair vision. Even if it does, the encounter is brief, and the soul must eventually leave the plain of truth.

5. Though the human cannot remain in the intelligible realm eternally, if she has followed the train of her god and once has beheld the truth, she will be unharmed and will resurrect in the next revolution of the spheres.

6. Though the Platonic model held that there was judgment after death and each soul went to either "houses of correction" or "places of joy in heaven" according to the degree of its righteousness on earth (determined

by the degree of caste fulfillment), the Greeks did not believe in a concept of eternal punishment.

7. According to the Platonic model, after correction the rehabilitated soul could choose the mode of its resurrection on Earth. The soul had ultimate control of its destiny within the particular cyclical sphere.

8. According to Plato, the forms the reincarnated soul will choose to take on earth depends on how much of the truth it glimpsed while in immobile eternity.

9. Finally, Plato indicates that not even the soul of a philosopher who stood at the apex of the caste system could remain within the intelligible realm indefinitely.

We now turn to Chapter Three and an explanation of the worldview held by first-century Pharisaic Judaism. As we will see in Chapters Five and Six, Paul addresses the Jews directly in his letter to the Romans, and makes reference to certain ideas and beliefs of the Pharisaic Jews.

CHAPTER THREE

# THE WORLDVIEW HELD
# BY FIRST-CENTURY PHARISAIC
# JUDAISM

Pharisaism was a Jewish sect in existence prior to 70 C.E. which had some beliefs and practices similar to those of the ancient Greeks. In this chapter we will discuss the precise nature of the pre-70 Pharisaic worldview, which together with the pagan worldview was the immediate backdrop against which Paul's letter to the Romans was a direct response. This is important because Saul of Tarsus (St. Paul) was a Pharisee prior to his revelatory experience on the road to Damascus, which resulted in his conversion to Christ. Therefore, knowledge of the pre-70 Pharisaic worldview is fundamental to understanding Romans. To this end we must isolate those beliefs and practices that distinguished the Pharisees from other Jewish philosophical schools and sects.

Despite differences that exist within contemporary Judaism, today's Jews are often considered to be a homogenous or monolithic group sharing a basic overall worldview and approach to life. In the same way, many view ancient Judaism to have been a monolithic entity. Neither view is valid. Contemporary as well as ancient Judaism is and was composed of many groups holding diverse and even opposing points of view. According to Morton Smith:

> . . . Judaism to the ancient world was a philosophy. That world

*had no general term for religion.* It could speak of a particular system of rites (a cult or an initiation), or a particular
set of beliefs (doctrines or opinions), or a legal code, or
a body of national customs or traditions; but for the
peculiar synthesis of all these, which we call a "religion,"
the one Hellenistic word that came closest was "philosophy." So when Judaism first took shape and became
conscious of itself and its own peculiarity in the Hellenized world of the later Persian Empire, it described
itself with the Hellenic term meaning the wisdom of
its people (Deut. 4:6). To the success of this concept
within Judaism the long roll call of the wisdom literature bears witness. Further, the claim was accepted by
the surrounding world. To those who admired Judaism
it was "the cult of wisdom" (for so we should translate
the word "philosophy" that they used to describe it),
and to those who disliked it, it was "atheism," which is
simply the other side of the coin, the regular term of
abuse applied to philosophy by its opponents. (Italics
mine.)

Further,

It is . . . not surprising that Jews living, as Palestinian
Jews did, in the Greco-Roman world and thinking of
their religion as the practice of wisdom, should think of
the groups in their society which were distinguished by
peculiar theories and practices as different schools of
the national philosophy.[1]

Thus, prior to 70 C.E., several diverse schools of thought
existed under the auspices of Judaism. Pharisaism, the Jewish
sect from which much of Christian theology derived, was one
of these schools.

After the Roman destruction of Jerusalem in 70 C.E., all

other forms of Judaism virtually disappeared from the scene, leaving post-70 Pharisaism the undisputed representative of mainline Judaism.

In response to the destruction of Jerusalem, and possibly to the defection of some and/or many to the nascent Jewish/Christian sect, post-70 Pharisaism organized into two rabbinic schools. These schools were the conservative House of Shammai and the more liberal House of Hillel. The worldview of pre-70 Pharisaic Judaism from which Christianity derived is not easily accessible because the then existing ideas, beliefs and values have since been adapted and revised by rabbinical masters.[2]

Though all of Judaism was influenced by Greco-Roman culture, the beliefs and practices of the Pharisees in particular paralleled those characteristic of the ancient Greeks.[3]

Pharisaic piety was centered on the teaching of a philosophy that the Pharisees claimed was derived from Moses at Mount Sinai. The basis of their claim of authority rested on their insistence that they preserved a "chain of tradition" that was unbroken from antiquity down to their own day.[4] Smith says:

> Their claim to authority was put in the form of a chain of successors *by whom the true philosophy had been handed down.* Elias Bickerman ... has remarked that the Greek and Pharisaic lists differed from those of the priestly "philosophies" of the barbarians in being lists of teachers, not of ancestors. He also mentions, apropos of the "houses" of Hillel and Shammai, the fact that "house of so-and-so" is a regular form of reference to a philosophic school founded by so-and-so; and he showed that both the Greek and the Jewish philosophic schools justified their peculiar teachings by claiming accurate tradition from an authoritative master.[5] (Italics mine.)

Furthermore, Smith explains the relationship between

Pharisaism and ancient Greek philosophy:

> *Not only was the theory of the Pharisaic school that of a school of Greek philosophy, but so were its practices.* Its teachers taught without pay, like philosophers; they attached to themselves particular disciples who followed them around and served them, like philosophers; they looked to gifts for support, like philosophers; they were exempt from taxation, like philosophers; they were distinguished in the street by their walk, speech, and peculiar clothing, like philosophers; they practiced and praised asceticism, like philosophers; and finally—what is, after all the meat of the matter—they discussed the questions philosophers discussed and reached the conclusions philosophers reached.
>
> Here there is no need to argue the matter, for *Professor Wolfson, in his . . . classic study of Philo, has demonstrated at length the possibility of paralleling a philosophic system point by point from the opinions of the Rabbis.* Now one, or two, or two dozen parallels might be dismissed as coincidental: all men, by virtue of mere humanity, are similar and life presents them with similar problems; it is not surprising, therefore, that they should often and independently reach the same answers.
>
> But parallels of terminology are another matter, and here we come . . . to Professor Lieberman's demonstration that some of the most important terms of Rabbinic Biblical exegesis have been borrowed from the Greek. This is basic. . . . The existence of such borrowings can be explained only by a period of profound Hellenization, and once the existence of such a period has been hypothecated it is plausible to attribute to it also the astounding series of parallels which Professor Wolfson has shown to exist between the content of

philosophic and rabbinic thought.

In sum, then, the discoveries and research of the past twenty-five years have left us with a picture of Palestinian Judaism in the first-century far different from that conceived by earlier students of the period. We now see a Judaism which had behind it a long period of thoroughgoing Hellenization—Hellenization modified, but not thrown off, by the revival of nationalism and nationalistic and antiquarian interest in native tradition and classic language (an interest itself typically Hellenistic). *As the Greek language had permeated the whole country, so Greek thought, in one way or another, had affected the court and the commons, the Temple . . . the school and the synagogue.*

This period of Palestinian Jewish history, then, is the successor to one marked by great receptivity to outside influences. It is itself characterized by original developments of those influences. These developments, by their variety, vigor, and eventual significance, made this small country during this brief period the seedbed of the subsequent religious history of the Western world.[6] (Italics mine.)

Smith's characterization tells us much of the similarity with respect to the practices of the Pharisaic and Greek philosophical schools. The theory of the Pharisees was the same as that of the Greek philosophical schools. The teachers of both schools taught without pay, attaching to themselves particular disciples who followed them around and served them. They were supported by gifts, exempted from taxation, and were distinguished by their walk, speech and mode of dress. They practiced and praised asceticism. The Pharisees discussed the same questions, reached the same conclusions, and even used the same terminology as the Greek philosophers.

Smith's discussion leaves one unsatisfied. While Smith's characterization surmises that the theory of the two schools was the same, he does not tell us precisely what that theory was. Merely noting the superficial similarities of the Pharisaic and Greek philosophic schools does not explain their substantive similarities. In addition, it is one thing to know what the beliefs and practices of the Pharisees were. It is yet another to know why they held their beliefs and adhered to their practices. It is yet another thing still to know how cultures grounded in apparently different traditions could share common terminology and practices. Morton Smith's response to this last question has been to assume a thoroughgoing Hellenization of Pharisaism. However, that two cultures grounded in different traditions could hold terminology and practices in common down to minute detail strongly suggests the existence of a shared cross-cultural worldview indigenous to each culture, with which superficial similarity and cultural interchange is compatible. Such a common worldview could have been derived from prophets, seers, mediums and mystics indigenous to each group. It is unlikely that a culture, Pharisaic or otherwise, would adopt the modes, practices and terminology of another culture if fundamental compatibility did not exist.

A shared worldview between the Greeks and Pharisees would also explain the historical and political emergence and subsequent dominance of the Pharisaic school over other forms of Judaism within the Greco-Roman world after 70 C.E. It is more likely that a form of Judaism with similarities to the surrounding Greco-Roman culture at large would more easily ascend to prominence than a Jewish sect without such similarities. Our task, then, is to discover the underlying cross-cultural common ground on which the Pharisees and Greeks stood.

There are three sources on which we can draw for more specific information about the worldview held by pre-70 Pharisaism. The three sources are: (1) the Pharisaic *Tannaitic* literature, (2) the writings of Josephus, a first-century Pharisee and historian, and (3) the New Testament.

We will begin our quest for explanation of the pre-70 Pharisaic worldview with the *Tannaitic* literature.

## A. THE *TANNAITIC* LITERATURE

The *Tannaitic* literature is a prime source of knowledge about the Pharisees.[7] Like the writings of Josephus and the New Testament, it provides evidence for the construction of a definition of the pre-70 Pharisaic worldview. This worldview, like that of the Greeks, held that the soul was subject to a process of reincarnation that was governed by law.

The *Tannaitic* literature is not a single collection, but an array of highly diverse writings. It is composed of the *Mishnah*, the *Tosefta*, the *Tannaitic Midrash* and thousands of passages strewn throughout the *Babylonian Talmud* and *Palestinian Talmud*, a large portion of which were recorded anonymously.

The *Mishnah*, the most authoritative corpus within the *Tannaitic* literature, was promulgated around 100-110 C.E. by the head of the scholar class, Judah ha-Nasi (the Prince). It is primarily a collection of laws arranged into six major divisions that are further subdivided into chapters and sections. The opinions of individual scholars are frequently presented, although most of the laws are set down anonymously.[8]

The *Tosefta* is a collection of laws that differs from the *Mishnah* only in content. At times the laws are different from those contained in the *Mishnah*, though the form is not. Like the *Mishnah*, the *Tosefta* is almost exclusively a book of law.

The *Tannaitic Midrash* differs from both the *Mishnah* and the *Tosefta*. Although it contains law, this law is attached as a commentary to the *Pentateuch* (the five books of Moses). With the exception of Genesis and the first eleven chapters of Exodus, the *Tannaitic Midrash* is a collective, exegetical hermeneutical commentary to the *Pentateuch*.[9] Unlike the laws of the *Mishnah* and the *Tosefta,* which for the most part are arranged logically, the laws of the *Tannaitic Midrash* are frequently derived from biblical verses by resort to logical-deductive methods, and no effort was made to arrange the derivative laws in any kind of logical or categorical order.[10] Another marked difference in the *Tannaitic Midrash* is its inclusion of nonlegal material called the *aggadah* (lore). This nonlegal material seeks to derive doctrinal teachings by hermeneutic methods using the *Pentateuch* as its point of departure. Scholars do not consider the *Tannaitic Midrash* to be as authoritative as the *Mishnah,* even though the exegetes cited are the same as those cited in the *Mishnah* and the laws may be the same.

While the *Tannaitic* sources are diverse in form and unequal in authority, they nevertheless possess an intrinsic unity because they are the work of the same scholar class. Characteristics of this unity include anonymity of author, the citing of scholars, the nonexegetical legal form, the exegetical principles, the loyalties and the presuppositions. In short, the *Tannaitic* literature reflects, on unequal levels of authority and in different forms, the activity of an identical scholar class, albeit a class that continuously changed its laws and transformed its doctrines—the Pharisees.[11]

Biblical scholars have drawn on the *Tannaitic* texts as a prime source for information about the Pharisees.[12] However, they have faced many difficulties. They have been unable to comprehend the meaning of, or even to acknowledge, the "unwritten law," which is the source of Pharisaic power.[13] Furthermore, the *Tannaitic* texts contain law and lore that are infinite in scope, the oral tradition of which is reckoned in centuries.[14] The range for possible error for dating the *Tannaitic* literature is not less than 350 years, thus lending itself to subjective and arbitrary manipulation.[15]

Further complicating matters, the *Tannaitic* texts contain no systematic disciplined interest in history and, unlike the Bible, are concerned only with individual episodes, single events and disconnected moments. Historical continuity with respect to chronology or successive interconnected events is of no relevance. The literature embraces thousands of pages of law and lore, and while it was generated during centuries of tumultuous events (166 B.C.E.–200 C.E.), the texts remain oblivious to the passage of historical events or afford them scant notice. The literature never connects the events it addresses precisely in place or time or sets them in any historical continuum.[16] In short, the *Tannaitic* texts confound scholars with hidden treasures, offering only the barest clues as to where the locks may be found and subtle hints about the keys needed to unlock them.[17]

The two separate but interrelated clues found in the *Tannaitic* literature and relevant to our inquiry are its characteristic ahistoricty and the apparent scholarly confusion with respect to the meaning of the terms "Unwritten Law" and "unwritten law" as used in the texts. Ironically, one of the clues to understanding the *Tannaitic* texts is that very ahistoricity of the literature that has proven so puzzling to scholars.

The first clue is simply this: one of the characteristics of cultures that embrace a worldview of cyclical time and regeneration (reincarnation) is ahistoricity.[18] Therefore, the ahistorical character of Pharisaic literature supports the assertion that the Pharisees, like other peoples whose distinguishing philosophical characteristic was ahistoricity, believed in reincarnation.

The second clue, the ambiguous meaning of the terms Unwritten Law and unwritten law, hinges on the first—the ahistorical character of the *Tannaitic* literature. The two together suggest the possibility that we are faced with a more complex picture with respect to the Pharisaic meaning of the terms Unwritten Law and unwritten law prior to 70 C.E.

It is asserted that the pre-70 Pharisaic reference to the Unwritten Law (capitalized), which the Pharisees claimed was re-

ceived by Moses at Sinai, was, in principle, the Pharisaic counterpart to the aforementioned Greek Immutable Law of cyclical
time and reincarnation. It is further asserted that the Pharisaic
unwritten law (not capitalized, that law which was subject to
change, abrogation and/or restoration) was promulgated in light
of the immutable Unwritten Law and was contingent upon it.

Paul refers to "the law" in Romans, and the respective meanings
of Unwritten Law and unwritten law will become important in
the context of the illuminated version of Romans in Chapter Six.

The *Mishnah* is the most authoritative corpus within the
*Tannaitic* literature. Therefore, we will draw on *Mishnaic* texts
to obtain information about Pharisaic concepts regarding
resurrection and theology.[19] The following *Mishnaic* text illustrates the Pharisaic belief in the existence of more than
one world:

> All those who used to conclude blessings in the Temple
> used to say, "From everlasting." *But when the heretics per-*
> *verted the truth and said there is one world only*, they or-
> dained that they should say "from everlasting to ever-
> lasting." (*Ber.* 9:5)[20] (Italics mine.)

The Pharisees thus clearly believed that there was another
world. We are not told whether the world to which they refer
was thought to exist simultaneously with the world that is.
Neither are we told whether they believed that the world to
which they refer is like or different from the world that is.
However, reading the texts, it is possible to conclude that the
other world to which the Pharisees refer is not unlike the world
that is. It would be premature to draw conclusions at this point,
as they depend on texts as yet not analyzed.

Pharisaic belief in another world is clearly stated in the following *Mishnaic* text, in which the authority of Isaiah is cited in
support of Pharisaic claims.[21]

All Israel has a share in the world to come, as it is said (Isaiah 60:21), "And your people shall inherit the land. The branch of my planting, the work of my hands that I may be glorified." (*Sanh.* 10:1)[22]

The "other world" to which the Pharisees refer is yet to come. But it is implied in the text the world to come is very much like the world that is. The statement "And your people shall inherit the land. . . ." supports the possibility that the Pharisees believed that the Jewish people as a whole will inherit the land (*terra firma*) in the world to come. Scholarly confusion is evidenced by the comment by Rivkin: "There is no embarrassment here with the fact that the *Mishnaic* text says nothing of the world to come but only of the world that is." [23] It is asserted that the *Mishnah* says nothing of the world to come precisely because the Pharisees held the same belief about the world to come as the "believing" pagan. It appears that the Pharisees anticipated a return to a new and better life in the world to come—a world very much like the world that is!

Furthermore, the Pharisees believed in the centrality of knowing and following the written law of Moses as well as the oral unwritten law promulgated by the Pharisees (together, the "twofold law"), because of its influence on one's next life. Moreover, they believed that the purpose of following the twofold law was to make the soul good as well as to avoid sin (negative *karma*) lest one lose the opportunity for resurrection. These concepts are evident in the following *Mishnaic* text:

These are the things which a person eats the fruits thereof in the world, while the *principle remains enduring for him in the world to come*: Honoring father and mother, the doing of gracious acts, and the bringing of peace between man and his neighbor, but the study of the Torah outranks them all. (Peach 1:1)[24] (Italics mine.)

Within the context of belief in the Unwritten Law, the meaning of this text is simply that the individual reaps a good life in this world by honoring father and mother, doing gracious acts, bringing peace among men and studying the Torah (the written law of Moses). Moreover, the consequences of these things endure for him in the world to come (positive *karma*). There is no reason to assume that the world to come, the world anticipated by the Pharisees, was qualitatively different from the world that is. On the contrary, in the next world, the person is still governed by the principles that produced the fruits he ate in the last world (or life). The principles are constant between lives, and rewards in this life are rewards in the next.

The Jewish law, then, was the means by which a soul could enjoy renewed existence. The purpose of the Jewish law, i.e., to prevent the individual from sinning (incurring negative *karma*) and thereby losing the opportunity of a renewed existence, is inferred from the following text, which affords insight into Pharisaic theology with respect to those condemned to death:

> When the (condemned) was about ten cubits away from the stoning chamber, they would say unto him, "Confess," since it was the custom of those condemned to death to confess; for whoever confesses has a share in the world to come. (*Sanh.* 6:2)[25]

From the Pharisaic perspective within the context of belief in the Unwritten Law, this can only mean that disobedience of the twofold law can result in the loss of opportunity for resurrection and in the eternal punishment of one's soul. In other words, this particular *Mishnaic* text supports the view that only the good soul has the opportunity for return or resurrection. If one confesses his crime, the individual is guaranteed a share in the world to come, or resurrection into the new world to come and a new body. Of particular importance here is the affirmation of the Pharisaic idea that resurrection into a new body and the next world to come is not possible unless the individual dies relatively free from sin (negative *karma*).

Another crucially important point is the Pharisaic idea that if for some reason the sinner is unable to confess, upon his supplication, his own death can expiate the sins he committed during his lifetime.

> If the convicted one does not know how to confess, they say to him, "Say (the following): 'May my death be an expiation for all my transgressions.'" (Sanh. 6:2)[26]

The Pharisees considered it of paramount importance that one should die free of sin (negative *karma*). With this in view, they instituted ways in which a condemned sinner could erase the sin from his soul: confession and the offer of one's life in payment for his sins. As we shall see in Chapter Six, when Paul wrote that God allowed Christ's death to atone for the sins of all, he struck a chord familiar to the Pharisees.

Based upon analysis of the *Mishnaic* texts, we draw the following picture of pre-70 first-century Pharisaic belief in resurrection and sin:

1. The *Tannaitic* literature, a prime source of information about the Pharisees, is anti-historical or ahistorical in character. A characteristic of cultures that hold a worldview incorporating cyclical time is ahistoricity. Thus, it is likely that the Pharisees held a worldview incorporating cyclical time and cyclical regeneration.

2. The Pharisees believed in the world to come. There is no indication that "the world to come" expected by

the Pharisees was different in form from the world that is. Neither is there indication that life in the world to come was expected to be qualitatively different from life in the world that is. This supports the assertion that the Pharisees believed that souls reincarnated into the same world.

3. The Pharisees cited the *Pentateuch* (the five books of Moses) in support of their belief in resurrection. The Old Testament texts cited by the Pharisees describe states of being that are similar to those found in Greek philosophical thought regarding the natural law of the cosmos, or the natural law of cyclical time and bodily resurrection (the Immutable Law).

4. Within the context of belief in the natural law of bodily resurrection (reincarnation), the Pharisees believed that a residue of the acts performed in one's present life would carry over into one's next life in the world to come. Implicit in this belief is the idea that one's present life in some way reflects the natural law of justice through acts that were performed in one's past existence (or existences).

5. If the condemned confessed his crime (sin), it would be erased from his soul. He then had a share in the world to come, or an opportunity for resurrection.

6. If the condemned was unable to confess, his death (upon supplication) was considered to be expiation for his sin.

In conclusion, the *Tannaitic* literature's ahistorical character, the scholarly confusion with respect to the meaning of its terms Unwritten Law and unwritten law and its theological content all indicate that first-century Pharisees shared, in principle, the same worldview as their Greek counterparts, albeit a modified version. The shared worldview was belief in an Immutable Law (Greek)—the Unwritten Law (Pharisaic) of cyclical time and bodily resurrection (reincarnation) in a new world to come. An important difference, however, was the Pharisaic addition of personal responsibility to the mechanistic Greek worldview.

Though helpful, the picture drawn in the *Tannaitic* literature about the Pharisees is far from complete. Fortunately, we have the writings of Josephus, a first-century Pharisee and historian, to whom we will now turn for more specific information about first-century Pharisaic belief, practices and theology.

## B. JOSEPHUS (37 C.E.–100 C.E.)

The historical writings of Josephus greatly illuminate the worldview held by first-century Pharisaism. A discussion of these writings, along with clarification of the meaning of the terms unwritten law and Unwritten Law, support my thesis that the Pharisees held a worldview (the Unwritten Law) that was a counterpart to the ancient Greek worldview of cyclical regeneration (the Immutable Law). In addition, Josephus' work illustrates the profound influence of the Pharisees and their beliefs over both the leaders and the masses in the Roman first century.

Josephus was a Pharisee and a contemporary of Saul of Tarsus, who was a Pharisee who converted to Christianity (St. Paul). It is therefore reasonable to assume that Josephus and Saul of Tarsus shared a similar worldview prior to Paul's conversion on the road to Damascus.

Josephus' writings concentrate on political questions, and the theological points to which he alludes are primarily of a general character.[27] This is because it was not Josephus' intention to write a history of the Pharisees. He merely mentions the Pharisees in the course of narrating the history of the Jews in *The*

*Jewish War* and *Jewish Antiquities*,[28] and his references to them are infrequent and confined to events that followed the schism between John Hyrcanus and the Pharisees (134-104 B.C.E.). According to Josephus, the Pharisees played a major role in a rebellion against Alexander Janneus (104-76 B.C.E.) and in a subsequent reconciliation of the Jews with his wife, Salome Alexandra (76-67 B.C.E.). Following the death of Salome Alexandra, mention of the Pharisees in Josephus' works is sporadic. However, we are still able to extract information about them from sources that were available to Josephus.

Josephus' earliest reference to the Pharisees is found in *Antiquities*, where it was inexplicably inserted after quotations of a letter sent by Jonathan the Hasmonean to the Lacedaemonians. This seems to link the Pharisees to the Hasmonean epoch (167-76 B.C.E.).

> Now at this time there were three schools of thought (or ways of life, Haereseis) among the Jews, which held different opinions concerning human affairs; the first being that of the Pharisees, the second that of the Sadducees, and the third that of the Essenes. As for the Pharisees, they say that certain events are the work of fate, but not all; as to other events, it depends upon ourselves whether they shall take place or not. The Essenes, however, declare that fate is mistress of all things, and that nothing befalls men unless it be in accordance with her decree. But the Sadducees do away with fate, holding that there is no such thing and that human actions are not achieved in accordance with her decree, but that all things lie within our power, so that we ourselves are responsible for our well-being, while we suffer misfortune through our own thoughtlessness. Of these matters, however, I have given a more detailed account in the second

book of the Jewish History. (*Ant.* XIII:171-3)[29]

Josephus' reference is important because it indicates that Pharisaism is the leading sect by designating it as "the first" and because it sets forth the philosophies of the three schools of thought with respect to fate and free will. The Pharisees believed that certain events are the work of fate, but not all. The Essenes held that fate is mistress of all things. The Sadducees did not believe in fate.

The next time Josephus mentions the Pharisees, it is with respect to the split between them and John Hyrcanus, who was a leader of the time. John Hyrcanus took pride in being a disciple of the Pharisees. However, sometime during his high priesthood an incident occurred that was of such a serious nature that he abrogated the unwritten laws the Pharisees had established for the masses and abandoned them for the Sadducees. The uprising that followed the abrogation of the unwritten laws indicates the strong influence the Pharisees had over the masses and the importance of the unwritten laws.[30]

> ... At this Hyrcanus became very angry and began to believe that the fellow had slandered him with their approval. And Jonathan in particular inflamed his anger, and so worked upon him that he brought him to join the Sadducean party and desert the Pharisees, and to abrogate the laws which they had established for the people, and punish those who observed them. Out of this, of course, grew the hatred of the masses for him and his sons, but of this we shall speak hereafter. For the present I wish merely to explain that the Pharisees had passed on to the people certain laws handed down by former generations and not recorded in the Laws of Moses, for which reason they are rejected by the Sadducean group who hold that only those laws should

be considered valid which were written down [in Scrip-
ture], and that those which had been handed down by
former generations should not be observed. And concerning these matters the two parties came to have con-
troversies and serious differences, the Sadducees having
the confidence of the wealthy alone but no following
among the populace, while the Pharisees have the support of the masses. But of these two schools and of the
Essenes a detailed account has been given in the second
book of my *Judaica. (Ant.* XIII:288-98)[31]

Josephus makes it clear that the Pharisees are philosophers of
religion, advocates of pleasing God, instructors as to the just
way of life, teachers of justice and underwriters of virtue.[32]
Moreover, we learn that the Pharisees are lenient in matters of
punishment and are especially averse to taking human life.[33]

Of greatest importance is Josephus' explanation of the essential difference that divided the Pharisees from the Sadducees.
The root disagreement revolved around the authority of the
unwritten law.

The Pharisees claimed that the Unwritten Law had been
transmitted in unwritten form and hailed back to the "Fathers."
The masses accepted these laws as authoritative. The Sadducees
rejected the unwritten law on the grounds that only the written laws in the *Pentateuch* were binding.[34]

Thus, according to Josephus, fundamental differences over
the law divided the Pharisees from the Sadducees. Here is where
confusion regarding the meaning of the two terms (unwritten
law and Unwritten Law) begins to complicate analysis.

We are told that abrogation of the unwritten law that the
Pharisees had established for the masses caused them to hate
John Hyrcanus and his sons. But questions arise: What was the
overall context or worldview that prompted the Pharisees to
promulgate the unwritten law? Why was the unwritten law so

important to the masses? The Pharisees were philosophers of religion, advocates of pleasing God, instructors as to the just way of life, teachers of justice, underwriters of virtue, lenient in matters of human punishment and averse to taking human life—but why? What was it they believed that gave rise to these particular attitudes and actions?

If we are to discover the dynamics behind first-century Pharisaic beliefs and practices, we must determine the meaning that the terms Unwritten Law and unwritten law held for the Pharisees and the masses. I have previously posited that the Unwritten Law was the Pharisaic counterpart to the Greek Immutable Law of cyclical regeneration (reincarnation) discussed above, and that the unwritten law was promulgated in light of the Unwritten Law.

In academic scholarship, we see confusion with respect to the meaning of the terms Unwritten Law and unwritten law. Ellis Rivkin's confusion with respect to the meaning of the Law/law is reflected by the inconsistent way in which he alternates the upper and lower cases when writing about the Law/law throughout his book:[35]

> The Unwritten Law thus emerges from the pattern of action as the core of Pharisaism. Yet Josephus never tells us, nor does he explicitly draw on sources that would tell us, what specifically these laws happened to be. Nor does he enlighten us as to how they had been transmitted, or as to who the "Fathers" had been. He gives us no clue as to whether the Pharisees had some institution that preserved and administered these laws; nor does he inform us as to whether the Pharisees also legislated Unwritten laws.
>
> The only example of how an Unwritten law might differ from a written law is Josephus' reference to the fact that the Pharisees considered flogging to be a suffi-

cient punishment for calumny since the Pharisees, according to Josephus, were naturally lenient in matters of punishment. The implication is clear that the Sadducees would have meted out the death penalty to the slanderer of a High Priest.[35]

The interchange of the terms "Unwritten Law," "Unwritten laws," "Unwritten law," and "unwritten law" suggests the possibility that Rivkin, following a long line of scholarly misinterpretation, simply followed suit, thereby propagating the error of interpreting two discreet, yet related, concepts of law to be one and the same.[36]

It is submitted, *a priori*, that the terms Unwritten Law and unwritten law were held by first-century Pharisees and the masses to be discreet but related concepts, the former of which they shared with the Greek philosophers. Furthermore, the Pharisees called the components of sin, fate, and divine retribution, "God's Law of Justice." Placed within the context of a cross-cultural belief in the existence of an Immutable Law of cyclical time and reincarnation (bodily resurrection-Greek) and/ or God's Law of Justice (Pharisaic), the distinction between the terms Unwritten Law and unwritten law appears quite clear: The term Unwritten Law would refer (cross-culturally) to both the Immutable Law of cyclical time and bodily resurrection (Greek), and to God's Law of Justice (Pharisaic). The term unwritten law, which is uniquely Pharisaic, would refer to those mutable laws that the Pharisees promulgated and imposed upon the masses in light of their belief in the Unwritten Law.

Another source of confusion derives from the concept of the twofold law that, according to Pharisaic belief, included the written law of Moses (the *Pentateuch*) and the *paradosis*, which means "Tradition of the Fathers." Scholars have assumed that the unwritten Pharisaic oral law was the same as the Tradition of the Fathers, one half of the twofold law. In my view, *paradosis* was not the unwritten law, but rather the Unwritten Law, the cross-cultural certain knowledge of cyclical regeneration (reincarnation) handed down by mystics to various cultures from time immemorial. The Pharisaic unwritten law (oral law) was promulgated in light of this cross-cultural and overarching dynamic of the cyclical worldview.

The separate meanings of unwritten law and Unwritten Law can be illustrated further. The Pharisees thought the law to be immutable. Yet, evidence suggests that they considered neither the written law of Moses (the *Pentateuch*) nor their own unwritten oral law to be immutable. The following examples illustrate this point. The Pharisees altered the law of Moses when they determined the procedures the high priest was to perform on the Day of Atonement. In another instance they flew in the face of a literal reading of Num. 28:4 by their insistence that the costs of the daily sacrifice should be defrayed by the Temple treasury.[37] It is important to note that the Sadducees, unlike the Pharisees according to our argument, were literalists with respect to the Mosaic law. However, they followed the effective alteration that the Pharisees made to the Mosaic law when the Pharisees introduced the lunar-solar calendar.[38] In addition, the Pharisaic dictum "Holy Scriptures render the hands unclean" is not found in the law of Moses. These changes and additions with respect to the Mosaic law illustrate that the Pharisees did not consider the Mosaic law to be immutable.

As to the unwritten oral law of the Pharisees, many laws operative during the early years of John Hyrcanus were displaced by other oral laws.[39] Moreover, the unwritten oral law of the Pharisees was in constant threat of abrogation by this or that monarch. So the term Unwritten Law cannot be synonymous with the unwritten law of the Pharisees unless, of course, contrary to Pharisaic belief and practice, the unwritten law was immutable.

In view of the position that the Pharisees considered neither the written law of Moses, nor their own unwritten oral law to be immutable, to what law does the concept of immutability refer?[40] On the basis of the need to reconcile Pharisaic belief and action, it is suggested that the Unwritten Law to which the Pharisees referred was the same Immutable Law of the cosmos referred to by the Greek philosophers (see Chapter Two, Section C). Thus, the *paradosis*, the Jewish tradition that was inherited from the Fathers and transmitted orally, was the sure knowledge of the existence and dynamics of this immutable Unwritten Law. The mutable oral law was promulgated in light of the greater and immutable Unwritten Law. The Pharisaic law, mutable, is the unwritten law.

Later we shall see that the Pharisees interpreted sin, fate and divine retribution to be integral components of the Law that, according to Jewish tradition, was God's Immutable Law of Justice. If, as it is proposed, the Pharisees shared the Greek worldview of the Immutable Law in principle, and believed it to be one and the same as their Unwritten Law, they would be hesitant to perform an act (sin) in their present existence that would generate punishment in their present life or in the life to come. This concern explains the Pharisaic preoccupation with just action. Believing in the Immutable Law of Justice, they were hesitant to offend God lest they incur his wrath through his Law.

The structure of events following John Hyrcanus' death further confirms the view of the Pharisees as tenacious champions of the Unwritten Law and unwritten law. John had quelled the violence that followed his abrogation of the Pharisaic unwritten law[41] and his defection to the Sadducean camp. The hatred and sustained rebellion of the masses reemerged with the accession of Alexander Jannaeus to the throne and high priesthood as the Pharisees sought to recapture their authority.

The power of the Pharisees is illustrated in Alexander's deathbed advice to his wife, Salome (Alexandra), who was to become queen:

. . . she should yield a certain amount of power to the Pharisees, for if they praised her in return for this sign of regard, they would dispose the nation favorably toward her. These men, he assured her, had so much influence with their fellow-Jews that they could injure those whom they hated and help those to whom they were friendly; for they had the complete confidence of the masses when they spoke harshly of any person, even when they did so out of envy; and he himself, he added, had come into conflict with the nation because these men had been badly treated by him. "And do," he said, "when you come to Jerusalem, send for their partisans, and showing them my dead body, permit them, with every sign of sincerity, to treat me as they please, whether they wish to dishonor my corpse by leaving it unburied because of the many injuries they have suffered at my hands, or in their anger wish to offer my dead body any other form of indignity. Promise them also that you will not take any action, while you are on the throne, without their consent. If you speak to them in this manner, I shall receive from them a more splendid burial than I should from you; for once they have the power to do so, they will not choose to treat my corpse badly, and at the same time you will reign securely." With this exhortation to his wife he died, reigning twenty-seven years, at the age of forty-nine. (*Ant.* XIII:399-404)[42]

Thus, Alexander's deathbed advice attested to the power of the Pharisees, a power derived from the masses. As the rebellion had its roots in Alexander's ill treatment of them, a shift in policy to give the Pharisees a robust decision-making role was calculated to end the conflict. In return for such power, the Pharisees would give Alexander a splendid funeral, recognizing the legitimacy of the monarchy. In addition, they would convince the masses that Alexander had been a great ruler and rehabilitate his honor.

Josephus tells us that the Pharisees did just that:

> Thereupon Alexandra, after capturing the fortress, conferred with the Pharisees as her husband had suggested, and by placing in their hands all that concerned his corpse and the royal power, stilled their anger against Alexander, and made them her well-wishers and friends. And they in turn went to the people and made public speeches in which they recounted the deeds of Alexander, and said that in him they had lost a just king, and by their eulogies they so greatly moved the people to mourn and lament that they gave him a more splendid burial than had been given any of the kings before him. . . . As for the queen herself, she was loved by the masses because she was thought to disapprove of the crimes committed by her husband. (*Ant.* XIII:405-7)[43]

Josephus then tells how the Pharisees used their power:

> Alexandra . . . permitted the Pharisees to do as they liked in all matters, and also commanded the people to obey them; and *whatever laws introduced by the Pharisees in accordance with the tradition of the fathers had been abolished* by her father-in-law Hyrcanus, these she again restored. And so, while she had the title of sovereign, the Pharisees had the power. (*Ant.* XIII:408-11)[44] (Italics mine.)

The Pharisees, knowing what they wanted, had moved decisively to break up the anti-Pharisaic clique, which enjoyed Alexander's confidence. They appear to have had two aims: (1) to restore the unwritten law, introduced in accordance with the tradition of the fathers (the Unwritten Law), and (2) to crush opposition. The unwritten law, the Pharisaic oral law, was reintroduced with Salome Alexandra's support.[45]

The Pharisees also took other actions to consolidate their power. They released prisoners, brought back the exiled and were responsible for the death of many.[46]

The Pharisees were a particular group of Jews known for their piety and for their precise exposition of the law, even though it was sometimes contrary to Mosaic law. They did not appear to consider piety and administering the office of state a contradiction, nor did they see a contradiction in putting Diogenes to death and being the exact expositors of the law.

The Pharisees appeared to be amenable to building a strong nation, as they did not object to Salome Alexandra's concern with affairs of state such as hiring large numbers of mercenaries or doubling the size of the army. They were legal experts who sought to rule a people and were not averse to taking steps necessary to achieve their ends.[47] The Pharisees enjoyed deep loyalty and devotion among the masses. Beginning with the reign of John Hyrcanus and ending with that of Salome Alexandra, they affected the functioning of dynastic, political and military affairs.[48]

In addition to providing political information, the following excerpt from *War* provides another clue as to the source of Pharisaic power:

> Alexandra, . . . being herself intensely religious, . . . listened with great deference; while they . . . became at length the real administrators of the state, at liberty to banish and to recall, to loose and to bind, whom they would. . . . But if she ruled the nation, the Pharisees ruled her . . . and as she from superstitious motives always gave way, they proceeded to kill whomsoever they would. (*War* I:107–114)[49]

Alexandra listened with great deference to the Pharisees and always gave way to them from superstitious motives.

The theologically related term that emerges from Josephus' account is "superstitious."[50] What did Josephus mean when he said that Alexandra always gave way to the Pharisees from superstitious motives? We can deduce Josephus' meaning when he describes the Pharisees Samaias and Pollion, who shared a special relationship to Herod and impinged meaningfully on Herod's career through augury.

> When Herod assumed royal power, he killed Hyrcanus and all the other members of the Synhedrion with the exception of Samaias. Him he held in the greatest honour, both because of his uprightness and because when the city was later besieged by Herod and Sossius, he advised the people to admit Herod, and said that on account of their sins they would not be able to escape him. (*Ant.* XIV:175-176)[51]

The action of the Pharisee Samaias advising the people to admit Herod into Jerusalem because he foresaw that they would be unable to escape him because of their sins illustrates the meaning of the concept of sin within Pharisaic theology. Sin was a corporate matter, and sin begets retribution!

Josephus mentions the Pharisees again with reference to the trial of Herod for the unlawful killing of the insurrectionary leader Ezekias and many of his men. The Pharisee Samaias, "an upright man," urged the members of the council to convict Herod. Despite this fact, Pollion and Samaias were honored when Herod gained leadership of Judea because of Samaias' uprightness and because when later Herod and Sossius besieged Jerusalem, Samaias advised the people to admit Herod, saying that on account of their sins (the sins of the people), they would not be able to escape him.

When Herod had got the rule of all Judaea into his hands, he showed special favour to those of the city populace which had been on his side while he was still a commoner, but those who chose the side of his opponents he harried and punished without ceasing for a single day. Especially honoured by him were Pollion the Pharisee, and his disciple Samaias, for during the siege of Jerusalem these men had advised the citizens to admit Herod, and for this they now received their reward. This same Pollion had once, when Herod was on trial for his life, reproachfully foretold to Hyrcanus and the Judges that if Herod's life were spared, he would (one day) persecute them all. And in time this turned out to be so, for God fulfilled his words. (*Ant.* XV:2-4)[52]

The narrative provides a glimpse into pre-70 Pharisaic theology with respect to Pharisaic belief regarding sin, fate and divine justice. We see that culpability for sin was placed not on the individual, but on the group. We see too that the Pharisees believed that the commission of sin was inevitably followed by punishment that was divinely generated. Further, the instrument of punishment for sin (in this case Herod) need not be an upright individual or force of good.

Why did Herod spare Samaias and Pollion even though one of them had called for his execution? Undoubtedly, he was lenient partly because these Pharisees had secured and enhanced his power by siding with him at a crucial time rather than throwing their power behind the Hasmonean Antigonus. No doubt their influence made the difference. But, we might ask, what was the reason for their influence? What was it about the Pharisees that generated such loyalty from the masses? We have seen that the Pharisees believed in the influence of fate and that they viewed Herod as an instrument of justice through which the people would be punished for their sins. The masses must have embraced this concept of fate, sin and retribution. But why did they have such implicit trust in the Pharisees for knowledge in these matters?

The previous narrative provides a clue as to the reason why the Pharisees were considered authoritative in these matters as well as insight into their theology. According to this passage, the Pharisees possessed foreknowledge that they employed within the context of the dynamics of God's judgment. When Herod was on trial for his life, Pollion foretold that if Herod's life was spared, he would persecute all of them. God fulfilled his word in time. The Pharisees combined their concepts of sin, fate and divine retribution together with their powers of augury in an interdependent way.

I suggest that the Pharisaic influence over the masses can be explained by their position as keepers of the gnostic tradition in Judaism, and the related ability of some Pharisees to predict future events and couch these predictions in terms that struck fear in the hearts of the masses. This ability, together with the placement of these events within the cultural context of belief in sin, fate and retribution, inspired awe among the masses, guaranteeing their support in times of political crises.[53]

Josephus provides additional material for a definition of Pharisaic theology when he contrasts the beliefs of the Pharisees and the Sadducees in *War* and *Antiquities*:

> Of the two first-named schools, the Pharisees, who are considered the most accurate interpreters of the laws, and hold the position of the leading haeresis, attribute everything to fate and to God; they hold that to act rightly or otherwise rests, indeed, for the most part with men, but that in each action fate cooperates. Every soul, they maintain, is imperishable, but the soul of the good alone passes into another body, while the souls of the

wicked suffer eternal punishment. (*War* II:162-63)[54]

Moreover,

> Although the Pharisees believe that, by and large, all things are brought about by fate, they nonetheless allow some role for the human will. For they find it seemly that God should have allowed for some fusion of the council chamber of fate, on the one hand, and the virtue and vice of human conduct on the other.
>
> The Pharisees believe that souls are immortal and that men are punished or rewarded in the underworld in accordance with the virtue or the vice they practiced during their lifetime: eternal punishment being the lot of evil souls; the opportunity for resurrection the destiny of good souls. (*Ant.* XVIII 12-15)[55]

Josephus' narrative tells us that the "believing" Pharisee, like his Greek counterpart, held that there was a fusion between human conduct and the council chamber of fate. Like the Greeks, the Pharisees held that souls are immortal and men are punished or rewarded in the underworld in accordance with their actions during their lifetimes. Unlike their Greek counterparts, the Pharisees believed that the lot of evil souls is eternal punishment; the opportunity for resurrection was the destiny of good souls. Thus, Pharisaic and Greek beliefs were similar with respect to the immortality of the soul and the fusion of human action in the council-chamber of fate (Providence). They differed in that the Pharisees saw fate to be the instrument of God's justice, whereas the Greeks considered it to be a mechanistic process—a natural law.

Pharisaic belief that only the good soul would have the opportunity to resurrect and that the state of one's existence in the next life would be determined by virtue or lack thereof during one's lifetime resulted in a specific mode of Pharisaic behavior. This is apparent in Josephus' description of the social intercourse of the Pharisees:

> The Pharisees are affectionate to each other and culti-vate harmonious relations with the community. (*War* II:166)

> The Pharisees live modestly, forswearing luxury. They adhere devotedly to the doctrines which have been trans-mitted orally to them, holding to and prizing their own teachings. They show great respect to their elders, re-fraining from rashly contradicting what their elders have taught. (*Ant.* XVIII:12-13)[56]

The beliefs of the Sadducees differed markedly from those of the believing Pharisees and their Greek counterparts:

> The Sadducees, the second of the orders, do away with fate altogether, and remove God beyond, not merely the commission, but the very sight of evil. They main-tain that man has the free choice of good or evil, and that it rests with each man's will whether he follows the one or the other. As for the persistence of the soul after death, penalties in the underworld, and rewards, they will have none of them. (*War* II:164-165)[57]

The social intercourse of the Sadducees reflected their un-belief in the concept of an afterlife:

> . . . The Sadducees on the contrary, are, even among themselves, rather boorish in their behavior, and in their intercourse with their peers are as rude as to aliens. (*War* II:166)[58]

Thus far, Josephus' writings indicate that we are on the right track. There was more affinity between the practices of the philosophical schools of the Pharisees and the believing Greeks than between the practices of the Pharisees and the Sadducees. However, we are trying to show more than the existence of a similarity of practices between the Pharisees and the Greeks. We are trying to show that the Pharisees and the Greeks shared, in principle, the worldview of belief in the Immutable Law of cyclical time and bodily resurrection (Greek) and/or God's Unwritten Law of Justice (Pharisaic).

Josephus provides support for the above assertion in two key passages found in *Against Apion*. The first describes the reason why the Jews are loyal to Pharisaic law to the death; the second describes why suicide is repugnant to the Pharisees.

According to Josephus, Jews are loyal to Pharisaic law to the death because:

> For those ... who live in accordance with our laws the prize is not silver or gold, no crown of wild olive or of parsley with any such public mark of distinction. No; each individual, relying on the witness of his own conscience and the lawgiver's prophecy, confirmed by the sure testimony of God, is firmly persuaded that to those who observe the laws and, if they must needs die for them, willingly meet death, *God has granted a renewed existence and in the revolution of the ages the gift of a better life.* (*Against Apio*n II:218-219)[59] (Italics mine.)

The modern reader must be careful not to impose the Christian meaning of "a better life," that is, of eternal life, on the consciousness of first-century Pharisaism.

Recall that the broader Greek scientific worldview of the natural law of cyclical time and reincarnation held two views of time. Specifically, it allowed for (1) eternal life outside of time, and (2) immortality (resurrection or reincarnation) within mobile cyclical time. Consideration of the entire passage indicates that Josephus is referring to the Pharisaic belief in the latter of the two concepts. Further support for the view that Josephus wrote from a Pharisaic consciousness that integrated the Greek scientific worldview of the Immutable Law of cyclical time and resurrection (reincarnation) is evident by his use of the phrase "revolution of the ages," which is identical to the phrase "revolution of the ages" found in Plato's *Phadrus*. It appears, too, that Pharisaism incorporated the Platonic idea of the possibility of hierarchical reincarnation since Josephus mentions the hope of the "gift of a better life" from God as a reward for following the precepts of the Pharisaic law. The concept of hoping for a better life presupposes the possibility of a lesser life from which one could come and a better life to which one might go.

Uniquely Pharisaic, however, is the reference to God's part in the granting of a renewed existence and the gift of a better life to the individual who observes and, if need be, dies for the law. Uniquely Pharisaic too is the conceptual blending of God, law, justice, conscience and individual indebtedness to God for one's present life as well as individual responsibility for the status into which one would reincarnate in the life (world) to come.

Josephus also provides data that ties the Pharisaic worldview into the Greek worldview of belief in the Immutable Law of cyclical time and resurrection (reincarnation) when he explains why suicide is repugnant to the Pharisee:

> No; suicide is alike repugnant to that nature which all creatures share, and an act of impiety towards God who created us. Among the animals there is not one that deliberately seeks death or kills itself; so firmly rooted in all nature's law—the will to live. Know you not that they who depart this life in accordance with the law of

nature and repay the loan which they received from God, when He who lent is pleased to reclaim it, win eternal renown; that their houses and families are secure; that their souls remaining spotless and obedient, are allotted the most holy place in heaven, whence in *the revolution of the ages, they return to find in chaste bodies a new habitation?* (*War* III:370-375)[60] (Italics mine.)

This passage contains several concepts that leave no doubt that the first-century Pharisee, like the Greek, held a belief in the Immutable Law of cyclical time and resurrection (reincarnation).

The Platonic concept of the "revolution of the spheres" is again reflected in Josephus' phraseology the "revolution of the ages." Further, the Greek concept of hierarchical reincarnation is reflected in the Pharisaic belief that he who departs this life naturally wins eternal renown and that his house and family are secure. What can Josephus mean if he is not referring to a new and better earthly existence? Where else but on earth are individuals concerned with eternal renown and the security of their homes and families? Moreover, the Pharisee, like the Greek, believed that though the soul (only the good soul for the Pharisee) was "allotted the most holy place in heaven," the heavenly state was temporary. The souls would inevitably "return to find in chaste bodies a new habitation."

As a believing Pharisee, Josephus felt repugnance toward the idea of suicide. His warning to his friends against suicide, lest they risk losing their immortality (the opportunity to resurrect) within cyclical time, indicates the strong thrust toward this worldly existence inherent within Pharisaic philosophical thought. In view of Josephus' earlier statement that a renewed existence and a better life was a gift from God, his repugnance toward suicide is quite understandable.

Josephus' statement that Pharisaic and Greek institutions are

similar, together with the fact that many Greeks tried to adopt
Pharisaic laws, further supports the view that believing Pharisees and Greeks shared a fundamental worldview:

> From the Greeks we are severed more by our geographi-
> cal position than by our institutions, with the result that
> we neither hate nor envy them. On the contrary, many
> of them have agreed to adopt our laws; of whom some
> have remained faithful, while others, lacking the neces-
> sary endurance, have again seceded. (*Against Apion*
> II:123)[61]

What reason, other than a shared worldview, could explain
the apparent willingness of two culturally diverse groups to
cooperate in matters philosophical?

The importance of the Pharisaic modification to the Greek
worldview that only good souls are given the opportunity for
resurrection while evil souls suffer eternal punishment should
not be overlooked. It provides an explanation of the willingness
of the Pharisees to defend their laws even to the death as well as
the willingness of those Greeks who were concerned about
their status in the next life to adopt the constrictive Pharisaic
law. Most important for our understanding of Paul's letter to
the Romans, it is the concept within Pharisaism that shaped
the core from which Christianity evolved.

Josephus provides insight into the extremes to which the
Pharisees went to preserve their laws in contrast to the Greeks:

> We (in contrast to the Spartan) . . . notwithstanding the
> countless calamities in which change of rulers in Asia
> have involved us, never even in the direst extremity
> proved traitor to our laws; . . . The fact is that not iso-
> lated individuals only, but large numbers have frequently,
> in defense of the injunctions of their law, surrendered

in a body with their arms to the enemy. Has anyone ever heard of a case of our people, not I mean, in such large numbers, but merely two or three, proving traitors to their laws or afraid of death? I do not refer to that easiest of deaths, on the battlefield, but death accompanied by physical torture . . . To such a death we are, in my belief, exposed by some of our conquerors, not from hatred of those at their mercy, but from a curiosity to witness the astonishing spectacle of men who believe that the only evil which can befall them is to be compelled to do any act or utter any word contrary to their laws. (*Against Apion* II:228-238)[62]

Because the Pharisees believed that the evil soul suffers eternal punishment, they, unlike the believing Greek philosophers who viewed the Law mechanistically, went to great lengths to instill their law and doctrine within the consciousness of the Jewish masses. This sheds light on the Jewish propensity to view the people of Israel as a unity that would be saved *en masse*. Josephus, writing from the perspective of a first-century Pharisee, assumes that the unwritten law of the Pharisees derived from Moses.[63] Thus, he credits Moses with innovation of a Pharisaic system that informed the masses of the written law (law of Moses) and the oral (unwritten) laws of the Pharisees:

Our legislator . . . took great care to combine both systems. He did not leave practical training in morals inarticulate; nor did he permit the letter of the law to remain inoperative. Starting from the very beginning with the food of which we partake from infancy and the private life of the home, he left nothing, however insignificant, to the discretion and caprice of the individual. What meats a man should abstain from, and what he may enjoy; with what persons he should associate; what period should be devoted respectively to strenuous labour and to rest—for all this our leader made the Law the standard and the rule, that we might live under it as under a father and master, and be guilty of no sin through wilfulness or ignorance.

For ignorance he left no pretext. He appointed the Law to be the most excellent and necessary form of instruction, ordaining, not that it should be heard once for all or twice or on several occasions, but that every week men should desert their other occupations and assemble to listen to the Law and to obtain a thorough and accurate knowledge of it, a practice which all other legislators seem to have neglected. Indeed, most men, so far from living in accordance with their own laws, hardly know what they are. Only when they have done wrong do they learn from others that they have transgressed the law. Even those of them who hold the highest and most offices admit their ignorance; for they employ professional legal experts as assessors and leave them in charge of the administration of affairs. But, should anyone of our nation be questioned about the laws, he would repeat them more readily than his own name. The result, then, of our thorough grounding in the laws from the first dawn of intelligence is that we have them, as it were, engraven on our souls. A transgressor is a rarity; evasion of punishment by excuses an impossibility. (*Against Apion* II:173-178)[64]

Three important points emerge from the narrative. First, the laws promulgated by the Pharisees served as a practical tool of governmental organization. Second, the laws were promulgated for the express purpose that the people be guilty of no sin through wilfulness or ignorance. Third, it wasn't easy to be a Pharisee!

The Pharisaic system of informing the masses of the written and unwritten laws created an informed, unified and harmonious people of God:

> To this cause above all we owe our admirable harmony. Unity and identity of religious belief, perfect uniformity in habits and customs, produce a very beautiful concord in human character. Among us alone will be heard no contradictory statements about God, such as are common among other nations, not only on the lips of ordinary individuals under the impulse of some passing mood, but even boldly propounded by philosophers; some putting forward crushing arguments against the very existence of God, others depriving Him of His providential care for mankind. Among us alone will be seen no difference in the conduct of our lives. With us all act alike, all profess the same doctrine about God, one which is in harmony with our Law and affirms that all things are under His eye. Even our womenfolk and dependents would tell you that piety must be the motive of all our occupations in life. (*Against Apion* II:179–181)[65]

Apparently, first-century Pharisaic piety impressed Greek philosophers as well as the world at large:

> An infinity of time has passed since Moses, if one compares the age in which he lived with those of other legislators; yet it will be found that throughout the whole of that period not merely have our laws stood the test of our own use, but they have to an ever increasing extent excited the emulation of the world at large.
>
> Our earliest imitators were the Greek philosophers, who, though ostensibly observing the laws of their own

countries, yet in conduct and philosophy were Moses' disciples, holding similar views about God, and advocating the simple life and friendly communion between man and man. But that is not all. The masses have long since shown a keen desire to adopt our religious observance; and there is not one city, Greek or barbarian, nor a single nation, to which our custom of abstaining from work on the seventh day has not spread, and where the fasts and the lighting of lamps and many of our prohibitions in the matter of food are not observed. Moreover, they attempt to imitate our unanimity, our liberal charities, our devoted labour in the crafts, our endurance under persecution in behalf of our laws. The greatest miracle of all is that our Law holds out no seductive bait of sensual pleasure, but has exercised this influence through its own inherent merits; and, as God permeates the universe, so the Law has found its way among all mankind. Let each man reflect for himself on his own country and his own household, and he will not disbelieve what I say. (*Against Apion* II:281-284).[66]

Finally, it is noteworthy that the practice of adopting the laws of one nation over those of one's own apparently was commonplace in Josephus' day.

Indeed, serious proselytes are welcomed, since the ties that bind the community together are the laws, not birth. (*Against Apion* II:209-210)[67]

Such an attitude of openness with which individuals approached the concept of converting from one philosophical system to another further supports the assertion that the Greeks and Pharisees shared core beliefs. Moreover, the apparent differences between the groups do not indicate a difference in core belief, but are indicative of cultural differences that lead to variances in interpretation of how one should conduct oneself in light of the existence of a particular core belief.

In summary, Josephus' depiction of the Pharisees provides explicit and implicit data from which to draw a picture of first-century Pharisaism:

1. Pharisaism was one of several schools of thought under the umbrella of Judaism. It appears to have had great momentum as a philosophy as well as a political entity during the reign of John Hyrcanus (134–104 B.C.E.). After the fall of Jerusalem to the Romans in 70 C.E., Pharisaism emerged as the culturally dominant school of thought within Judaism.

2. The Pharisaic and Greek philosophical schools shared striking similarities. These similarities encompassed theory and practice as well as parallels in terminology.

3. The Pharisees taught a philosophy that they claimed was derived from Moses at Sinai. Their authority rested on their insistence that they preserved a "chain of tradition" (*paradosis*) from the "Fathers" that was unbroken from antiquity down to their own day. Evidence suggests that the "Tradition of the Fathers" was a sure knowledge of the dynamics of the Immutable Law of cyclical time and bodily resurrection (reincarnation) (Greek) God's Law of Justice/the Unwritten Law (Pharisaic). The term "Unwritten Law" refers to the Pharisaic counterpart to the Greek Immutable Law. Evidence also suggests that the Pharisees viewed the written law of Moses and the Pharisaic oral unwritten law to have been promulgated in light of the Unwritten Law.

4. The Pharisees, like their Greek counterparts, be-

lieved in the immortality of the soul and cyclical regeneration. However, unlike the Greeks, they held that only the good soul is given the opportunity to resurrect while the evil soul suffers eternal punishment. The Pharisees believed that the existence of an individual and the mode of an individual's resurrection in the life to come reflect the degree to which the soul of that individual attained righteousness in a previous existence. Implicit in this belief is the idea that justice prevails in the world despite appearances to the contrary.

5. Some Pharisees had the power of foreknowledge. The Pharisees combined their ability of foreknowledge with their ideas about sin, fate and retribution. This combination proved a potent force in winning the awe and support of the masses as well as the loyalty of "believing" monarchs.

6. The Pharisees organized places where the masses could congregate and hear both the written law of Moses and the oral, unwritten Pharisaic law. This was done specifically to prevent the masses from sinning through ignorance of the various laws.

7. The Pharisaic practice of organizing places where the masses could congregate and hear the written law of Moses and the oral, unwritten Pharisaic law created a unity of belief and practice among the Jewish people in matters pertaining to God and righteous conduct.

8. The Jewish masses, unlike the Greeks, took their law very seriously. This was probably largely due to the Pharisaic teaching that only the good soul is given the opportunity to resurrect, while the evil soul suffers eter-

nal punishment.

9. By the first century, many Greek as well as barbarian cities and nations embraced Pharisaic modes of belief and practice. This suggests that there must have existed a cross-cultural worldview within the context of which Pharisaic beliefs and practices were compatible with those of the Greeks. Josephus' writings indicate that the cross-cultural worldview was a belief in the Immutable Law of cyclical time and bodily resurrection/reincarnation (Greek), and/or the God's Law of Justice/The Unwritten Law (Pharisaic).

10. Though Pharisees and Greeks held that the good soul dwells with God (or within the intelligible realm), neither held that the soul remained with God indefinitely. Both cultures viewed bodily resurrection to be desirable and good.

A line indicating a fundamental conformity of worldview has been drawn beginning with the Hindu model through the Hebrew, Greek and Platonic models in Chapter One and first-century Pharisaism in Chapter Two. Each shared a cross-cultural worldview of belief in reincarnation, albeit each culture responded to the worldview according to its own traditions. We will now turn to our last source of information about the Pharisees, the New Testament.

## C. THE NEW TESTAMENT

Like the *Tannaitic* literature and the writings of Josephus, the New Testament provides insight into the worldview of first-century Pharisaism. But unlike these other writings, the New Testament records a cross-cultural revolution that began to coalesce among those first-century Greeks and Pharisees who believed in the Immutable Law (Greek) and God's Law of Justice/the Unwritten Law (Pharisaic). This change is described in the New Testament by the teachings of Jesus of Nazareth, who spoke of a radically new concept of resurrection. After Jesus' death, the converted Pharisee, Saul of Tarsus, preached the new concept of resurrection to the gentiles. Through Saul of Tarsus, and with the dawn of the Holy Roman Empire, the new concept of resurrection was destined to eclipse the old concept of immortality via cyclical regeneration as the culturally dominant worldview. As a record of this transition in process, the New Testament illustrates both the new and old concepts of resurrection that foil each other and thus provides a clearer understanding of each.

Like the *Tannaitic* literature and the writings of Josephus, the New Testament presumes, without explanation, a cross-cultural belief in the Unwritten Law (the Immutable Law) and God's Law of Justice. Despite this lack of direct mention, some aspects of the Pharisaic worldview and belief in reincarnation can be directly discerned from the text. Others are inferred.

The Gospel according to Matthew supports the existence of the pre-Christian Pharisaic view of resurrection in a depiction of a confrontation between Jesus and the Sadducees. Recall that according to Josephus, the Pharisees believed in resurrection, but the Sadducees did not. This difference in worldview was the source of constant animosity between the two groups. This animosity is reflected in Matthew by the sarcastic manner in which the Sadducees questioned Jesus about the resurrection, as well as the content of their questioning.

The questions the Sadducees ask Jesus reveal information about the Pharisaic belief in resurrection:

> The same day Sadducees came to him [Jesus], who say
> that there is no resurrection; and they asked him a ques-

tion, saying, "Teacher, Moses said, 'If a man dies, having no children, his brother must marry the widow, and raise up children for his brother.' Now there were seven brothers among us; the first married, and died, and having no children left his wife to his brother. So too the second and third, down to the seventh. After them all, the woman dies. In the resurrection, therefore, to which of the seven will she be wife? For they all had her."

But Jesus answered them, "You are wrong, because you know neither the scriptures nor the power of God. For in the resurrection they neither marry nor are given in marriage, but are like angels in Heaven. . . ." (Matt. 22:23-30)

But when the Pharisees heard that he had silenced the Sadducees, they came together. (Matt. 22:34)[68]

First, the Pharisees believed that the next life would be one of mortal or bodily existence, where individuals would be in a similar or same relationship with those with whom they had shared a past life. This is illustrated when the Sadducees ask, "In the resurrection, therefore, to which of the seven will she be wife? For they all had her."

Second, the Sadducees assumed that Jesus' concept of resurrection was the same as that of the Pharisees; thus they confronted him with the same arguments they had been accustomed to presenting to the Pharisees.

But Jesus had another kind of resurrection in mind, a resurrection that did not include rebirth into a renewed bodily existence. Jesus spoke of a new resurrection in which individuals neither marry nor are given in marriage, but are like angels in heaven. Careful analysis of these Gospel passages demonstrates that Jesus and the Pharisees ascribed to belief in resurrection, but that in this instance each referred to a different kind of resurrection.

Other passages illuminating the concept of resurrection held by first-century Pharisaism are recorded in Acts. These depict Paul being brought before the Jewish counsel by a Roman tribune curious to know why the Jews accused one of their own:

> But on the morrow, desiring to know the real reason why the Jews accused him, he unbound him, and commanded the chief priests and all the council (Sanhedrin) to meet, and he brought Paul down and set him before them. (Acts 22:30)

> But when Paul perceived that one part were Sadducees and the other Pharisees, he cried out in the council, "Brethren, I am a Pharisee, a son of Pharisees; *with respect to the hope and the resurrection of the dead I am on trial.*" And when he said this, a dissension arose between the Pharisees and the Sadducees; and the assembly was divided. For the Sadducees say that there is no resurrection, no angel, nor spirit, but the Pharisees acknowledge them all. (Acts 23:6-8)[69] (Italics mine.)

These passages indicate that first-century Pharisees believed in resurrection, angels and spirits. As a Pharisee, Paul would have held these same beliefs. In fact, as a follower of Christ converted from Pharisaism, it is likely that he held both the Pharisaic and Christian concepts of resurrection (this will be discussed in the section on Paul) and yet considered the Christian concept to be infinitely more desirable,[70] as it led to eternal life with God.

Finding himself in a tight spot in this particular public debate, Paul seized the moment and identified himself with the Pharisees and with the Pharisaic concept of resurrection. His diplomacy served his purpose, as the Pharisees and Sadducees began to argue, dividing the assembly.

The following incident is recorded in the Gospel according to John and involves Jesus' encounter with Nicodemus ". . . a man of the Pharisees, . . . a ruler of the Jews" (Jn.3:1). Jesus says to Nicodemus:

> Truly, truly, I say to you, unless one is born anew, he cannot see the kingdom of God. (Jn.3:3)

Nicodemus then said:

> How can a man be born when he is old? Can he enter a second time into his mother's womb and be born? (Jn.3:4)

What are we to make of this? Can it be that this instance of Jesus speaking to Nicodemus indicates that there were Pharisees in first-century Palestine who, unlike other Pharisees, did not believe in the concept of reincarnation?[71] What Nicodemus' question does indicate with certainty is that the concept of a man entering his mother's womb for a second time to be re-born was not only in existence during the first century, but was considered central enough to depict Jesus holding a discussion about it.

The following Biblical passage is recorded in the Gospel according to Mark. It concerns King Herod's curiosity about who Jesus was and further supports the view that the idea of bodily resurrection to a renewed earthly existence was understood among the Jews of first-century Palestine:

> King Herod heard of it; for Jesus' name had become known. Some said, "John the baptizer has been raised from the dead; that is why these powers are at work in him." But others said, "It is Elijah." And others said, "It is a prophet, like one of the prophets of old." But when

> Herod heard of it he said, "John, whom I beheaded, has been raised." (Mk.6:14-16)[72]

The speculation that Jesus might possibly have been the resurrected John the Baptizer or Elijah indicates: (1) that one of the meanings of resurrection during the first-century included the concept of the transmigration of souls, meaning that the spirit of a dead person (John the Baptist) could enter the body of a living person (Jesus of Nazareth), and (2) that one of the meanings of resurrection during the first-century included the concept of reincarnation (the rebirth of the spirit of Elijah in the body of Jesus of Nazareth). Finally, all of the above indicates that the New Testament was written within the context of, and is relevant to, belief in reincarnation and related concepts. Evidence from the above passage indicates that Jesus, his disciples, King Herod and some of the general populace were immersed in a cultural milieu that was well acquainted with ideas of the supernatural.

Another passage in Mark in which Jesus' knowledge with respect to the supernatural is depicted is when Jesus and his disciples are going to the villages of Caesarea Philippi. Jesus asked them:

> Who do men say that I am? And they told him, "John the Baptist; and others say, Elijah; and others one of the prophets." And he asked them, "But who do you say that I am?" Peter answered him, "You are the Christ." And he charged them to tell no one about him. (Mk.8:28-30)

Again, the evidence that some people believed that Jesus was John the Baptist, Elijah or one of the prophets indicates a first-century belief in reincarnation and the transmigration of souls. This particular passage has an added dimension. When Jesus asked his disciples who they thought he was, Peter answered, "You are the Christ."[73]

The testing of John the Baptist by the priests and Levites from Jerusalem is recorded in the Gospel according to John and further indicates that those to whom the persons and events recorded in the New Testament were relevant believed in reincarnation:

> Who are you? He confessed, he did not deny, but confessed, "I am not the 'Christ.'" And they asked him, "What then? Are you Elijah?" He said, "I am not." "Are you the prophet?" (Jn.1:19-21)

That some first-century Jews believed in reincarnation is again indicated in the Gospel according to Matthew. Though John denied being (having been) Elijah, Jesus states that John is (was) in fact Elijah:

> For all the prophets and the law prophesied until John; and if you are willing to accept it, he is Elijah who has come. (Matt.11:13-15)

Again in Matthew, Jesus states that John the Baptist is Elijah who has come:

> And the disciples asked him, "Then why do the scribes say that first Elijah must come?" He replied, "Elijah does come, and he is to restore all things; but I tell you that Elijah has already come, and they did not know him, but did to him whatever they pleased. So also the Son of man will suffer at their hands." Then the disciples understood that he was speaking to them of John the Baptist. (Matt.17:10-13)[74]

To conclude, the New Testament indicates the following regarding the first-century cross-cultural familiarity with and belief
in the supernatural with respect to resurrection and the transmigration of souls. First, there was belief in a concept of resurrection such that the disembodied spirit of the dead could enter the body of the living. Second, some Pharisees (not necessarily all) and the masses who followed them believed in reincarnation and referred to it as resurrection. Moreover, the New
Testament informs that the Pharisees believed that relation-
ships from one's past existence carried over into one's afterlife
(Matt. 22:23-28, Mk. 6:14-16). Third, Jesus understood the
Pharisaic concept of resurrection, which was reincarnation (Matt.
11:13-15, Matt. 17:10-13). Fourth, Jesus held a concept of
resurrection that was new and different from the Pharisaic concept (Matt. 2:29,30).

The New Testament as a record of cultural transition records
Jesus the man and Jesus the prophet. We see Jesus the man when
he acts and speaks in the present tense—when his words and/
or actions do not contradict the traditions and cultural context
in which he moved and taught. At these times, he expresses the
Pharisaic view of resurrection as well as other aspects of Judaism.

We see Jesus the Anointed One when he acts and speaks in
the future tense—when his words and/or actions can be partially or completely differentiated from the Jewish cultural milieu. During these moments he performed acts and made pro-
nouncements that flew in the face of Jewish tradition, such as
when he assumed the authority to forgive sins (the future Church
would assume this authority) and preached a new form of resurrection.

In summary, analysis of the New Testament indicates that
first-century Pharisees held the following beliefs:

1. The Pharisees believed in resurrection/reincarna-
tion.

2. The Pharisees believed that the next life would be one of mortal or bodily existence (reincarnation) in which individuals would stand in relationship to those with whom they had shared a past life.

3. The Pharisees believed that the soul of the dead could enter the body of the living (transmigration of souls).

4. The Pharisees believed in angels and spirits.

5. Jesus spoke of a new concept of resurrection: a resurrection in which "they neither marry nor are given in marriage, but are like angels in Heaven."

Thus, the New Testament, like parts of the *Tannaitic* literature and the writings of Josephus, supports the posited view of first-century Pharisaic belief. But the New Testament also records a point in time when Jesus of Nazareth emphasized a concept of resurrection different from that of first-century mainline Pharisaism.

The New Testament attests that Jesus embodied in word and deed a combination of concepts, some but not all of which were familiar to first-century Jews. Ultimately, as foretold, after his crucifixion and after the Gospel of his resurrection had taken hold within the broader Greco-Roman culture, the new concepts gained cultural ascendancy through the power of the kingdom of God, which is synonymous with the Holy Roman Empire and the Church.

How did this happen? A cross-cultural subculture had been simmering below the surface of paganism and Judaism for some time prior to the first century. At its core was a negative attitude toward the Immutable Law and God's Law of Justice. In some rare (and some not so rare) Jewish and pagan documents, we can see evidence of the existence of this subculture. Unhappy with the idea of incessant regeneration on earth and/or some other world similar to earth, these believers viewed the saving power of Jesus Christ as the means to break the cycle of sin (negative *karma*) and death.

We will now turn to Chapter Four, a discussion of select Jewish and pagan writings that indicate the existence of this pre-Christian subculture, a subculture that naturally embraced the gospel of Christ as a means of salvation.

# CHAPTER FOUR

# VOICES OF DESPAIR IN PHARISAISM AND PAGANISM

This chapter will discuss select Jewish and pagan writings that indicate the existence of a pre-first-century cross-cultural subculture of believers in the Immutable Law and God's Law of Justice. This subculture held at its core a negative view of the process of reincarnation. Unlike the culturally dominant mainline Greek and Pharisaic perspectives, this view held the cyclical process to be the "Wrath of God"—the instrument by which God judged the world. In his letter to the Romans, Paul reached to these people who viewed the progressive process of reincarnation as the Wrath of God. Their worldview fostered the flourishing of Christianity, which lifted their hearts by providing a way out of the cycle.

We will begin our discussion of this negativism as it manifested within Judaism. Having done so, we will proceed to discuss its pagan manifestation, including a discussion of the Gnostics.[1]

## A. *KOHELETH* (ECCLESIASTES)

The cross-cultural negative attitude toward the Immutable Law and God's Law of Justice that emerged in late antiquity is reflected in a certain malaise, weariness and wishful longing for things to be otherwise. One of the finest literary examples expressing Pharisaic sentiments of weariness, despair and futility

in light of God's Law of Justice is found in the Hebrew book
*Koheleth* (Ecclesiastes).

*Koheleth* is of a genre known as Wisdom Literature or Hebrew *Hokmah*, which includes the books of Proverbs, Job, Ben
Sira and the Wisdom of Solomon. It has been discovered that
Hebrew *Hokmah* reflects the broader Oriental culture-pattern
of Syria, Babylonia and Egypt. The greatest similarity exists between Hebrew and Egyptian Wisdom.[2] Like Hebrew Wisdom,
Egyptian Wisdom offers practical advice on life, narrates tales
of oppression, often purports to originate from a king or prophet
and is concerned with the transitoriness of life.[3] Interestingly,
Egyptian Wisdom suggests the source of tradition of the Stoic
philosopher and Roman emperor Marcus Aurelius. The Stoics
were pagans who believed in the circular recurrence of time
and in Natural Law, which predetermined events within cycles.[4]
According to Josephus, the Pharisaic School of thought had
points of resemblance to the Greek Stoic School.[5] This is significant because it suggests a basis on which to postulate that
Stoicism, Pharisaism and *Koheleth* shared a common worldview
from which their respective traditions derived.

The style and language of *Koheleth* reflect the latest stage in
the development of Hebrew and the text closely approximates
words found in the *Mishnah*.[6] Except for a small part of the
introduction and the epilogue, *Koheleth* was written in Hebrew
around 250 B.C.E. by a Jew living in Hellenistically (Greek)
penetrated Jerusalem who was familiar with basic Greek ideas.[7]

The title *Koheleth* is derived from the Hebrew word *kahal*,
which means community or congregation. The Greek equiva-
lent Ecclesiastes means a member of the *ecclesia*, the citizens'
assembly in Greece. Later *ecclesia* designated the Church. Some
translators render *Koheleth* as "the Preacher."[8]

Robert Gordis suggests that the two fundamental themes of
*Koheleth* are the essential unknowability of the world and the
divine imperative of joy. While these themes are indeed impor-

tant, they are referred to relatively few times in the text.[9] Moreover, they are eclipsed by the larger and much more frequently mentioned theme of the irony of life and man's misery "under the sun," which inevitably ends in death. Thus, in the *Koheleth* the themes of the essential unknowability of the world and the divine imperative of joy are secondary to the theme of the essential vanity (futility) of earthly existence.

The controversy over the canonization of *Koheleth* at the Council of Jamnia in 90 C.E. by the Pharisees (rabbinic Judaism) has puzzled scholars. The book consists of heterodox, skeptical material that apparently had been glossed in an effort to make it acceptable to orthodox readers, thereby rendering it acceptable for canonization. Even after the book of *Koheleth* was canonized, debate as to its canonical worthiness continued. The argument most widely accepted today is that *Koheleth* was canonized because the canonizers believed that it was written by the much-revered King Solomon.[10] Significantly, Gordis suggests that *Koheleth* took on the guise of Solomon as a literary ploy by which to make a point. I concur, but what is the point?[11]

The key to the interpretation of *Koheleth*, like that of the *Tannaitic* literature, the writings of Josephus and the New Testament, rests not only upon knowing its sources and content, but also upon understanding the author(s) worldview, presupposed and therefore unmentioned, in light of which the book has relevance. In the case of *Koheleth*, analysis is complicated by the following factors: (1) The contradictory points of view in *Koheleth* indicate a division of sources from which the book was written and (2) the canonicity of *Koheleth*, officially recognized at the Council of Jamnia in 90 C.E., was the subject of controversy between the two rabbinic (Pharisaic) schools of Hillel (more liberal) and Shammai (more conservative).[12] These added dimensions necessitate a multidimensional approach to the interpretation of the book, which must also consider the following: (1) the Roman destruction of the temple at Jerusalem in 70

C.E. and (2) the conflicts and historical events that existed internally within Judaism and externally within the larger pagan culture with which the contents of *Koheleth* interfaced before, during and even after the time of its canonization in 90 C.E.

First presented will be the presupposed worldview within the context of which *Koheleth* was written and had relevance as well as peripheral matters related to it. Then, bearing the worldview in mind, the passages in *Koheleth* that appear to contain skepticism and heresy in light of the presupposed worldview will be extracted and analyzed. Having done our homework in this regard, we may then present a likely source for the controversy long associated with the book of *Koheleth*, a controversy that came to a head at the Council of Jamnia in 90 C.E., as well as the reason for the work's ultimate canonization.

It is asserted that *Koheleth* was a Pharisaic subcultural and despairing response to the mainline Pharisaic worldview, which according to Josephus was not only belief in, but a joyful acceptance of the dynamic of God's Law of Justice (reincarnation). This despairing attitude is what rendered the book heterodox.

The identity of the speaker in *Koheleth* is important. The words of *Koheleth* are purported to derive from the mouth of no less a personage than King Solomon, and reflect the Pharisaic mainline worldview of belief in the Immutable Law and God's Law of Justice—with a twist.

The choice of the personage of the illustrious King Solomon as spokesman for this bittersweet view of God's law and the state of mankind under the sun is significant if one considers that: (1) the pagans and Pharisees shared the same worldview with respect to belief in the Immutable Law and God's Law of Justice and (2) the attributes traditionally ascribed to King Solomon in Jewish tradition were the same as those ascribed to the highest earthly manifestation of the soul possible in Greek tradition. These attributes were those of philosopher, king, lover and warrior. Recall that Plato held that the soul that had seen the most truth passed into a philosopher (or a lover who had philosophy). The soul that had seen truth in the second degree passed into a king or warrior. King Solomon, then, embodied the Greek (and Pharisaic) ideal of ultimate wisdom and earthly achievement. In view of this, what better choice than King Solomon to express the voice of believers who were grateful to God for the gift of life yet disheartened by the prospect of incessant birth and death?

Within the context of the Pharisaic worldview of belief in the Immutable Law and God's Law of Justice, the best that Solomon, already a philosopher, king, lover and warrior, could hope for was to return again as a philosopher king. Believing himself to have reaped his lot in life from a past existence, and knowing that fulfilling his current caste requirements would ensure his return to the highest possible human manifestation, a philosopher king, he proceeds to do what philosopher kings were destined to do—philosophize. Belief in the Immutable Law and God's Law of Justice is implicit in the following passage:

> So I turned to consider wisdom and madness and folly;
> *for what can the man do who comes after the king? Only what*
> *he has already done.* (Ecc. 2:12) (Italics mine.)

Gordis notes that this is a "difficult final clause," because it does not appear to make sense standing alone, nor does it appear to relate logically to the surrounding text.[13] However, it does make sense and relate to the text if one superimposes the Pharisaic worldview—belief in the Immutable Law and God's Law of Justice—together with the existence of Pharisaic law, which delineated the terms of right action toward caste fulfillment.

The *Catalog of Seasons* further expresses Solomon's belief in the fixed and, broadly speaking, predetermined and repetitive quality of life's pattern, in light of which nothing ultimately is gained by human activity:[14]

For everything there is a season,
and a time for every matter under heaven:
a time to be born, and a time to die;
a time to plant, and a time to pluck
up what is planted;
a time to kill, and a time to heal;
a time to break down, and a time to build up;
a time to weep, and a time to laugh;
a time to mourn, and a time to dance;
a time to cast away stones, and a
time to gather stones together;
a time to embrace, and a time to
refrain from embracing;
a time to seek, and a time to lose;
a time to keep, and a time to cast away;
a time to rend, and a time to sew;
a time to keep silence, and a time to speak;
a time to love, and a time to hate;
a time for war, and a time for peace.
What gain has the worker from his toil?
(Ecc. 3:1-9)

The following clauses indicate the tedium and repetition that in Solomon's view are endured by man under the sun:

What has been is what will be, and what has been done is what will be done; and there is nothing new under the sun. Is there a thing of which it is said, "See, this is new"? It has been already, in the ages before us. (Ecc. 1:9,10)

I know that whatever God does endures forever; nothing can be added to it, nor anything taken from it; God has made it so, in order that men should fear before

him. That which is, already has been; and God seeks
what has been driven away. (Ecc. 3:14,15)

The Platonic (and later Stoic) worldview of belief in the
Immutable Law/the Law of Nature (Stoic) is implicit in every
phrase. The uniquely Pharisaic modification to the cross-cultural worldview is implicit in the reference to a single God and
the inference that God's Law of Justice, which endures forever,
was made by God in order that men should fear before him.

Solomon offers many reasons for his disheartened attitude
with respect to existence "under the sun." Wisdom was highly
valued in Jewish culture, and Solomon observes that the acqui-
sition of wisdom has an ironic twist in that it causes vexation:

> I said to myself, "I have acquired great wisdom, surpass-
> ing all who were over Jerusalem before me; and my
> mind has had great experience of wisdom and knowl-
> edge." And I applied my mind to know wisdom and to
> know madness and folly. I perceived that this also is but
> a striving after wind. For in much wisdom is much vexa-
> tion, and he who increases knowledge increases sorrow.
> (Ecc. 1:16-18)

Irony accompanies the possession of wealth as well, for the
man who loves wealth is never satisfied:

> He who loves money will not be satisfied with money;
> nor he who loves wealth, with gain: this is also vanity.
> (Ecc. 5:10)

The purpose of money is to satisfy man's appetite. But man
remains empty:

> All the toil of man is for his mouth, yet his appetite is
> not satisfied. (Ecc. 6:7)

Often the wealthy man does not get to enjoy his money because he has many dependents:

> When goods increase, they increase who eat them, and what gain has their owner but to see them with his eyes? (Ecc. 5:11)

Others who are wealthy lack an ability to enjoy their wealth:

> There is an evil which I have seen under the sun, and it lies heavy upon men: a man to whom God gives wealth, possessions, and honor, so that he lacks nothing of all that he desires, yet God does not give him power to enjoy them, but a stranger enjoys them; this is vanity; it is a sore affliction. If a man begets a hundred children, and lives many years, so that the days of his years are many, but he does not enjoy life's good things, and also has no burial . . . (Ecc. 6:1-3)

Furthermore, even if a man has everything he desires and the power to enjoy it, he can lose it to chance:

> There is a grievous evil which I have seen under the sun: riches were kept by their owner to his hurt, and those riches were lost in a bad venture; and he is father of a son, but he has nothing in his hand. (Ecc. 5:13,14)

King Solomon then considers pleasure, concluding that it has no ultimate use and that the pursuit of pleasure is futile:

> I said to myself, "Come now, I will make a test of pleasure; enjoy yourself." But behold, this also was vanity. I said of laughter, "It is mad," and of pleasure, "What use is it?" I searched with my mind how to cheer my body

with wine—my mind still guiding me with wisdom—and how to lay hold on folly, till I might see what was good for the sons of men to do under heaven during the few days of their life. I made great works; I built houses and planted vineyards for myself; I made myself gardens and parks, and planted in them all kinds of fruit trees. I bought male and female slaves, and had slaves who were born in my house; I had also great possessions of herds and flocks, more than any who had been before me in Jerusalem. I also gathered for myself silver and gold and the treasure of kings and provinces; I got singers, both men and women, and many concubines, man's delight. So I became great and surpassed all who were before me in Jerusalem; also my wisdom remained with me. And whatever my eyes desired I did not keep from them; I kept my heart from no pleasure, for my heart found pleasure in all my toil, and this was my reward for all my toil. Then I considered all that my hands had done and the toil I had spent in doing it, and behold, all was vanity and a striving after wind, and there was nothing to be gained under the sun. (Ecc. 2:1-11)

Solomon did hold that some things in life were worth having more than others:

A good name is better than precious ointment ... (Ecc. 7:1) and ... wisdom excels folly as light excels darkness. (Ecc. 2:13)

Yet the same fate comes to all. Solomon concludes that life under the sun is really not worth living. It is a struggle from which nothing is gained because it must of necessity end in death. The following are some of the most vivid passages that express this view:

A good name is better than precious ointment; and the day of death, than the day of birth. It is better to go to the house of mourning than to go to the house of feasting; for this is the end of all men, and the living will lay it to heart. (Ecc.7:1, 2)

Everything before them is vanity, since one fate comes to all, to the righteous and the wicked, to the good and the evil, to the clean and the unclean, to him who sacrifices and him who does not sacrifice. As is the good man, so is the sinner; and he who swears is as he who shuns an oath. This is an evil in all that is done under the sun, that one fate comes to all. (Ecc. 9:1-3)

Then I said to myself, "What befalls the fool will befall me also; why then have I been so very wise?" . . . How the wise man dies just like the fool! (Ecc. 2:13-16)

For the fate of the sons of men and the fate of beasts is the same; as one dies, so dies the other. (Ecc. 3:19)

And I thought the dead who are already dead more fortunate than the living who are still alive; but better than both is he who has not yet been, and has not seen the evil deeds that are done under the sun. (Ecc.4:1-3)

I say that an untimely birth is better off than he. For it comes into vanity and goes into darkness, and in darkness its name is covered; moreover it has not seen the sun or known anything. (Ecc.6:3-5)

The above passages appear straightforward. Solomon believes all to be vanity (futility) since death comes to all. However, within the context of what we have learned about the Pharisaic worldview, death and rebirth is not final but continual. Following this line of thought, Solomon knows he will be reborn into the same futile state of existence that will inevitably again end in death. In Solomon's case, the best possible outcome is rebirth again as a philosopher king:

" . . . for what can the man do who comes after the king? Only what he has already done." (Ecc. 2:12)

Solomon is dog tired of the emptiness of life and implicitly the process of cyclical return. There's no doubt about it:

All things are full of weariness; a man cannot utter it; the eye is not satisfied with seeing, nor the ear filled with hearing. (Ecc. 1:8)

Generally speaking, it is human nature to believe that one will be happy once one has achieved everything one has hoped for in life. King Solomon, the epitome of worldly success, informs that nothing truly satisfies, not even the exalted position of philosopher king. Moreover, all ends in death. What hope, then, is there for the common man who toils incessantly for mere existence "under the sun"?

The following passage indicates that superficially it appears that justice does not prevail in the world:

There is a vanity that takes place on earth, that there are righteous men to whom it happens according to the deeds of the wicked, and there are wicked men to whom it happens according to the deeds of the righteous. (Ecc. 8:14)

Nevertheless, King Solomon has faith in the ultimate triumph of Justice, which according to the promise of mainline

Pharisaic theology is inherent in God's Law of Justice, if not apparent in the universe. (One reaps what one sows.)

> Then I saw the wicked buried; they used to go in and out of the holy place, and were praised in the city where they had done such things. This also is vanity. *Because sentence against an evil deed is not executed speedily*, the heart of the sons of men is fully set to do evil. Though a sinner does evil a hundred times prolongs his life, yet I know that it will be well with those who fear God, because they *fear before him*; but it will not be well with the wicked, neither will he prolong his days like a shadow, because he does not *fear before God*. (Ecc. 8:10-13) (Italics mine.)

"Solomon" knows that it will be well for those who fear before God. What does he mean? Implicit in the phrase "those who fear before God" is the Pharisaic concept of indebtedness to sin/negative *karma*. The debts for sins committed in one's present existence might be collected before the death of the sinner, or they might be collected in one's next life. Thus, "sentence against an evil deed is not executed speedily." Within the context of the Pharisaic worldview, the meaning of the phrase to "fear before God" could be that one should refrain from sin in one's present existence (before) for fear of God's judgment within one's present lifetime or the next (after).

Again, *Koheleth* reflects the Pharisaic mainline worldview when "Solomon" states that God's Law of Justice is inescapable:

> Rejoice, O young man, in your youth, and let your heart cheer you in the days of your youth; walk in the ways of your heart and the sight of your eyes. *But know that for all these things God will bring you into judgment*. (Ecc. 11:9) (Italics mine.)

The passages discussed in this section of *Koheleth* strongly indicate the presupposition by the author of what was shown in Chapter Three to have been the orthodox Pharisaic worldview that was characterized by: (1) belief in the Immutable Law and God's Law of Justice, (2) belief that justice prevailed in the world despite appearances to the contrary, and (3) belief that the opportunity for life (resurrection/reincarnation), one's lot in life and the ability to enjoy life were God's gifts, which were predicated on the degree of one's obedience to the Jewish law during a past existence.

Because man is destined to immortality, of a sort, within perpetual cyclical regeneration and cannot choose otherwise, and because he is subject to the Immutable Law and God's Law of Justice in light of which the Pharisaic (two-fold) law was promulgated, King Solomon counsels that one should enjoy what one has within the parameters of one's caste because one's lot is a gift of God.

> What I have seen to be good and to be fitting is to eat and drink and find enjoyment in all the toil with which one toils under the sun the few days of his life which God has given him, for this is his lot. Every man also to whom God has given wealth and possessions and power to enjoy them, and to accept his lot and find enjoyment in his toil—this is the gift of God. (Ecc. 5:18-19)

King Solomon advises moderation in daily life. He apparently thinks that moderation will prevent the accumulation of sin/negative *karma*. Interestingly, he advises against too much zeal in seeking to attain positive *karma* as well: "Be not righteous overmuch."

> In my vain life I have seen everything; there is a righteous man who perishes in his righteousness, and there is a wicked man who prolongs his life in his evil-doing.

Be not righteous overmuch, and do not make yourself over wise; why should you destroy yourself? Be not wicked overmuch, neither be a fool; why should you die before your time? It is good that you should take hold of this, and from that withhold not your hand; for *he who fears God shall come forth from them all.* (Ecc. 6:15–18) (Italics mine.)

In light of the hopeless state of mankind, doomed at best to immortality within the process of cyclical regeneration and death, at worst to eternal punishment, the epilogue emphasizes the inevitability of judgment and the importance of keeping God's commandments.

The end of the matter; all has been heard. Fear God, and keep his commandments; for this is the whole duty of man. *For God will bring every deed into judgment, with every secret thing, whether good or evil.* (Ecc. 12:13, 14) (Italics mine.)

Thus, the presupposed worldview within the context of which *Koheleth* was written and had relevance was mainline Pharisaism's belief in, and joyous acceptance of, the Immutable Law and God's Law of Justice, together with the Pharisaic law which was promulgated in light of the Immutable Law and God's Law of Justice. The passages in *Koheleth* indicating skepticism and heresy in light of the presupposed worldview have been extracted and analyzed. Generally speaking, these passages reflect an accepting but despairing view of life in general, which by implication included the Immutable Law and God's Law of Justice since it was its dynamic to which mankind was inextricably bound that maintained the perpetual life and death cycle.

We are now in a position to answer the heretofore puzzling

questions regarding why the book of *Koheleth*, which clearly contained heterodox ideas, was not consigned to destruction,[15] but was rather preserved for three hundred and forty years only to meet opposition to its canonization in 90 C.E. The answer lies in the interface of the heterodox contents of the book with events that occurred internally within Pharisaism and externally within the broader pagan culture prior to and during the first century.

It is asserted that the historical events that prompted the canonization of Hebrew Scripture as well as the controversy over the appropriateness of the book of *Koheleth* for canonization were the following: (1) the Roman destruction of Jerusalem in 70 C.E., which left the Jews without a temple and thus made it more important to preserve and interpret what had passed before[16] and (2) the nascent Jewish/Christian threat, which it is asserted, *a priori*, consisted of those Pharisees who despaired of both the Immutable Law and God's Law of Justice and the Pharisaic law promulgated in light of such law.

It must have been apparent to mainline Pharisees that *Koheleth's* despairing acceptance of the Immutable Law and God's Law of Justice, together with its irony that accompanied the attainment of the most exalted and fortunate position possible for man, had the potential to undermine mainline Pharisaism by fueling the fires of the new Judaism/Christianity.

We shall see that they were right!

The preservation of the book of *Koheleth* for 350 years despite controversy over its content indicates the presence, long before the Christ event, of a strong Pharisaic element that questioned the value of cyclical immortality and, by implication, the efficacy of the Immutable Law and God's Law of Justice espoused by mainline Pharisaism. The fact that the book of *Koheleth* was canonized in 90 C.E. indicates that at that time, the same strong opposition to the Pharisaic mainline worldview held sway within Pharisaic circles.

Pharisaism was not the only quarter from which voices of despair and resignation rang forth in light of the Immutable Law and God's Law of Justice. The same laments echoed in pagan sources in light of the Immutable Law.

Toward the end of antiquity, instead of admiration for the divine order originally found in paganism, we find expressions of melancholy, weariness and an intense feeling of anguish and servitude. Some pagan believers held that the inflexible order of time that periodically repeats itself without beginning or end was monotonous. They felt that their lives were not unique; they had lived many times before and might return many times again. History revolves around itself, and things are forever the same. The pagans saw life as controlled in a deterministic, pre-destined fashion by the position and movements of the stars and planets.[17] Because the Immutable Law is immutable and eternal, the rational approach is to submit and, in face of the inevitable, to cultivate frugal, self-sufficient wisdom (albeit with an aftertaste of bitterness).[18]

The Roman emperor Marcus Aurelius (121-180) was a Stoic, and he thus believed in the circular recurrence of time. Like King Solomon in *Koheleth*, Marcus Aurelius combined his belief with a keen and often-expressed sense of the transience and fragility of things and events. In *Confessions*, he muses over the vanity and nullity of man's state on this "clod of earth" that is the world. Still, he tries to "love" this poor and heavy destiny that is man's.[19]

To conclude, the book of *Koheleth* expressed the subcultural Pharisaic voices of despair and disillusionment with the process of reincarnation and, implicitly, life. Furthermore, there were pagan counterparts to these Pharisaic voices. The despairing view of existence "under the sun" and implicitly under the Immutable Law and God's Law Justice, in light of which the Pharisaic law was promulgated, flew in the face of mainline Pharisaism which construed life, the Immutable Law and God's Law of Justice and the

Pharisaic law in a positive way.

We have seen that some Pharisees as well as some pagans voiced despair in light of the Immutable Law and God's Law of Justice. However, these voices were mere whispers compared to the voices of the Gnostics, whose cries of mortal anguish were destined to usher in a new world order.

## B. *GNOSIS*, GNOSTICS AND GNOSTICISM

The Gnostics of the early Christian era were individuals who, no matter their mainline religious or cultural membership, shared a belief in and a distaste for the cycle of reincarnation. Furthermore, they understood that Christ was the means to break the cycle. The Gnostics shared in the subcultural despair outlined in Section A of this chapter, as well as an interest in mysticism. In his letters Paul used terms familiar to various Gnostic schools in order to share with them the new hope in Christ. This will be further discussed in Chapters Five and Six.

There is much confusion about the precise origin, definition and influence of Gnosticism. This confusion has been perpetrated in scholarly texts because of the failure to define and distinguish between the meaning and relationship of the terms *gnosis*, gnostic and Gnosticism.[20] Consequently, there is confusion about whether Gnosticism predated or antedated Christianity,[21] as well as whether Gnosticism was a heresy of early Christianity.[22] In order to clarify the confusion we must define the meaning and establish the relationship of the terms *gnosis*, gnostic and Gnosticism.

According to *Webster's* dictionary, the word *gnosis* is derived from the Greek. It means "knowledge" or "to know." It is a term that " ... implies superior wisdom; knowledge of mysteries or spiritual truth mystically acquired." *Webster's* defines a Gnostic as " ... one of a class of rationalists in the early Christian church; also any believer in Gnosticism." Finally, *Webster's* defines Gnosticism as a system of mystical religious and philosophical doctrines combining Christianity with Greek and Oriental philosophies, propagated by early Christian sects that were denounced as heretical.[23]

Writing from experience, I take issue with *Webster's* definition of a Gnostic. A Gnostic is any individual who has a gnostic mind. The Gnostic may have knowledge or experience with all or part of phenomena included under the definition of *gnosis*. The knowledge may or may not be confined in time and space, and it may or may not be situation-specific. The Gnostic is not necessarily a believer in reincarnation (though most are). He may be a deist, atheist or an agnostic. He may or may not adhere to a moral or ethical code.[24] He may keep his knowledge to himself, or he may join groups whose members share similar talents and interests. Some Gnostics conduct private psychic, astrological or numerological readings. Others write books or have books written about them.[25]

The knowledge of *gnosis* may occur out of the blue or as a result of practices that have traditionally been employed to induce the phenomenon. Such practices have included the refinement of character, meditation, fasting or the use of drugs. *Gnosis* can occur to anyone in any place at any time. Its occurrence and the knowledge it reveals may or may not make sense within a particular religious or cultural context, nor is it necessarily situation-specific.[26]

Historically, the visions, prophecies, teachings and lives of great gnostic minds have catalyzed significant cultural shifts.[27] Judaism and Christianity—indeed, all revelatory religions—sprang from the gnostic mind. The Old Testament references to the Holy One of Israel reflect the gnostic tradition of the mystic vision of the One (see below). In addition to references to the Holy One, the Bible also contains implicit or explicit references to lesser forms of *gnosis*. These include mental telepathy (1 Sam.15:19, Matt.9:3,4; 12:25), clairvoyance (1 Sam.15:20, Mk.11:2, Matt.21:1-3), "supernatural" healing (Matt.12:22; 15:21-28), foreknowledge (Mk. 11:2,3;

13:1,2; Matt. 24:1,2; 26:20-25; 26:33-35; 26:69-75; 1 Sam.10:1-9), mediumship (1 Sam. 28:3-19), foreknowledge communicated from the dead via a medium, (1 Sam. 28:15-19), astral projection (Ezek.8:1-8) and the sacred quality of dreams (Gen. 37:5-11; 40:5-23; 41:1-36). (This list is not all-inclusive.)

The word Gnosticism presupposes *gnosis* and Gnostics. I would expand *Webster's* definition (above) and assert that Gnosticism refers to various cross-cultural and (within particular cultures) subcultural pre-Christian Gnostic philosophical schools and cultic traditions that constellated around Gnostic/charismatic Jewish/Christian and pagan teachers after the Christ event.These cross-cultural groups consisting of Pharisees and pagans from the various traditions and/or mystery cults within the Roman Empire were distinguished from others not by their overall worldview, but rather by their attitude toward that worldview and the issues that they thought relevant to that worldview. It is asserted, *a priori*, that the bonds that the Gnostics shared in common were:

1. Belief in the Immutable Law and God's Law of Justice (reincarnation).

2. Abhorrence and/or a general distaste regarding the Immutable Law and God's Law of Justice and, by association, the Jewish law.

3. The belief that the Christ event was the means by which to attain salvation from the tyranny of the cycle of reincarnation.

4.Various degrees of giftedness with respect to knowledge (*gnosis*) and/or interest in the esoteric arts and sciences.

Consensus ended there. Differing opinions on issues relevant to the Christ event divided Gnostics on the group as well as the individual levels. The groups existed side by side, each stressing various forms of *gnosis* and teaching contradictory interpretations of the meaning of the Christ event and the nature of Christ.

*Gnosis* can be broadly divided into three categories, two of which can be further subcategorized. These are: (1) mystical union with the One, (2) prophecy (the foretelling of future events) and (3) the occult (esoteric) arts and sciences.[28]

1. *Mystical union with the One.* This form of *gnosis* cannot be subcategorized. It consists of an experience of self-awareness that leads to a mystical union with the One, which is referred to variously (depending on the mystical/gnostic tradition) as the Holy One, the One, Enlightenment, the All, God or the Saviour and/or the Christ. (This list is not all-inclusive.) The union experience has a timeless quality that cannot be communicated in words because, unlike the experience, language is sequential and time-bound. Mystical union with the One comes instantly, at one stroke, springing from the immediate perception of a transformed consciousness.[29] Mystical union with the One is the highest form of *gnosis* because the experience is not time-bound, cannot be subcategorized and cannot be taught.

2. *Prophecy.* This form of *gnosis* occurs in a vision, voice or idea and can be further sub-categorized as follows:

a. The knower loses consciousness and speaks words of which he is unaware.[30]

b. The knower is in a state of normal consciousness in which his vision is clarified. His understanding is instructed without any suspension of free will.[31]

c. The knower is given insight into past or future events while in a conscious state.[32]

d. The knower is given insight into future events while in the dream state. (Gen.37:5-11; 40:5-23; 41:1-36)

3. *The Occult Arts and Sciences.* This form of *gnosis* includes the following: healing, astrology, numerology, hypnotism, the hidden virtues of sound, love potions, aphrodisiacs, sorcery, magic, clairvoyance, talismans, seals, spells and strange mind states that can bring about possession and post-mortem experience.[33] (This list is not all inclusive.)

Prophecy and the occult arts are generally considered to be lesser forms of *gnosis*. There are two main reasons for this:

1. Prophecy does not necessarily relate to higher *gnosis*. Typically it predicts future events, which strictly speaking are time-bound and earth-bound.

2. The occult arts and sciences that relate to past, present and/or future events are time-bound. Examples would be tarot cards, astrology, numerology, palm reading, etc. This type of *gnosis* can be taught to a certain extent through practices that develop the psychic faculty.

Having defined the meaning and relationship of the terms *gnosis*, Gnostic and Gnosticism, we will proceed to examine the worldview, beliefs and practices held by some Gnostics before and during the early Christian centuries. While the variety of gnostic thought prohibits complete disclosure, it is possible to indicate the main features common to most Gnostic schools and relevant to our discussion of Paul's letter. As we will see in Chapters Five and Six, Paul, a Gnostic himself, makes references to some of these features as he appeals to the Gnostics in his Romans audience.

## THE ONE/GODHEAD/TRINITY

To the Gnostics, the One is eternal. That which is known of the One is derived from direct mystical experiences that are ineffable and inscrutable. The concepts of time, space, matter and substance cannot be applied to the One. It is nothingness and does not exist in terms of existence as we know it. It is beyond good and evil and cannot be considered in terms of any moral quality. In complete repose, it is before all origins and events.

Paradoxically, the indivisible and undifferentiated One contains three fundamental divine aspects. Despite the limitations of language in describing this paradox, attempts at explanation have been made. Some Gnostic schools explained the One in terms of a trinity of three persons within the unitary essence. These persons were equated with three fundamental divine aspects referred to as *Nous,* "mind," *Logos,* "word" or "reason," and *Ennoia,* "thought" or "idea." Other schools referring to the same concept in colloquial terms equated *Nous* with God the Father, *Logos* with God the Son and *Ennoia* with God the Holy Spirit. As we will see in Chapters Five and Six, Paul refers to these three gnostic concepts in Romans and other letters.

God the Father (*Nous* or mind), as distinguished from the One, is the active principle that manifested as a result of the movement of divine being. The other qualities of the One, pre-existence, indivisibility and self-begottenness, are associated with God the Father. He is uncaused yet causes all, unmoved yet moves all, sourceless yet the source of all. He needs nothing, yet all things need of him.

The Son (*Logos* or word) is divine, uncreated and of one substance with the Father yet paradoxically is begotten of the Father, before all worlds. Some Gnostic schools considered Him to be co-eternal and co-equal with the Father. Others distinguished between the Father and the Son, attributing divinity to the Father alone. However, most Gnostics held that the Son, though divine, uncreated and of one substance with the Father, is not self-begotten, but begotten of the Father before all worlds. The Son is God's revealed expression, or the word of God. In Gnosticism, the word manifested itself in the world as the Christ, the Lord's anointed one. Gnostics held that God's involvement with the world is through the Son and that man may experience the love of God only through the mediation of the Son.

The Holy Spirit (*Ennoia*, "thought" or "idea") is the presence of God, the exhorter and comforter. He is the tongue of God and shares in the qualities of both the Father and the Son. Some Gnostic sects gave the Holy Spirit a female personification. In any case, it was thought that those who spoke from God were moved by the Holy Spirit.[34]

Knowledge of the One could hold great significance in the destiny of the soul. Some Gnostic schools held that he who achieves mystical union with the One (the highest form of *gnosis*), regardless of ethical or moral considerations, is freed from the bondage of creation and becomes Christ, or anointed by the Lord. Others held that salvation is attained not by knowledge of the One, but by adherence to a moral code, by doing good works and by having faith in Jesus Christ.

A fundamental cosmological concept of many Gnostic schools was commonly known as emanation. Emanation related the creation of things in existence to a projecting forth of qualities from the divine Unity/Trinity. By a unique manifestation, God generated a paradoxical chain of being, forming a descending hierarchy of spiritual entities.[35] I have outlined the gnostic hierarchy, a mythology of sorts, below.

### THE HEAVENS

The heavenly region and the entities that inhabit it belong to the divine perfection. They make up the earliest and most pure manifestation of the emanatory process.

The celestial sphere contains various heavens that are hierarchically arranged and attended by corresponding angels. The highest heaven, sometimes referred to as the seventh heaven, is eternal and holy. It is the true heaven, the heaven beyond heaven. Only the "angels of the presence," the "angels of the throne" and "the angels of the chariot" serve in this supercelestial heaven. The word (manifested as the Christ) came from this heaven. Adam, the prototype of man, was formed in the fourth or perhaps the third heaven. St. Paul experienced the third heaven (2 Cor. 12:2), Enoch and Elijah went to the second heaven. The *archons* (evil angels) come from the first or lowest heaven.

Some gnostic cosmologies included multifarious paradises for the elect, which were considered to be lower heavens (not to be confused with the heavens of the divine realm). Included among them were the Fortunate Isles, the Elysian Fields, the stellar and planetary spheres and other traditional paradises of pagan mythology. These symbolized the passing pleasures offered to human beings by evil angels in exchange for worship and homage. These heavens are destined to be rolled up like a scroll at the end of time. (Isa. 34:4)[36]

### THE ANGELS

The word "angel" is a generic term that means messenger. It refers to those entities that emerged from the emanatory process. Angels are invisible and cannot eat or drink, but when they visit the earth, they may assume an apparently physical body. Their individual qualities, the regions they occupy, the dimensions in which they operate and the time span of their functions all exist independently and form links in the chain of emanation.

### THE AEONS

The word *aeon* designates a good angel. Originally, all angels were "good" and manifested those abstract qualities associated with the Father. The host of angelic entities included in the heavenly hierarchy are archangels, cherubim, seraphim, amens, voices, virtues, marks, guardians, splendors, reasons, authentics and others.

### THE HOROS (BOUNDARY)

Within the lower part of the heavenly region, sometimes treated as existing between the spiritual and the material realms, there is a region referred to as the boundary (*horos*). The *horos* conceals what occurs in the higher realm and admits only the elect. The *horos* is a point of paradox. It lies outside the cosmic system and as such is beyond time and space. It is closely associated with the *Logos* (word). A great *aeon* guards the *horos*, which is referred to variously as the Limit-Setter, the Across-Taker, the Guide or Leader, the Emancipator or the Redeemer.[37] Sometimes he is identified with Christ. A curtain stretches across the *horos* that bears the archetypal images or the original concepts of the *Logos* (word). Their imperfect distorted reflections exist as shadows in the phenomenal world below.[38]

The *horos* is referred to variously as a wall, a turnstile, a portal, a palisade. Because it is the region between the spiritual and material realms and protects against violation, it is known as the barrier, the frontier, the partition, the suburbs. The *horos* is encircled by a barricade of dazzling white light known as the Flaming Walls or the Ring-pass-not. The angels carry messages from the divine realm to mortals below via a long narrow bridge, the Rope of Angels.

Significantly, the cross, or *stauros*, a symbol known worldwide, is perhaps the most significant descriptive analogy used for this mystical boundary. Generally, the cross symbolized salvation through suffering. For some Gnostics the cross represented the crossbeam or yoke that the Son (*Logos* or word) willingly took upon himself and asked his followers to bear (Matt. 11:29). Other Gnostics viewed the cross as a stake or crossed beams for punishment.

Many mystical systems included a concept of a spiraling cruciform figure, signifying the transit point between the real (above) and the unreal (below). In the Greek system the soul stuff of the universe is referred to in terms of two circular strips joined together like the Greek letter *chi* (X). Similarly, the last letter of the Phoenician and Old Hebrew alphabets, *tau*, which was believed to be a supernatural protective emblem, is shaped like a cross. It is said that the enigmatic nature of the cross is alluded to in the Old Testament reference to the "line of confusion" (Isa. 34:11) and in the phrase "line upon line" (Isa. 28:13).

In Gnosticism, souls can enter into eternal life only through the cross, or *stauros*. It is the axis of a mighty vortex at which the cosmic order is reversed. It takes man from the unreality and emptiness of the lower world (flux, change), to the reality and fullness of the upper (changelessness). Without the *stauros*, or cross, men are held captive to time, fate and reincarnation. Through the *stauros*, man is redeemed.[39]

### THE UNIVERSE/WORLD

Some Gnostic schools held that the material order in which man lives emerged as a continuation of the emanatory process. As the process continued, degenerative elements manifested, becoming less and less perfect expressions of God and becoming more and more material. Thus, the heavenly and material realms are interrelated and contain a progressively graded series of beings. Other Gnostic schools held that the material order resulted from a fall that followed the exercise of free will. This view bears striking similarity to the Hebrew model discussed in Chapter Two. In this gnostic view, God created the *aeons* out of love and gave them the power of free choice. To implement this he withdraw his will from them, letting them determine their own destiny. The process of withdrawal (emptying) left a place for the exercise of free will. This void became the natural universe (dimension) of space and time that we know. Where the Father withdrew his will, evil prevailed. Love and Providence were superseded by the Immutable Law of reincarnation and fatality. Yet nothing can exist without God. Traces of His presence are evident in the mixture of good and evil, of dark and light, that constitutes the world.[40]

## THE ARCHONS

In contrast to the *aeons* and in constant opposition to them are the wicked, evil and disobedient *archons*.

Though there was considerable variation within gnostic thought regarding *archons*, most agreed that there was a fall of certain members of the angelic host. This event played a special role in the creation of the world and the fate of mankind. Among the fallen angels were Satan (Satanel); Adam (Adamel), the prototype of man; and the female *aeon* Sophia. The matter is a mystery, but each fell because of adherence to a primordial sin. Satan fell through pride, Adam fell through disobedience, and Sophia fell through curiosity.

Western orthodoxy included the gnostic tradition of the fall of Satan and Adam and excluded the fall of Sophia. In the Bible, words like "chief," "ruler," "prince," or "magistrate" are often used to translate the word *archon*.[41]

## SATAN/THE DEMIURGE

In the Bible, Satan, also referred to as the Demiurge, is the monarch of the demons and embodies all evil. His chief agents are death and Hell (Rev. 6:8). He is described as the lord of the universe, with the power to dispose of the world's goods (Luke 4:6). He is the god of this world (2 Cor. 4:4) and the old serpent (Rev. 12:9). In speaking of Satan, Jesus refers to him as the "prince of this world" (Jn. 12:31). In these contexts, the interpretation of "world" is "age," so that Satan is god of the present age.

The Gnostics advanced several theories for Satan's fall. In one account, boredom with his state caused him to rebel. In another he became jealous of the importance accorded Adam. Regardless of the reason, Satan revolted and was joined by a number of other *aeons*. They were all overcome and expelled from the heavenly region. In the Jewish gnostic view, Satan, desiring to emulate the Father, exalted himself above God (Isa. 14:13).

Some Gnostic schools were dualistic. Equating matter to be co-eternal with evil, they held that God the Father did not create the material order and is entirely remote from it. Instead, creation of matter was attributed to Satan, who formed it out of the substance that appeared in the place that God had vacated. In the void lay the potential of time and space, the integral elements of the phenomenal world. The Jewish cabalists teach that the void became filled with degenerate entities. It was their pollution, abortions and afterbirths that constituted the fundamental ingredients of matter.

Generally these believers held that Satan attempted to create a perfect and eternal world like that of the Father by trying to obtain the archetypes that were in heaven. Unable to do so, he proceeded to imitate divine perfection as best he could. Out of space he created the world and all living creatures which, like the beings of the heavens, formed a hierarchy of entities, albeit on the material plane. Time too, with its segments of seconds, minutes, days, seasons and ages, was made in imitation of the sacred ever-now that prevailed in heaven.[42]

Subordinate to Satan was Ialdabaoth, who represents the "fate" aspect of the cosmos. Subordinate to Ialdabaoth were lesser administrators, including the powers, principalities and other world rulers mentioned in the New Testament (Eph. 6:12). Some of these agents are responsible for the division of time and the dimensions of space. Others supervise the pathways of the stars, planets and constellations through which fate and destiny (*heimarmene*) are dispensed.

The elemental powers (Gal. 4:3), some good, some evil, rule various aspects of nature. As such they exercise control over the human body and its functions. The elements of earth, air and water are closely associated with terror, ignorance, grief and bewilderment. The earth element is physical matter and belongs to the Demiurge. The lower waters are the sources of the water element. As for the air element, St. Paul says that Satan is the "prince of the power of the air" (Eph. 2:2). The tyrannical spirits of the elements, star spirits and demonic powers guide the forces of nature, govern the passage and division of time and supervise temporal events. The Gnostics held that besides the elemental spirits who rule the natural order, there are also other unseen entities that try to influence man. Spirits, some good, some evil, dwell in man and struggle for possession of his soul. Others record what the individual thinks, says and does.[43]

## The Cosmos

Gnostics describe the cosmos created by the Demiurge in many ways. Generally, they held the cosmos to be geocentric. It is helpful to think of the earth as located at the center of eight transparent bubbles, each enclosing the other. The seven "planets" of the ancient world, the Moon, Sun, Mercury, Venus, Mars, Jupiter and Saturn, immediately surround the earth. These planets comprised the zones of the *hebdomad*. Between the bubble of the last planet and the outermost bubble of the cosmos lay the zodiac and all the fixed stars. This is the zone of the *ogdoad*, or "eight," and *Ialdabaoth* controls the powers exerted in this zone that dispense fate *(heimarmene)*. Enclosing the zone of the ogdoad, and encircled by the world serpent with its tail in its mouth, making eight zones in all, was the great firmament. The eighth sphere marks the end of the cosmos.

Contained in the cosmos are the visible natural world in which we live as well as an invisible dimension of incorporeal beings. These include etheric and astral entities, spirits, demons and all the dark powers and principalities that fall under the dominion of the "god of this world"[44] (2 Cor. 4:4).

### MAN

We will see when analyzing Romans that Paul refers to gnostic concepts relating to the fall of man. Adam (man), the archetypal progenitor of mankind, is central to the designs of God as well as those of the Demiurge. Conceived in the divine mind, he pre-existed in the upper world of light before he was born. Eve was created from him. The Son *(Logos)* formed man in the fourth (in some accounts the third) heaven in His own image and gave him dominion over heaven. Resplendent and androgynous, he was the pride of the Son.

In Gnosticism there are three explanations of how archetypal man lost his eternal life. Some Gnostics held that Satan was responsible for the fall. Others blamed Adam alone. In one version, Satan tempted Adam to fall into disobedience through Eve. As punishment God gave them fleshly bodies, or "coats of skins" (Gen. 3:21) and banished them to the world of Satan, where mortal generation and death began (Gen. 4:1, 2). In this way the soul of man became enmeshed in the plane of matter.

In another version, Satan made a physical image of man from the distorted form of the archetypal pattern of Adam, which was reflected from the celestial curtain onto the world below, and animated him by breathing upon him. This imitation of primordial man, unable to stand upright, crawled like a worm.

As a remedy, Satan decided to provide it with a soul. By enticing the spirit with earthly delights, he lured the spirit down from the heavenly realm and trapped it within the body of Adam.

In a variation on this last version, the Son, seeing this imitation of life wriggling on the ground, had compassion. He sent forth a spark of light, a soul, from heaven that enabled the man-plasm to stand upright. Even so, the spirit escaped bondage by passing out of the big toe of Adam's right foot or through his anus. At last, Satan was able to anchor the soul within the body, and the plasm was able to stand upright and develop limbs.

In the gnostic view, the soul cannot be removed from the heavens and immediately trapped within a gross material body because, even after it is incarnated in human form, it remembers its heavenly home and is reluctant to remain in such a degraded state. To ensure that the soul will forget its original bliss and be less reluctant to remain in its mortal state, Satan sees to it that each soul makes a gradual "descent through the spheres." First, it passes through the sphere of the stars. Each *archon* ruling this sphere engraves its seal upon the soul. These seals determine the nature and disposition of the particular individual. Second, it passes through the seven spheres of the planets. The *archons* ruling each sphere prepare a mask (*persona*) for it, so that it receives in varying degrees the astrological characteristics associated with each planet (the astrological signs). In this way the memory of heaven is gradually effaced and the soul is subjected to the authority of the planets, which thereafter rule its destiny.

Man receives intimations of his divine origin from time to time. He may experience this directly by revelation, or he may receive it from another who has had a revelatory experience. Paul understood the gnostic ideas regarding the divine light of the soul. Thus St. Paul urges, "Awake, thou that sleepest" (Eph. 5:14), "cast off the works of darkness and put on the armour of light" (Rom. 13:12). The world-ruling *archons* have a vital interest in preventing the liberation of the soul of man because the entire world-structure created by the Demiurge depends on the continued entrapment of the sparks of light that lie within mankind.[45] The concept of spiritual armour plays an important part in certain gnostic systems. Man is a warrior and must fight the *archons*, who are ever striving to weaken his armour and capture the light. He must fight for victory so that he might return to his own country.

## ESCHATOLOGY

To the Gnostic, the body disintegrates upon death and its components return to the elements of earth, air, fire and water.

All souls descend to hell for chastisement, purification and self-realization. Then there is a parting of the ways. The destiny of each soul is determined by the type of person that it became while imprisoned within a body on earth. Gnostics held that mortal man is made of three basic elements: body, mind and spirit. The essence of one or other of these elements predominates in each person, which establishes the person's type and determines his post-mortem destiny.

The man of flesh (*sarkikos*) is one in whom the body or carnal desires predominate. The body, because it is composed of matter, belongs to the works of the Demiurge and nature. It is the robe covering the psyche. The physical life and physical consciousness with which the body is endowed constitute the etheric body. This non-rational instinctive element (animal soul) is characteristic of all animals. Though he borders on eternal damnation, *sarkic* man is unaware of his need for salvation. He is deaf to the call that comes from the realm of light (Matt. 13:13, 14). He knows only the world of illusion and flux. His soul is shrouded in grave clothes. Upon death, *sarkic* man will not be saved. His etheric body is relegated to the Demiurge. After being swallowed and digested by a dragon-like *archon*, the soul is spit into one of many lower hells, where it suffers appropriate torments with other similarly damned souls. At times it is sent out as an evil spirit to afflict mankind.

The mind (psyche), regarded as female, governs the mental, intellectual or rational side of humanity. It is the outer covering or the vehicle of the divine soul. Mind and thought constitute the astral body and contribute to the ego or personality. Man alone among species possesses this rational element (human soul). The psychic man (*psychikos*) is one in whom the rational element predominates. As such his actions are self-determined— he is responsible for what he does. As the mind lies between the carnal and spiritual, psychic man can identify with the upper realm and be transformed, or with the lower and perish. He hears the call but chooses whether or not to listen (Matt. 13:13, 14). He must take care not to be misled by intellectualism and disbelief. Having free will, he tends to good as well as evil. He must choose the direction toward which he will move.

Upon death, psychic man has hope of salvation. If he listened and responded to the call of heaven during life, tipping the scales in his favor, he is sent to one of the milder hells. He may then be reincarnated as many as three or four times, and during these lifetimes he will have an opportunity for salvation. If he fails continuously, he ultimately shares the destiny of *sarkic* man. But if he continues to strengthen his faith, to do good works and to strive for knowledge (*gnosis*), he will ascend toward heaven through the spheres where he will face the hazards of the return journey.

The soul (*nous*), or pure spirit (*pneuma*), is regarded as male. It is composed of the divine essence and is termed the divine soul. The body is produced through sexual intercourse, but the soul does not spring from other souls. Souls are made by God for the bodies produced by human copulation. Descending from the heavenly realm, the soul is first blanketed by the garment of the mind and then wrapped in the shroud of the flesh, each of which is expendable (Matt. 5:40).

The spiritual or noetic man (*pneumatikos*) is one in whom the spirit dominates. He has spiritual understanding and responds to the highest aspirations of the soul. Recognizing the light, he aspires toward heaven. Upon death, *pneumatikos* or noetic man "is saved by nature" (his own nature). Free from the influence of fate and beyond the operation of sacred and moral laws, he is the "elect," the "perfect," "a saint." After passing through hell, where he is purged of his physical state, he proceeds heavenward. Like psychic man, noetic man must pass through several stages where he must contend with malevolent *archons* who will try to prevent his ascension through the next higher sphere. The first part of the journey is through the seven planetary spheres. Here he returns to the *archon* of each zone, where he had previously been endowed with evil inclinations. Second, he passes through the sphere of the stars, which also has its hostile *archons*. He must be able to answer questions, make the correct signs and pronounce the appropriate formulas. The Gnostic will have knowledge of these matters from instruction and ritual practice learned in his mortal state. Finally, the soul must trample the head of the *archon* Sabaoth as a sign of triumph over him. Now the soul is like an *aeon*, free of the delusion of ego, personality and psyche, and is ready to pass into the timeless divine sphere of the One and only God.

All Gnostics agreed on the unique status of noetic man. But they disagreed on the criteria that placed one among the "elect." For some, having experienced "enlightenment" or the "One" while in the body was a sure sign of resurrection or salvation. Indeed, many held that if a man did not attain such resurrection while in the body, he could not receive it after death. The Gnostic teacher Theodotus alludes to this view when he states that all members of the spiritual church belong to the "chosen race." In contrast is the gnostic view (early orthodox Christian view) that "outside the Church there is no salvation," which referred to the institutional Church and therefore allowed less breadth in the salvation process. The Christian position is that God calls to every soul and offers salvation through the Church. But the choice to be among the chosen is not with God, but with each individual who possesses free will to choose.[46]

Though the mind is partially and the body is completely under the domination of destiny, the soul can be a free agent if it can rid itself of the weakness of the flesh. Both the rite of baptism and the experience of *gnosis* can release man from the bondage of fate and achieve this end. In the gnostic view then, fate is affective until baptism. Astrology is no longer relevant to the baptized, for the writ of Ialdaboath ceases to run, and the individual is no longer subject to the Immutable Law of the cosmic agencies. Of course, the heavenly bodies continue to exercise power over the unbaptized. Though the Gnostics believed that the baptized soul is no longer subject to time after death, they nonetheless consulted the stars and drew lots to arrive at important decisions that were time-bound.[47]

### Evil and the Soul's Anguish

Some Gnostics believed that the anguish of the soul's incarnation and cycle of suffering in mortal form was a product of Satan. An explanation of the gnostic concept of evil, coupled with illustrations from Gnostic texts, support this proposition. The two main gnostic theories about the origin of evil are the Oriental (Persian, Zoroastrian, Manichaean) and the Occidental (Alexandrian, Palestinian, Syrian).

1. *The Oriental View:* In the beginning there were two supreme and co-eternal powers. Good (God) ruled the light. Evil (Satan) ruled the darkness. These two primordial principles are in everlasting opposition and exist eternally.

2. *The Occidental View:* Evil is not an absolute in itself, but arises out of the absence or weakening of the divine will.

Gnostics did not think of evil in terms of its manifestations, such as murder or adultery, but rather that evil or sin is the dynamic activity of Satan and his legions that gives rise to evil thoughts or deeds. Thus the sin/negative *karma* that instigates murder is wrath. Adultery is instigated by lust. This dynamic or generative force abides along with the good in man.[48]

For the Gnostic, time and matter are quintessential and inseparable elements of the pseudo-reality that is the world. This reality has its life in the heart of man that is inherently evil. Change the heart of man, and time, matter and mortal existence are no more. Indeed the word "heart" evokes the essence of Gnosticism.[49]

Two texts reveal the extent to which mortal existence was anguish for the Gnostic. One text is Manichaean,[50] the other Mandaean, and each expresses the deep longing of a bewildered and exiled soul.[51] Certain texts of the Manichees liken the process of reincarnation to the Hindu *samsara*; these texts view existence like a "growth of death."[52]

The following are passages from Manichaean hymns. The first three lines are from a "Psalm of Jesus," in which the son of the Primordial Man evokes all that he and every man endures in the hell that is this world. Note the references to previously described gnostic concepts, such as "powers and principalities," the dark elements of the visible and natural world, which Paul makes reference to in Romans:[53]

> Since I went forth into the Darkness,
> I was given a water to drink
> which (was bitter) to me.
> I bear up beneath a burden which is not mine.
> I am in the midst of my enemies,

the beast surrounding me;
the burden which I bear
is of the powers and principalities.
They burned in their wrath,
they rose up against me,
they run to (seize) me
like sheep that have no shepherd.
Matter and her sons
divided me up amongst them,
they burnt me in their fire,
they gave me a bitter likeness.
The strangers with whom I mixed,
me they know not;
they tasted my sweetness,
they desired to keep me with them.
I was life to them,
but they were death to me.... [54]

Further:

Deliver me from this profound nothingness,
From the dark abyss which is a wasting away,
Which is all torment, wounds until death,
And in which there is neither helper nor friend!
Never, never is salvation found here;
All is full of darkness . . .
All is full of prisons; there is no issue,
And those who arrive here are struck with blows.
Parched with drought, burned by torrid wind,
And no green . . . is ever found here.
Who will deliver me hence, and from all that wounds,
And who will save me from infernal anguish?
And I weep for myself: "Let me be delivered hence,
And from the creatures who devour one another!
And the bodies of humans, the birds of space,

And the fishes of the seas, the beasts, the demons,
Who will remove me from them and free me
From the destroying hells, without detour or issue?"[55]

This last poem, which is incomplete, refers to other terms Paul uses in Romans and other letters, such as "child of light" and "demons":

Child of the Light and of the gods,
Behold, I am in exile, separated from them.
My enemies fell upon me,
And carried me off among the dead.
Blessed be he and find deliverance,
Who will deliver my soul from anguish!
I am a god and born of the gods,
Glittering, resplendent, luminous,
Radiant, perfumed and beautiful,
But now reduced to suffering.
Hideous devils without number
Seized me and deprived me of strength.
My soul lost consciousness.
They bit me, dismembered me, devoured me.
Demons, yakshas and peris,
Somber inexorable dragons,
Repulsive, stinking and evil,
They made me see pain and death.
Roaring they rush upon me,
Pursue me and assail me . . . .[56]

The following Mandaean text expresses sentiments similar to those found in the texts of the Manichees:

In this world (of Darkness)
I lived for a thousand myriad years
and no one knew that I was there. . . .

The years followed the years,
the generations followed the generations:
here I was and they did not know
that I was living here, in their world[57]

and:

Now, O gracious Father, innumerable myriads
of years have passed since we were separated
from Thee![58]

Earthly existence perpetuates our slavery to time brought
about by our birth, as our earthly instinct to generate and mul-
tiply engenders new slaves, who in turn engender others, ad
infinitum. The Gnostics found unbearable the subjugation within
time, matter, the body, and the exposure to temptations and
their degradation. They believed that Satan instituted human
reproduction. Lust was Satan's most formidable contrivance, a
wonderful weapon for gaining captives to his kingdom of perpetual death. The Gnostics saw woman as a decoy whose womb
cries out to be filled. Conception was the descent into death
for some miserable soul.[59]

### JEHOVAH

Some Gnostics believed that Satan (the Demiurge), creator
of the cosmos and responsible for the doom of the cycle of
reincarnation, was Jehovah, the God of the Old Testament.[60] To
these Gnostics, Satan, or Jehovah, imposed the tyrannical Jewish law (in light of the Immutable Law) on his people, by which
they were kept earthbound. These Gnostics rejected the Greek
and mainline Pharisaic concept of salvation (resurrection into a
new body and a better earthly existence) by continuous and
necessary degrees[61] through the practice of morality and good
works.

Some Gnostics condemned the Old Testament because they

felt it contained elements that were only relevant to Jews. Others, criticizing the hymns, said that though some were partly inspired by Jehovah, most were adopted from non-Jewish peoples. The Commandments were similarly viewed. Some Gnostics claimed that the injunctions against murder, bearing false witness and adultery were common to most peoples in early times and thus not particular to the Old Testament. In contrast, these Gnostics rejected as ordinances of Satan aspects of the twofold law endemic to Judaism, such as the Sabbath observance, dietary regulations, circumcision, fasting and the like, on the grounds that they were primarily related to material ritualism and social observances. For these Gnostics, such concerns were time-bound and irrelevant to the superior world.[62]

Furthermore, for these Gnostics, the way to find God was not to preserve and execute the cosmic Immutable Law by obedience to the Jewish twofold law espoused by mainline Pharisaism, but rather to intervene and destroy the entire system.[63] They argued that salvation was attainable in this life and dependent upon knowledge alone. This knowledge was obtained by divine grace through the instantaneous revelation (*gnosis*) of the Saviour.[64]

The extreme hatred with which some Gnostics viewed Jehovah, the material order, the Immutable Law, the Jewish twofold law (promulgated in light of the Immutable Law) and the prophets wreaked havoc among the ranks of believers. While the Christian canon was being formed, some argued for preclusion of the Hebrew Scriptures (the Old Testament).[65] This position was unacceptable to others, who saw the entire pattern of Christian revelation and the legitimizing of Jesus Christ as the long-awaited Saviour to have been prefigured and foretold in Hebrew Scriptures. As a result, Marcion, a Gnostic from Sinope who championed the exclusion of the Hebrew Scriptures, left the Church of Rome in 144 C.E.[66] Untold others with similar ideas likewise went their separate ways to join or form new sects espousing their particular points of view.

## ANTISOCIAL BEHAVIOR

The revulsion that some Gnostic extremists felt toward the process of reincarnation, which they believed was instituted by Jehovah, resulted in antisocial behavior, including active participation in the world in a manner contrary to Jehovah's intent. The practices of Gnosticism ran the gamut between asceticism and libertinism, but the intent was always the same—to stop the process of cyclical regeneration.[67]

Gnostics who took the ascetic approach showed their contempt for Jehovah by spurning the pleasures the world had to offer. They reasoned that it would frustrate the Demiurge if one abstained from what he has made or instituted in order to keep man bound to him. Moderate ascetics frequently remained unmarried and avoided sexual activity. Strict ascetics left family and friends, renounced property and lived alone, devoting themselves to prayer and contemplation. The most drastic form of asceticism was voluntary castration.[68]

In contrast, libertine Gnostics showed their contempt through licentiousness. They believed that one should take note of the law of the Demiurge (the Pharisaic law) and then undermine it through deliberate excess or perversion. It appears that the rationale behind the theory of excess was that constant abuse of the Pharisaic law would desensitize the individual, thus rendering the conscience (heart) invulnerable. The libertine, like the ascetic, objected to marriage. However, unlike the ascetic, he preferred concubinage and prostitution because these were not permanent and, unlike marriage, generally did not lead to the procreation of human beings. If a woman became pregnant, the Phibionite sect would abort the fetus and smash it with a pestle and mortar. Then, after mixing it with condiments to avoid nausea, each member with his fingers would eat a morsel of the mangled fetus.

In order to nullify the commandment against adultery, some libertine Gnostics committed adultery. The males of the Levitici sect had intercourse only with men; others practiced sodomy with both sexes. Members of certain other groups did not consort with women but instead masturbated. Because intercourse with children did not lead to procreation, it was permissible. Some consumed the seminal fluid of men and the menstrual flow of women along with drugs in order to attain ecstasy. In a state of ecstatic frenzy they would stand up naked and smear the semen everywhere, praying that by this means they "may obtain free access to the presence of God."[69]

This concludes Chapter Four, which described the existence of a cross-cultural subculture prior to and during the first century. This subculture consisted of Pharisees as well as pagans (both of which undoubtedly included gnostic Pharisees and/or gnostic pagans among their ranks) who held a negative view of God's Immutable Law and the Immutable Law of Justice and, implicitly, the Jewish law. The degree of negativity toward such law ran the gamut from a despairing acceptance to outright anger, resentment and disgust. In some cases the negative view led to socially abhorrent behavior.

We will now proceed to Chapter Five, where we will discuss the socioeconomic and philosophical structure of the Roman Empire, the Jews within the Roman social order and the letters of the Apostle Paul, who, as we shall see, was indeed "all things to all men."

# CHAPTER FIVE

# THE CULTURAL MATRIX OF THE ROMAN EMPIRE

## A. THE SOCIOECONOMIC AND PHILOSOPHICAL MATRIX OF THE ROMAN EMPIRE

The Roman worldview also had the belief in reincarnation as a tenet. Understanding the socioeconomic and political structure of the Roman Empire is important to our inquiry because the nature of the Romans, as Paul's audience, is the explicit manifestation of implicit philosophical cultural assumptions. It follows, then, that the unmentioned philosophical assumptions of a culture can be deduced from its socioeconomic and political organization.[1] This chapter will illustrate how the work of contemporary sociology and archaeology supports the position that the Roman worldview was characterized by belief in reincarnation.

First, the progressive caste system of the Roman social structure reflects a belief in reincarnation. Sociological studies of the Roman Empire have shown that the fundamental criterion that determined class or rank on the Roman social ladder was birth or heredity.[2] The Roman social order consisted of seven categories, each of which was subcategorized into a hierarchy of ranks. These categories were:[3]

Language and place of origin

> Formal *ordo* (position in government)
> Personal liberty or servitude
> Wealth
> Occupation
> Age
> Sex

The household was subcategorized as follows:

> Male
> Female
> Parents
> Masters
> Slaves

Though these categories related specifically to Rome, similar criteria prevailed throughout the provinces.[4] There was little movement across social lines, nor was there expectation of movement among the Roman non-elite.[5] Moreover, though education, intelligence, skills, wealth and power were valued, they were not considered criteria by which to advance in social status.[6]

The determination of class or rank by birth or heredity, the rigid social categorization that allowed little movement across social lines, and the devaluation of individual attributes as a means of social mobility and classification indicate a Roman social structure based on a caste system not unlike that of Hinduism. It then seems likely that the Romans, like the Hindus, believed in reincarnation. This assumption is based on the logical deduction that cultures that share similar principles of social organization, though separate in time and space, are likely to share a similar worldview.

The nature of the trade and professional associations of Rome further support the notion that the Romans believed in reincarnation, and illustrate the extent to which this belief permeated everyday life. The purpose of these associations, though organized according to trade or profession, was unlike that of medieval guilds or trade unions which centered around business activity.[7] Inscriptional evidence indicates that although the Roman guilds were organized on the basis of trade or profession, they seem to have been purely social bodies, unconcerned with the particular business activities of their members.[8]

What, then, is the principle underlying the establishment of homogenous trade or professional organizations for purposes other than business? It appears that belief in reincarnation is the answer. If one's occupation, determined by birth, was thought to be a direct manifestation of the Immutable Law (pagan) or God's Law of Justice (Pharisaic) and indicative of one's invisible spiritual state, it follows that social organizations based on trade or profession would be organized to foster interaction among those on the same spiritual level. It also explains why these groups, though formed on the basis of trade or profession, functioned as purely social bodies. Furthermore, the formation of cultic associations of merchants and artisans who worshiped deities associated with their particular business or art[9] also indicates the caste mentality and implies a belief in reincarnation and its inextricability from occupation and spirituality. The coupling of business and art (trade) with corresponding deities indicates the strong connection thought to exist between one's occupation, one's lot in life and the divine order. The fact that these associations provided for the proper burial and commemoration of the dead[10] further supports this view.

The traditional social categories began to weaken during the late Roman Republic, making social advancement possible.[11] This disruption resulted in a complicated interweaving of class categories in which certain distinctions in status could override others. For instance, the inequality of the sexes could be overridden by the distinction between slave and free person. Thus tombstone inscriptions indicate the name of a freed woman before that of her husband who had remained a slave. Similarly, the name of a freeborn son (born to a free woman married to a slave) would be placed ahead of both mother and father.[12]

One's relative position within the categories of slave and freedman depended on the relative status of one's patron. Thus, imperial slaves and imperial freedmen as a group had greater opportunities for social mobility than others who were of the same caste but unconnected to the imperial household.[13] Unlike the rest of society, slave-born members of the imperial household married freeborn wives.[14] Other than in Caesar's household, it was more common for slave-born women to marry free men. Indeed, this was one of the most common means by which female slaves gained freedom, importance and status.[15]

The freed individual occupied a curious niche in the Roman social hierarchy. He was superior to the slave, but nevertheless obligated to his patron (former owner) in many ways, both legal and informal. Despite his freed status he was stigmatized because he was born a slave, and would carry this stigma to the grave despite any accumulation of wealth or other acquired insignia of prosperity.[16] This deep, almost obsessive sense of status consciousness also characterized higher levels of Roman society.[17]

The question arises: what was the cultural assumption with respect to which legal status was considered more important than material wealth? The answer is clear if one assumes belief in reincarnation, which equated birth, rank and social class with spiritual status—and by extension death and the afterlife. The inscriptions on tombstones indicating legal/social status and the means by which it was obtained[18] testify to this conclusion.

The picture that emerges of first-century Greco-Roman culture is, in principle, not unlike that of Hinduism. Both were philosophical and socioeconomic-cultic systems based on belief in reincarnation and the justice component that was believed to be integral to it.

The letter Paul wrote to the Romans was addressed to a community consisting mainly of gentile Christians. However, it is estimated that the Jews made up ten to fifteen percent of the total population of the Greco-Roman cities—in Alexandria, perhaps even more.[19] The Jews held a special place in Roman history, and there were converts to Judaism as well as ethnic Jews. Moreover, Saul of Tarsus (St. Paul), a Pharisee before he became a follower of Christ, had much to say about Jews in his letter to the Romans. Therefore, understanding the social status of the Jews within the Roman Empire is critical to our inquiry.

## B. THE JEWS WITHIN THE ROMAN SOCIAL ORDER

When Israel lost her independence at the Babylonian exile in the sixth century B.C.E.,[20] the prophets reestablished the old aristocratic order of the patriarchs. This order was gradually supplanted by the rule of the Sadducees, who were the priestly caste. Thus, Jewish society was organized hierarchically, with the high priest at its apex[21] and the invisible God as king.[22] All government functions, excluding the administration of justice (which remained in the hands of the priests) were executed by the foreign power; in this way, Israel ceased to be a nation and became a church.[23]

The Persian emperor Cyrus restored the Jews from exile and in 444 B.C.E. commissioned Ezra to establish the Jewish Church State. Therefore, Israel became at once a church and a national community. Israel derived its cohesion as a nation through preservation of its past traditions in rituals that included circumcision and the observation of the Sabbath.[24] This basic organizational structure prevailed through most of the first century.

The Romans destroyed the temple of Jerusalem in 70 C.E. The important thing for our inquiry is that like virtually all pre-Christian cultures before the destruction of the temple, Israel was organized according to the principles of the caste system. The differences between Judaism and other contemporaneous cultures lay not in principle or overall structure, but rather in criteria endemic to the traditions of each respective culture. For example, the emperor stood at the top of the Roman social order. Along with the other "gods," he was an object of worship. The imperial laws relevant to the Roman caste system flowed from the top, and the people were expected to obey them. Similarly, in Israel the high priest reigned supreme along with an imageless God whose law was relevant to the Jewish caste system, and this law was to be obeyed. This is reflected in Paul's statement that he was "as to the law a Pharisee" (Phil. 3:5).

After the Roman destruction of the temple at Jerusalem, the Jews were scattered outside of Palestine. The formidable task of the resulting Jewish diaspora communities was to maintain their integrity (caste requirements under the Jewish law) while simultaneously adopting and integrating those aspects of the Roman system that were socially and economically advantageous.[25] This explains why some, but not all, aspects of the social organization of the urban synagogue paralleled those of the Roman clubs, guilds and cultic associations.

The Romans classified the Jewish groups in each city as collegia. Like their Roman counterparts, Jews gathered in a particular place, a synagogue (*synodos*) for both cultic and social functions. They depended on wealthy and influential non-Jews as well as congregants who were rewarded by honorary titles like "Father" or "Mother of the Synagogue." Both the Jews and the Romans rewarded benefactors with inscriptions and special seats in their assemblies. They had officers with titles that imitated those of the city and also provided for the burial of their dead.[26] According to a tradition preserved in the *Tosefta*, special places were set apart in the Great Synagogue of Alexandria for guilds of blacksmiths, silversmiths, carpet makers, weavers and such. There is also evidence connecting guilds with synagogues in Hierapolis (Phrygia) and Corcyros (Cilicia). Stephen (St. Stephen) was a Hellenistic Jewish Christian associated with the Synagogue of the Freedman in Jerusalem (Acts 6:9), indicating that this synagogue was serving the caste of the freedman.[27] This illustrates the connection between spirituality and caste with respect to personal liberty and servitude and/or the trades.

The functions of the synagogues that were different from functions of non-Jewish collegia highlight the aspects of Judaism that could not be conceded without jeopardizing community cohesiveness. For example, the Jews avoided "idolatry" and maintained dietary rules and Sabbath observance.[28] Another difference was the automatic acceptance of membership in the synagogue for a Jew by right of birth without question of admission or enrollment. This practice illustrates the special spiritual status Jews acknowledged in one another because of the mere fact of having been born into Judaism. Moreover, membership was exclusive to Jews and proselytes. This was in sharp contrast to other collegia that were corporations with voluntary, open membership.[29] These practices of the Jewish collegia effectively prevented Jews from integrating with non-Jews or participating in civic cults; however, the Jews sought at every opportunity to acquire rights identical to those of citizens. As a result, some citizens developed an impression that the Jews were arrogant and self-righteous. These issues were the source of strained relations between the Jews and the local citizens.[30] Nevertheless, Judaism won admiration among many pagans, leading some to become sympathizers, proselytes or formal adherents to the synagogue.[31]

What could explain the apparent arrogance and self-right-eousness of the Jews? What could explain the attraction and avoidance syndrome operative between Jews and non-Jews? It appears that the answers lie in the cross-cultural belief in rein-carnation that existed during the first century. From this per-spective, the believing Jew considered himself and his fellows as a whole to make up a privileged caste—"The chosen people." Further, the Jews believed that this status was ordained by the will of the God of Israel. It therefore makes sense that Jews were accepted as members of the synagogue by right of birth. This perspective implicitly placed the Jews, as a group,[32] in a superior position to all non-Jews regardless of other social or caste considerations. Because the Jews did relatively well in terms of worldly success and status,[33] the truth of this spiritual superiority would have been confirmed in their own eyes as well as in those of non-Jews who also believed in reincarnation and the justice component inherent in the caste system.

Hypothetically then, if Jews were materially more successful than their pagan counterparts, believers in the caste system would conclude that the Jewish God and His law were responsible for the discrepancy. Along these same lines, it is also important to remember that according to Jewish tradition, the Hebrews were delivered from slavery (the lowest social caste) by Moses, who, it was believed, gave them the law of God by which they were made a people.

The shared perception that the Jews made up a privileged caste was undoubtedly the result of the cross-cultural belief in reincarnation and the justice component of the Immutable Law and God's Law of Justice, which decreed that one's lot in life was a reflection of one's spiritual status.

There are two ways in which a believing non-Jew could respond to the situation. The mean-spirited might respond with resentment and jealousy. The more ambitious and fair-minded might respond by trying to get in on the act. Wayne Meeks believes that the "imageless" worship, strict monotheism and strong cohesion of the Jews won admiration, sympathy and even converts among many non-Jews. James Dunn notes the " . . . understandable if exaggerated pride of the widespread desire among Greek and barbarian to adopt Jewish customs and laws."

I do not think it was an exaggeration. If having the spiritual status of a Jew was perceived to mean material prosperity in one's present life or in the life to come, it is perfectly understandable that there would be a "run" on Judaism during the time in which the Roman/Jewish caste system was in a state of collapse and caste/cultic crossing over was thus possible. I concur with Meeks' suggestion that sympathizers and converts saw that the worldly prosperity of the Jews coincided with the Jewish cultus and way of life[34] and understood such worldly prosperity to indicate that their cultus (which included the Jewish law) led to reincarnation into a better worldly existence. Thus, the Jewish God and the Jewish law, in the eyes of believers in reincarnation and its relationship to the caste system, were simply means to an end. Such believers felt that the Jews appeared to have the best system by which to reincarnate into a better life; therefore, it would be wise to follow it. This explains the appeal that the concept of one God and the Jewish law held for the pagan. Why else would anyone change his cultic practices and be willing to take on the yoke of the Jewish law?

As will be discussed in Chapter Six, it is asserted that those of the Roman Church who "called themselves Jews and boasted of their relation to God" (Rom. 2:17) were precisely those pagans who had adopted Judaism in the hope of receiving the benefits promised under the law (Rom. 2:7) but had fallen short of the mark (Rom. 2:21-24). This may explain why many non-Jews became sympathizers of Judaism as well as proselytes and "godfearers" (semiproselytes). The presence of "godfearers," those of pagan origin who lived as sympathizers on the margin

of the synagogues, and proselytes indicates that the Jewish social order, like that of the Roman Empire, was more flexible
than it had been in the past, when birth into Judaism was the
only means by which one was considered to be a Jew. It also
could explain why, contrary to popular belief, official Rome
was often evenhanded in its dealings with the Jews.[35] The believing pagan official who disrespected the Jewish caste system
was, in effect, undermining the system on which the Roman
Empire, indeed the whole world, stood. This is because the
worldview of reincarnation and the caste system on which the
hierarchy of Rome was justified was, in principle, the same as
that which justified the unique social status of the Jews.

By the first century the two cultures intermingled, especially
in the large cities of the Roman Empire. The extent of this
cultural interchange is indicated in the writings of Josephus
(see Chapter Three, Section B) as well as those of Philo, a first-
century Alexandrian Jewish philosopher (ca. 25 B.C.E.-40 C.E.)
who wrote a series of elaborate commentaries and paraphrases
on the *Pentateuch*: "He read Plato in terms of Moses, and Moses
in terms of Plato to the point that he was convinced that each
had said essentially the same things."[36] The comparison of the
teaching of Moses to that of Plato as well as Philo's reference to
"disembodied spirits" indicates that Philo believed that the
teachings of both Moses and Plato were grounded in belief in
reincarnation as well as other aspects of gnostic thought.

It has been demonstrated that during the first-century Pharisaic and pagan cultures interacted to a degree barely conceiv-
able from the modern perspective. A cultural interchange of
such magnitude could not have developed unless both cultures, despite traditions endemic to each, shared the same fundamental worldview. This worldview was belief in the Immutable Law (pagan) and/or God's Law of Justice (Pharisaic), which
is inextricably bound with belief in reincarnation.

## C. The Apostle Paul and the Churches
### "All Things to All Men"

We have outlined the cultural matrix within which Paul's letter to the Romans was written and to which it was a response. We now turn to an analysis of the person of Paul, his worldview and the worldview assumed by the churches to which he wrote. We will also see how Paul's letters reflect the presence of the cross-cultural reincarnation worldview, and contain references and ideas that speak directly to the beliefs of the Jewish, pagan and Gnostic people we have reviewed. Paul hears the anguish of all men, spreading the word that Christ has ended the cycle.

Innumerable scholarly attempts to answer the questions raised by Paul's letter by setting him against the background of various kinds of Judaism have failed.[37] This should alert us to the fact that something quite "other" and fundamental has been missing from analysis.

Paul was an immensely complex individual. He epitomized all aspects of the cultural milieu within which he preached his gospel. He also possessed extraordinary spiritual gifts. Any serious exegete of Pauline texts must bear this continuously in mind.

The earliest sources pertinent to Paul and the early churches are found in the New Testament. According to his own testimony, Paul was of the people of Israel, a descendant of Abraham, of the tribe of Benjamin, a Hebrew. As to the law, he was a Pharisee. He was circumcised on the eighth day according to the law and was blameless under the law (Rom. 9:3,4; 11:1, Phil. 3:5,6). However, Paul was no ordinary Jew. Recalling his former life in Judaism before his conversion, he says that he was so zealous for the traditions of his Fathers that he advanced beyond many of his own age among his people (Gal. 1:13,14).

As a defender of Judaism, he persecuted the Church violently and tried to destroy it (Gal. 1:13).

But Paul was distinguished from his peers in more than the quantitative sense, for he had the quintessential gnostic experience. According to his own testimony, the gospel Paul received did not come from man, but through a direct and instantaneous revelation of Christ (Gal. 1:11,12). Describing this experience, Paul describes being caught up to the third heaven (2 Cor. 12:2). He states that he did not know whether he was in or out of his body at the time (2 Cor. 12:3). He heard things that cannot be uttered (2 Cor. 12:4). After this, Paul did not confer with anyone, nor did he go to Jerusalem to confer with those who were apostles before him. Instead he went to Arabia and then returned to Damascus (Gal. 1:16,17).

It is on the basis of this obviously gnostic revelatory experience of the One, the Christ, the Son, the Saviour, and/or the Lord, depending on one's particular cultic tradition and frame of reference, that Paul, who never knew Jesus in the flesh, claimed the authority of an apostle of Christ, called by the will and grace of God (1 Cor. 1:1, Gal 1:15). Paul also stated that after Christ was revealed to him (Gal. 2:1,2), he went to Jerusalem by revelation and laid the gospel he had preached to the pagans before other Jewish/Christian leaders (Gal. 2:1,2).

Paul was therefore a Gnostic and a Pharisee. He was also a Roman citizen[38] familiar with Roman and Oriental customs and ideas.

Because of his eclectic and cosmopolitan nature, Paul was able to understand the perspectives and spiritual capacities of Jews and pagans and thus could effectively communicate with them. As a Gnostic, he could relate to those Jews and pagans who, like himself, were Gnostics—as well as to those who were familiar with gnostic thought.

Sociological studies about the urban environment of the Greco-Roman empire provide important clues about the overall worldview of the Pauline congregations. Language in particular is an excellent means to identify groups or movements. Language is also a means by which groups draw boundaries between themselves and "others."[39] Study of words and phrases used by Paul and understood by his audience illustrates that he was familiar with gnostic, Jewish, and pagan ideas of the Roman world he addressed. For example, the word "body" was commonly used as a metaphor for society in ancient rhetoric, especially by the Stoics. It was adopted by Jewish writers with reference to Israel. Paul adopts it and speaks of the Church as "the body of Christ" (1 Cor. 12:12-27).[40]

Pagan clubs and cult associations, as well as Jewish organizations, used family terms such as "brother" (1 Thess. 4:6) and "sister," "children" (Gal.4:19, 1 Cor. 4:14, 2 Cor. 6:13, 12:14), "child" (Philem. 10, 1 Cor. 4:17), "son," "father" (Phil. 2:22) "children of God" (Rom. 8:16,21; 9:8, Phil. 2:15), and "sons of God" (Gal. 3:26) as well as the notion of adoption.[41]

Analysis reveals that Paul's letters are replete with key words and phrases drawn from Jewish and/or pagan gnostic thought which have been discussed. Included among these are "saints" or "holy ones" (1 Cor. 1:2; 2 Cor. 1:1; Phil. 1:1; Rom. 1:7), the "elect" (Rom. 8:33), the "chosen" (1 Thess. 1:4; 1 Cor. 1:27), "wake from sleep" (Rom. 13:11), "making no provision for the flesh to gratify its desires" (Rom. 13:14), "Satan" (Rom. 16:20), "death, life, principalities, powers, height and depth" (Rom. 8; 38, 39), "angels" (Rom. 8:38, 1 Cor. 6:3), "demons" (1 Cor. 10:20,21), the "third heaven" (2 Cor. 12:2) and the "elemental spirits of the universe" (Gal. 4:3). The few places in the Pauline corpus in which Christians are urged to separate themselves as "children of light" from the "children of darkness" are particularly interesting. The language is best known from the Essene writings found at Qumran.[42] This indicates the possibility that the Essene community was rooted in gnostic thought as well.

In addition, Paul and the churches were cognizant of the lesser forms of *gnosis*. This is illustrated in Paul's first letter to the Corinthians, in which he refers to the spiritual gifts. Among the gifts identified as coming from the Spirit are healing, the working of miracles, prophecy, the ability to distinguish between spirits, various kinds of tongues and the interpretation of tongues (1 Cor. 12:4-11). These spiritual gifts are similar to some of the lesser forms of *gnosis* discussed in Chapter Three. The matter-of-fact manner in which the gifts of the Holy Spirit are described indicates that *gnosis* in its many forms was understood by and integral to the Pauline congregations.[43]

Paul's use of words and phrases such as "Jesus Christ," "God," his "son," the "Spirit of holiness" (Rom. 1:1,3,4), "God the Father" (1 Cor. 1:3) and "God our Father" (Gal. 1:3, 2 Cor. 1:2) blends the concepts of the Gnostic Trinitarian and paradoxical aspects of the unitary godhead, as well as Jewish monotheism. This language could be expanded or contracted to include the whole constellation of beliefs held by those in the churches who were undoubtedly familiar with various schools of gnostic thought.[44]

In his first letter to the Corinthians, Paul says, "For although there may be so-called gods in heaven or on earth—as indeed there are many 'gods' and many 'lords'—yet for us there is one God, the Father . . ." (1 Cor. 8:5,6).[45] These passages are interesting in two respects. First, by indicating "gods" and "lords" in lower case and putting them in quotation marks, Paul indicates that he, like other pagans and Jews familiar with the gnostic strain within their respective traditions, recognized the existence of disembodied entities other than God. However, Paul did not think of these entities as gods. Second, Paul's skill in avoiding offending those of the church who were being weaned from polytheism is apparent when he concedes that though there are many "gods" and many "lords," believers are to set their minds on the one God. The weaning from polytheism is also evident when Paul reminds the Thessalonians of their calling "and how you turned to God from idols, to serve a living and true God" (1 Thess. 1:9).

Paul's letters also indicate references to the Jewish tradition. Interestingly, the Jewish code of strict sexual morality is reflected when Paul urges Christians not to take a wife in "the passion of lust like heathens who do not know God" (1 Thess. 4:5).

The form of Christian revelation had its roots in the forms of Jewish apocalyptic. This form, important in the speech of Christians, is echoed in First Corinthians:

> Yet among the mature we do impart wisdom, although it is not a wisdom of this age or of the rulers of this age, who are doomed to pass away. But we impart a secret and hidden wisdom of God, which God decreed before the ages for our glorification. None of the rulers of this age understood this; for if they had, they would not have crucified the Lord of glory. But, as it is written, "what no eye has seen, nor ear heard, nor the heart of man conceived, what God has prepared for those who love him," God has revealed to us through the Spirit. (1 Cor. 2:6-10)

The Christian belief that revelation was an experience unique to believers was also part of Jewish tradition.

Furthermore, Jewish and/or gnostic cosmology is impressionistically blended in Paul's explanation of how sin came into the world. Recall that both the Jews and the Gnostics believed that Adam was involved in the establishment of man's regenerative cycle on earth. According to Paul, sin/negative *karma* and death through sin/negative *karma* came into the world through the sin/negative *karma* of Adam, archetypal man. Death spread to all men because they, like Adam, sinned (Rom. 5:12,14).

Paul expresses the gnostic view that the creation was subject to futility, as it is bound to decay and cyclical regeneration (Rom. 8:20, 21). According to Paul, all creation and mankind have been groaning in travail together, waiting for the redemption of their bodies (Rom. 8:22,23). Paul's reference to the body as an earthly tent in which we live (2 Cor. 5:1) is also consistent with the gnostic view. While in this bodily tent, we groan and long to put on our heavenly dwelling (2 Cor. 5:2). We sigh with anxiety so that what is mortal may be swallowed up by life (2 Cor. 5:4). We know that while in the body, we are away from the Lord (2 Cor. 5:6).

Paul's heartfelt conviction that none of the angels, principalities, powers, heights and depths (astrological powers that try to prevent the resurrection body from ascending through the spheres) could separate believers from the love of God in Christ. Paul's words in Romans 8:38-39 illustrate the commingling and reinterpretation of gnostic and/or Jewish concepts in light of the Christ event. The uniquely Christian interpretation is that these powers, which affected all of mankind before the coming of Christ, were rendered powerless against those who believe in His saving power. This meant that after physical death the resurrected body of the believer was no longer subject to time and thus no longer subject to reincarnation, which was, in the gnostic view, co-eternal with sin/negative *karma*, bondage, decay and regeneration.

Referring to those who are "perishing," Paul says that the "god of this world" has veiled the gospel to them; that he has blinded unbelievers (2 Cor. 4:3,4). Recall that some Gnostics were dualists who held that the creator god was not the true god, but was rather an imposter. Further, they identified this lesser god with the Jewish creator God and referred to Him variously as the "god of this world," "Satan," the Demiurge and "Jehovah." Paul the Pharisee believed in one god, the creator of heaven and earth.[46] Nevertheless, Paul the Gnostic believed in the existence of the entity Satan, whom he referred to as a god. It is reasonable to assume that he used such terms in order to relate to those familiar with gnostic thought who were accustomed to thinking of Satan as well as other "gods" and "lords" in terms of gods (1 Cor. 8:5,6). There is no doubt, however, that like other Gnostics, Paul believed that until the Christ event, the entity Satan was ruler of the age and the fate of mankind.

For Paul, the gnostic view that the creation is subject to bondage and decay (Rom. 8:20,21) and the gnostic/Jewish/Christian view that this state of affairs was brought to an end for believers with the advent of the Lord Jesus Christ, who gave himself for sinners to deliver them from the present evil age according to the will of God the Father (Gal. 1:4), are all of one piece.[47] Paul was indeed all things to all men that by all means he might save some (1 Cor. 9:22).

Comparison of the words, phrases and concepts of the biblical and extra-biblical pagan and Jewish literature presented earlier with the words, phrases and concepts obtained from extracts of Paul's letters indicates that Paul and the churches to whom he wrote shared a nebulous and fluid blend of gnostic concepts and language derived from pagan and Pharisaic traditions. The same words, phrases and concepts were integral to the discrete belief systems of those pagans and Jewish Gnostics who believed in reincarnation. It follows, then, that the early Christian churches consisted of individuals from these various traditions who, despite innumerable differences and apparent disorganization, shared a core belief in reincarnation[48] as well as other cosmological beliefs characteristic of pagan and Jewish gnostic thought.

Language analysis of extracts of the Pauline letters also indicates that the core of the churches to whom Paul wrote (as opposed to those who came to consider the gospel message) shared a belief in the unique significance of the birth, death and resurrection of Jesus Christ. These teachings were superimposed over the pre-existing understanding and beliefs of the church members, which were presumed by Paul and therefore unexplained in the letters.[49] The superimposition of one thing over another implies continuity as well as difference between that which pre-exists and that which is added. Belief in reincarnation was the pre-existent overall cross-cultural worldview over which early Christian teachings were superimposed, and as such it is the overall context within which Romans, and presumably all Pauline texts, can be understood.

Sociological studies also provide invaluable information about the socioeconomic constitution of the Roman churches, which included Jews and Gnostics as well as other pagans. The constitution of the churches in Rome, in contrast to the strict social/spiritual stratification of Roman society, generally reflected a cross-section of urban society. People of various social levels as well as of divergent rankings within the caste system were included. These were slaves, artisans, small traders, freedmen or descendants of freedmen as well as members of Caesars' household. Absent were the extreme top and bottom of the Greco-Roman social scale.[50] Significantly, there were wealthy artisans and traders who had high income yet were low in occupational prestige. There were wealthy women and wealthy Jews as well. The Roman churches therefore stood in sharp contrast to traditional Roman groups, which were segregated—"organized along strict categorical lines"[51]—and equated social categorization with spiritual status.

The myriad composition of the Roman churches is significant, as the message of Christ delivered by Paul eliminated the significance of earthly social/spiritual stratification with respect to the destiny of the soul. Paul's letter to Philemon, a slave owner and fellow Christian, illustrates the uniquely Christian view that caste or social status, the gauge for one's spiritual state outside of Christ, is irrelevant for those who are in Christ. While Paul was under house arrest in Rome, he converted the runaway slave Onesimus and persuaded him to return to his master, Philemon. Though Onesimus' outward status as a slave remained unchanged (Paul returned Onesimus to Philemon), Paul appealed to Philemon for leniency toward Onesimus on the basis that as Christians, master and slave were spiritual equals:

> Perhaps this is why he (Onesimus) was parted from you for a while, that you might have him back forever, no longer as a slave but more than a slave, as a beloved brother, especially to me but how much more to you, both in the flesh and in the Lord. So if you consider me your partner, receive him as you would receive me. (Philem. 15-17)

It is tempting to say that Paul intended to equalize social differences. However, his letter to Philemon (and 1 Cor. 7:20-24) indicate that this was not the case. The change to which Paul referred was not outward and physical but inward and spiritual. No doubt the perceived threat to the caste system generated by the Gnostic/Jewish Christian disregard of caste is probably why Christians were persecuted by the Roman state from time to time.

This concludes Part II, Chapters Two through Five, in which biblical and extra-biblical sources were presented to establish the existence of a pre–first-century cross-cultural belief in reincarnation—a worldview consistent with the caste system of social structure. The various subcultural elements in existence at the time and their ideas and tenets were also explained. Finally, how Paul's letters presumed this worldview was illustrated.[52] Indeed, we have established that this presumption is that very element of Romans which is, as Ernst Kasemann described it, the " . . . central concern and . . . remarkable inner logic that may no longer be entirely comprehensible to us."[53]

We will now present Paul's letter to the Romans, which has been illuminated to better reflect the cultural matrix within which it was written. Romans can now be understood.

# PART III

## CHAPTER SIX

# PAUL'S LETTER
# TO THE ROMANS

Paul wrote his letter to the Romans from Corinth at the height of his career (between C.E. 54 and 58). It is the first of his letters in the canonical order. It is also the longest, most theological and most influential.

Rome, as the capital of the Roman Empire, was a microcosm of the far-flung and disparate macrocosm of the Roman Empire. It follows that virtually all pre-Christian cults were represented in Rome. Thus, what was philosophically true and/or relevant for believers in Rome was philosophically true and/or relevant for those out in the provinces. This answers the much-debated scholarly question with respect to the reasoning behind the premier position of Romans in the canonical order.

The following scenario with respect to the constitution of the Roman churches and the various issues that Paul addresses is offered on the basis of the socioeconomic and philosophical matrix of Paul's audience presented in Part II, Chapters Two through Five of this work.

The subject matter of Paul's letter to the Romans is universal and as such is all-inclusive. It addresses the various pre-Christian cults, including Pharisaic Judaism, existing within the Roman Empire during the first century. It also reflects the cross-cultural disintegration then in process of the caste system that was the socioeconomic and philosophical underpinning of virtually all of the ancient world. Indeed, Romans supports Josephus' claim (the extent of which is disputed by some scholars) that many pagans adopted the Jewish law (a process that was virtually unheard of when the respective caste systems were intact), but were unable to keep its precepts.

The common bond between virtually all of the cults within the Roman Empire was belief in reincarnation (resurrection/immortality). What distinguished each from the other was their respective attitudes toward cyclical regeneration and the philosophical and/or cultic means by which they attempted to control their individual and/or group destiny within the parameters of the process of cyclical regeneration.

It is important to not think of the Roman churches in contemporary terms. Unlike the contemporary Church, which is established, has buildings with distinctive architectural styles and is constituted of people who are in general agreement with respect to the deity and the correct process of worship, the Roman churches (and probably virtually all the churches of the first century) were points of missionary activity that, most scholars agree, operated from individual homes.

Based on the socioeconomic and philosophical matrix that prevailed within the Roman Empire prior to and during the first century, the fact that the cross-cultural caste system was in its death throes, and the interpretation of Paul's letter to the Romans, the churches at Rome were probably founded by gentiles who had converted to Judaism—and subsequently to Christianity (gentile Jewish Christians). Hence Paul's reference to them as brethren (Rom. 7:1)—those who, like himself, were Jews, but who now followed Christ—and as those who "know the law." What ethnic Jew did not know the law? Paul deliberately distinguished the gentile Jewish Christians (Rom. 7:1) from the ethnic Jews—his brethren/kinsmen by race (Rom.

9:3). Through great diligence these dedicated gentile Jewish converts to Christianity (Rom. 1:8-13) brought into their circles other believers in resurrection, reincarnation and immortality who were willing to listen to the gospel message and perhaps be persuaded to follow Christ as a means by which to be saved from the cyclical process. Among those to be persuaded were pagan gentiles who converted to Judaism, proselytes to Judaism, half-proselytes to Judaism and all possible gradations in between.

In Romans Chapter 3, Paul's rhetoric appears to be a response to a question anticipated from some gentiles who were weighing the advantages and/or disadvantages of adhering to and/or adopting Judaism as opposed to Christianity. Further complicating the matter is that the "Jews" Paul addresses in Romans Chapter 2 were not ethnic Jews. When the caste system was intact, one was either a Jew by birth or not a Jew. One could not call oneself a Jew at will. These "Jews" addressed in Chapter 2 were apparently gentiles who had adopted Judaism (gentile Jews) in order to gain the advantage of the Jewish law as a means by which to ensure their resurrection and control their socioeconomic and spiritual destiny within the parameters of cyclical return. But according to Paul, these "Jews" who called themselves Jews were not protected under the law because they didn't obey the universal precepts of the law (Rom. 2:17-29).

Thus, among those who were brought into the churches' circles for the benefit of Paul's persuasive rhetoric were gentile Jews as well as Jewish proselytes in all their gradations. The others consisted of gentiles of various pre-first-century pagan traditions. It is difficult to know, but my impression is that the majority brought in for conversion to Christianity were gentile Jews. Perhaps I feel this way because of my strong conviction that the founders of the churches at Rome were gentile Jews before their conversion. This scenario answers the often-debated scholarly question as to why Paul was eager to visit the Roman churches before going to Spain, especially in light of his policy not to preach where Christ had already been named. If the majority of those listening to Paul's Christian message were gentile Jews, what could be more politically astute than a visit by the apostle, an exemplary ethnic Jew who, though perfect under the law, was chosen by revelation to preach the gospel to the gentiles—an undertaking for which he risked his life?

To the gentiles, Paul would be a persuasive force in winning for Christ those who were ambivalent about whether to adopt Pharisaic Judaism or Christianity (Rom. 3:1-20). To the gentile Jews who had adopted the Jewish law but were not protected under it because they didn't obey its universal precepts (Rom. 2:17), adopting Christianity would have made perfect sense. After all, Paul himself, who was "perfect under the law," opted for faith in Christ over the Pharisaic law, didn't he? Why shouldn't they? As to those committed and faithful Christians, he wanted to strengthen their resolve (Rom. 1:11). These were the committed gentile Jewish Christians who probably founded the churches and were spreading the good news. He also wanted to reap harvest among them (Rom. 1:13), those gentile Jews whom the committed gentile Jewish Christians brought within their circles, and the rest of the gentiles, Greeks and barbarians, the wise and the foolish (Rom.1:13,14). But Paul had so far been prevented from visiting Rome. Indeed, the very existence of Romans indicates that he was beginning to doubt whether he would ever do so.

Thus, Paul's letter to the Romans is a substitute for a personal visit by the apostle during which he intended to win for Christ those gentiles who were considering the advantages of adopting Pharisaic Judaism as well as Christianity and gentile

Jews who were still enslaved to sin/negative *karma* and death because they did not obey the universal precepts of the Jewish law. To do so he had to explain the advantages of the Jewish law (Rom. 3:1-19), of which these potential converts were undoubtedly well aware, as well as its ironic quality (which was effectively like that of a two-edged sword), of which they were not. In addition, he had to relate the Christ event to the particular traditions of the various pre-Christian cults, including Pharisaic Judaism, to which many gentiles had converted. To this end, Paul responded to those in his audience in terms of their own philosophical/cultic systems while at the same time weaving in the significance of the Christ event as it related to their shared belief in resurrection, reincarnation and immortality—a belief that Paul and his audience took for granted.

In order to be effective by letter, Paul had to anticipate and answer questions that would have been raised and fielded were he actually addressing his audience in person. This explains the careful construction of Romans, its unmistakable rhetorical and apologetic tone, as well as those instances in which Paul appears to be inconsistent and fragmented. It also explains why Romans comes closer than all of Paul's other letters to being a theological treatise.

It is necessary to clarify two points before proceeding with our illuminated reading of Romans. First, in Romans, Paul uses the phrase the "Wrath" and/or the "Wrath of God." These phrases express the negative connotation given to the Immutable Law (Greek) or God's Immutable Law of Justice (Pharisaic) by those pagans, Pharisees and Gnostics who held a negative view of it. Second, the word "sin" as it appears in Romans is to be understood as being synonymous, in principle, with the concept of negative *karma* in Hinduism.

In summary, Paul's letter to the Romans presented below is to be read within the logical parameters of the interpretive matrix established in Part II, Chapters Two through Five—a pre-first-century and first-century cross-cultural belief in reincarnation—a worldview consistent with the caste system of social organization then in existence. The illuminated version of Romans to follow represents what Paul might have written had he known that the interpretive matrix within which his letter to the Romans was conceived, and to which it is a response, would be obscured to future generations. The essential content of the letter has not been changed.

Notes at the end of this book provide important scholarly input (I am particularly indebted to Kasemann) and additional analysis, and should be read along with The Letter of Paul to the Romans.

# THE LETTER OF PAUL TO THE ROMANS

### *Illuminated* text

1 Paul, a servant of Jesus Christ, called to be an apostle, set apart *by revelation*[1] for the gospel of God 2 which he promised beforehand through his prophets in the holy scriptures, 3 the gospel concerning his Son, who was descended from David according to the flesh[2] 4 and designated Son of God in power according to the Spirit of holiness by his resurrection from the dead,[3] Jesus Christ our Lord, 5 through whom we have received grace[4] and apostleship to bring about the obedience of faith for the sake of his name among all the nations, 6 including yourselves who are called to belong to Jesus Christ;

7 To all God's beloved in Rome, who are called to be saints:[5]

Grace to you and peace from

### Standard text

1 Paul, a servant of Jesus Christ, called to be an apostle, set apart for the gospel of God, for the gospel of God 2 which he promised beforehand through his prophets in the holy scriptures, 3 the gospel concerning his Son, who was descended from David according to the flesh 4 and designated Son of God in power according to the Spirit of holiness by his resurrection from the dead, Jesus Christ our Lord, 5 through whom we have received grace and apostleship to bring about the obedience of faith for the sake of his name among all the nations, 6 including yourselves who are called to belong to Jesus Christ;

7 To all God's beloved in Rome, who are called to be saints:

Grace to you and peace from

God our Father and the Lord Jesus Christ.[6]

8 First, I thank my God through Jesus Christ for all of you, because your faith is proclaimed in all the world. 9 For God is my witness, whom I serve with my spirit in the gospel of his Son, that without ceasing I mention you always in my prayers, 10 asking that somehow by God's will I may now at last succeed in coming to you. 11 For I long to see you, that I may impart to you some spiritual gift to strengthen you, 12 that is, that we may be mutually encouraged by each other's faith, both yours and mine. 13 I want you to know, brethren, that I have often intended to come to you (but thus far have been prevented), in order that I may reap some harvest among you as well as among the rest of the Gentiles.[7] 14 I am under obligation both to Greeks and to barbarians, both to the wise and to the foolish:[8] 15 so I am eager to preach the gospel to you also who are in Rome.[9]

16 For I am not ashamed of the gospel *that Christ died for sinners once and for all and is resurrected from the dead*: it is the power of God for salvation to every one who has faith,[10] to the Jew first and also to the

God our Father and the Lord Jesus Christ.

8 First, I thank my God through Jesus Christ for all of you, because your faith is proclaimed in all the world. 9 For God is my witness, whom I serve with my spirit in the gospel of his Son, that without ceasing I mention you always in my prayers, 10 asking that somehow by God's will I may now at last succeed in coming to you. 11 For I long to see you, that I may impart to you some spiritual gift to strengthen you, 12 that is, that we may be mutually encouraged by each other's faith, both yours and mine. 13 I want you to know, brethren, that I have often intended to come to you (but thus far have been prevented), in order that I may reap some harvest among you as well as among the rest of the Gentiles. 14 I am under obligation both to Greeks and to barbarians, both to the wise and to the foolish: 15 so I am eager to preach the gospel to you also who are in Rome.

16 For I am not ashamed of the gospel; it is the power of God for salvation to every one who has faith, to the Jew first and also to the Greek. 17 For in it the righteousness of God is revealed through faith for faith; as it is

Greek.[11] 17 For in it the righteousness of God is revealed through faith for faith; as it is written, "He who through faith is righteous shall *not be regenerated unto death.*"[12]

18 For the wrath of God/*the Immutable Law/God's Law of Justice*[13] is revealed from heaven[14] against all ungodliness and wickedness of men who by their wickedness suppress the truth.[15] 19 For what can be known about God is plain to them, because God has shown it to them *in their present lot in life.* 20 Ever since the creation of the world his invisible nature, namely, his eternal power and deity, has been clearly perceived in the things that have been made.[16] So they are without excuse; 21 for although they knew God they did not honor him as God or give thanks to him, but they became futile in their thinking and their senseless minds were darkened. 22 Claiming to be wise, they became fools, 23 and exchanged the glory of the immortal God for images resembling mortal man or birds or animals or reptiles.

24 Therefore God gave them up in the lusts of their hearts to impurity, to the dishonoring of their bodies among themselves, 25 because they exchanged the

written, "He who through faith is righteous shall live."

18 For the wrath of God is revealed from heaven against all ungodliness and wickedness of men who by their wickedness suppress the truth. 19 For what can be known about God is plain to them, because God has shown it to them. 20 Ever since the creation of the world his invisible nature, namely, his eternal power and deity, has been clearly perceived in the things that have been made. So they are without excuse; 21 for although they knew God they did not honor him as God or give thanks to him, but they became futile in their thinking and their senseless minds were darkened. 22 Claiming to be wise, they became fools, 23 and exchanged the glory of the immortal God for images resembling mortal man or birds or animals or reptiles.

24 Therefore God gave them up in the lusts of their hearts to impurity, to the dishonoring of their bodies among themselves, 25 because they exchanged the

truth about God for a lie and worshipped and served the creature rather than the Creator, who is blessed for ever![17]Amen.

26 For this reason God gave them up to dishonorable passions. Their women exchanged natural relations for unnatural, 27 and the men likewise gave up natural relations with women and were consumed with passion for one another, men committing shameless acts with men and receiving in their own persons the due penalty for their error.[18]

28 And since they did not see fit to acknowledge God, God gave them up to a base mind and to improper conduct. 29 They were filled with all manner of wickedness, evil, covetousness, malice. Full of envy, murder, strife, deceit, malignity, they are gossips, 30 slanderers, haters of God, insolent, haughty, boastful, inventors of evil, disobedient to parents, 31 foolish, faithless, heartless, ruthless. 32 Though they know God's decree that those who do such things deserve to die *ad infinitum*,[19] they not only do them but approve those who practice them.

2 Therefore you have no excuse, O man, whoever you are,[20] when you judge another; for

truth about God for a lie and worshipped and served the creature rather than the Creator, who is blessed for ever! Amen.

26 For this reason God gave them up to dishonorable passions. Their women exchanged natural relations for unnatural, 27 and the men likewise gave up natural relations with women and were consumed with passion for one another, men committing shameless acts with men and receiving in their own persons the due penalty for their error.

28 And since they did not see fit to acknowledge God, God gave them up to a base mind and to improper conduct. 29 They were filled with all manner of wickedness, evil, covetousness, malice. Full of envy, murder, strife, deceit, malignity, they are gossips, 30 slanderers, haters of God, insolent, haughty, boastful, inventors of evil, disobedient to parents, 31 foolish, faithless, heartless, ruthless. 32 Though they know God's decree that those who do such things deserve to die, they not only do them but approve those who practice them.

2 Therefore you have no excuse, O man, whoever you are, when you judge another; for

in passing judgment upon him you condemn yourself, because you, the judge, are doing the very same things. 2 We know that the judgment of God rightly falls upon those who do such things. 3 Do you suppose, O man, that when you judge those who do such things and yet do them yourself, you will escape the judgment of God? 4 Or do you presume upon the riches of his kindness and forbearance and patience *in allowing a renewed existence to those who are undeserving*? Do you not know that God's kindness is meant to lead you to repentance? 5 But by your hard and impenitent heart you are storing up wrath for yourself on the day of wrath when God's righteous judgment will be revealed 6 *at which time he will no longer exercise forbearance, but* will render to every man according to his works: 7 to those who by patience in well-doing seek for glory and honor and immortality, he will give eternal life;[21] 8 but for those who are factious and do not obey the truth, but obey wickedness, there will be wrath and fury. 9 There will be tribulation and distress for every human being who does evil, the Jew first and also the Greek, 10 but glory and honor and peace for every one

in passing judgment upon him you condemn yourself, because you, the judge, are doing the very same things. 2 We know that the judgment of God rightly falls upon those who do such things. 3 Do you suppose, O man, that when you judge those who do such things and yet do them yourself, you will escape the judgment of God? 4 Or do you presume upon the riches of his kindness and forbearance and patience? Do you not know that God's kindness is meant to lead you to repentance? 5 But by your hard and impenitent heart you are storing up wrath for yourself on the day of wrath when God's righteous judgment will be revealed. 6 For he will render to every man according to his works: 7 to those who by patience in well-doing seek for glory and honor and immortality, he will give eternal life; 8 but for those who are factious and do not obey the truth, but obey wickedness, there will be wrath and fury. 9 There will be tribulation and distress for every human being who does evil, the Jew first and also the Greek, 10 but glory and honor and peace for every one who does good, the Jew first and also the Greek. 11 For God shows no partiality.

who does good, the Jew first and also the Greek. 11 For God shows no partiality.

12 All who have sinned without the *Jewish* law will also perish without the law, and all who have sinned under the *Jewish* law will be judged *by the extent to which they do or do not follow its precepts*. 13 For it is not the hearers of the law who are righteous before God, but the doers of the law who will be justified. 14 When Gentiles who have not the *Jewish* law do by nature what the *Immutable Law/God's Law of Justice* requires, they are a law to themselves, even though they do not have the *Jewish* law. 15 They show that what the *Jewish* law requires is written on their hearts, while their conscience also bears witness and their conflicting thoughts accuse or perhaps excuse them[22] 16 on that day when, according to my gospel, God judges the secrets of men by Christ Jesus.[23]

17 But if you *have adopted Judaism and, therefore,* call yourself a Jew and rely upon the law and boast of your relation to God[24] 18 and know his will and approve what is excellent, because you are instructed in the law, 19 and if you are sure that you are a guide to the blind, a

12 All who have sinned without the law will also perish without the law, and all who have sinned under the law will be judged the law. 13 For it is not the hearers of the law who are righteous before God, but the doers of the law who will be justified. 14 When Gentiles who have not the law do by nature what the law requires, they are a law to themselves, even though they do not have the Jewish law. 15 They show that what the law requires is written on their hearts, while their conscience also bears witness and their conflicting thoughts accuse or perhaps excuse them 16 on that day when, according to my gospel, God judges the secrets of men by Christ Jesus.

17 But if you call yourself a Jew and rely upon the law and boast of your relation to God 18 and know his will and approve what is excellent, because you are instructed in the law, 19 and if you are sure that you are a guide to the blind, a light to those who are in darkness, 20 a corrector of

light to those who are in darkness, 20 a corrector of the foolish, a teacher of children, having in the law the embodiment of knowledge and truth—21 you then who teach others, will you not teach yourself? While you preach against stealing, do you steal? 22 You who say that one must not commit adultery, do you commit adultery? You who abhor idols, do you rob temples? 23 You who boast in the law, do you dishonor God by breaking the law? 24 For, as it is written, "The name of God is blasphemed among the Gentiles because of you."

25 Circumcision indeed is of value if you obey the law *to the letter*; but if you break the law, your circumcision becomes uncircumcision. 26 So, if a man who is uncircumcised keeps the precepts of the law, will not his uncircumcision be regarded as circumcision? 27 Then those who are physically uncircumcised but keep the *universal precepts of the law* will condemn you who have the written code and circumcision but break the law. 28 For he is not a real Jew who is one outwardly, nor is true circumcision something external and physical. 29 He is a Jew who is one inwardly, and real circumcision is

the foolish, a teacher of children, having in the law the embodiment of knowledge and truth—21 you then who teach others, will you not teach yourself? While you preach against stealing, do you steal? 22 You who say that one must not commit adultery, do you commit adultery? You who abhor idols, do you rob temples? 23 You who boast in the law, do you dishonor God by breaking the law? 24 For, as it is written, "The name of God is blasphemed among the Gentiles because of you."

25 Circumcision indeed is of value if you obey the law; but if you break the law, your circumcision becomes uncircumcision. 26 So, if a man who is uncircumcised keeps the precepts of the law, will not his uncircumcision be regarded as circumcision? 27 Then those who are physically uncircumcised but keep the law will condemn you who have the written code and circumcision but break the law. 28 For he is not a real Jew who is one outwardly, nor is true circumcision something external and physical. 29 He is a Jew who is one inwardly, and real circumcision is a matter of the heart, spiritual and not literal.

a matter of the heart, spiritual and not literal. His praise is not from men but from God.[25]

3 Then what advantage has the Jew? Or what is the value of circumcision? 2 Much in every way. To begin with, the Jews are entrusted with the oracles of God.[26] 3 What if some were unfaithful? Does their faithlessness nullify the faithfulness of God? 4 By no means! Let God be true though every man be false, as it is written,

"That thou mayest be justified in thy words, and prevail when thou art judged."[27]

5 But if our wickedness *is a manifestation of our just punishment from a past existence which is not within our control*, what shall we say? That God is unjust to inflict wrath/*sin* on us? (I speak in a human way.) 6 By no means! For then how could God judge the world? 7 But if through my falsehood/*sin* God's *justice is manifested* to his glory, why am I still being condemned as a sinner? 8 And why not do evil that good may come?—as some people slanderously charge us with saying.[28] Their condemnation is just.

9 What then? Are we Jews any better off? No, not at all; for

His praise is not from men but from God.

3 Then what advantage has the Jew? Or what is the value of circumcision? 2 Much in every way. To begin with, the Jews are entrusted with the oracles of God. 3 What if some were unfaithful? Does their faithlessness nullify the faithfulness of God? 4 By no means! Let God be true though every man be false, as it is written,

"That thou mayest be justified in thy words, and prevail when thou art judged."

5 But if our wickedness serves to show the justice of God, what shall we say? That God is unjust to inflict wrath on us? (I speak in a human way.) 6 By no means! For then how could God judge the world? 7 But if through my falsehood God's truthfulness abounds to his glory, why am I still being condemned as a sinner? 8 And why not do evil that good may come?—as some people slanderously charge us with saying. Their condemnation is just.

9 What then? Are we Jews any better off? No, not at all; for

I have already charged that all men, both Jews and Greeks, are under the power of sin,[29] 10 as it is written:

"None is righteous, no, not one;

11 no one understands, no one seeks for God.

12 All have turned aside, together they have gone wrong; no one does good, not even one."

13 "Their throat is an open grave,[30] they use their tongues to deceive."
"The venom of asps is under their lips."

14 "Their mouth is full of curses and bitterness."

15 "Their feet are swift to shed blood,

16 in their paths are ruin and misery,

17 and the way of peace they do not know."

18 "There is no fear of God before their eyes."

19 Now we know that whatever the law says it speaks to those who are under the law, so that every mouth may be stopped, and the whole world may be held accountable to God.[31] 20 For no human being will be justified in his sight by works of the law, since through the law comes

knowledge of sin/*guilt*.[32]

21 *With the coming of Christ, the righteousness of God is manifested in a different way than it is under the law, though* the law and the prophets bear witness to it, 22 *through faith in Jesus Christ for all who believe*.[33] *This means that the spiritual distinctions made manifest in caste which, for the Pharisee, were regulated by the law are no longer relevant with respect to justification;* 23 *because all fall short of the glory of God and are, therefore, equal*,[34] 24 they are justified by his grace as a gift, through *a new dynamic which is not realized by works of the law but is rather in Christ Jesus*, 25 whom God put forward as an expiation by his blood, to be received by faith. *In the past God showed his righteousness by passing over former sins which were stored up*.[35] *He sustained us in life even though we did not deserve the opportunity to resurrect.* 26 *This was done to show his divine forbearance in order to assure us* at the present time that he himself is righteous and that he *will justify* him who has faith in Jesus.[36]

27 Then what becomes of our boasting? It is excluded. On what principle? On the principle of

knowledge of sin.

21 But now the righteousness of God has been manifested apart from law, although the law and prophets bear witness to it, 22 the righteousness of God through faith in Jesus Christ for all who believe. For there is not distinction; 23 since all have sinned and fall short of the glory of God, 24 they are justified by his grace as a gift, through the redemption which is in Christ Jesus, 25 whom God put forward as an expiation by his blood, to be received by faith. This was to show God's righteousness, because in his divine forbearance he had passed over former sins; 26 it was to prove at the present time that he himself is righteous and that he justifies him who has faith in Jesus.

27 Then what becomes of our boasting? It is excluded. On what principle? On the principle of

works? No, but on the principle of faith. 28 For we hold that a man is justified by faith apart from works of the law. 29 Or is God the god of Jews only? Is he not the God of Gentiles also? Yes, of Gentiles also,[37] 30 since God is one; and he will justify the circumcised on the ground of their faith and the uncircumcised through their faith.[38] 31 Do we then overthrow the law by this faith? By no means! On the contrary, we uphold the law *but we do not rely on it for the purpose of justification.*

4 What then shall we say about Abraham, our forefather according to the flesh? 2 For if Abraham was justified by works, he has something to boast about *before men* but not before God.[39] 3 For what does the scripture say? "Abraham believed God, and it was reckoned to him as righteousness." 4 *Now one who by works—the requirements of which are embodied in the law—fulfills the law has in the past, and will in the future, receive precisely their due (wages/reward) with respect to caste/status and/or justification. That which is earned is not a gift.*[40] 5 *But he who does not fulfill his caste requirements (works/law),*

works? No, but on the principle of faith. 28 For we hold that a man is justified by faith apart from works of the law. 29 Or is God the god of Jews only? Is he not the God of Gentiles also? Yes, of Gentiles also, 30 since God is one; and he will justify the circumcised on the ground of their faith and the uncircumcised through their faith. 31 Do we then overthrow the law by this faith? By no means! On the contrary, we uphold the law.

4 What then shall we say about Abraham, our forefather according to the flesh? 2 For if Abraham was justified by works, he has something to boast about, but not before God. 3 For what does the scripture say? "Abraham believed God, and it was reckoned to him as righteousness." 4 Now to one who works, his wages are not reckoned as a gift but as his due. 5 And to one who does not work but trusts him who justifies the ungodly, his faith is reckoned as righteousness.

*but trusts him who justifies the ungodly, will receive as a gift more than that which under the law would have been his due. Indeed that which is received through faith is qualitatively different from that which is received through works/law. The gift for faith (and of faith) is not a renewed and better mortal existence which of necessity must end in death, but righteousness (innocence).* 6 So also David pronounces a blessing upon the man to whom God reckons righteousness apart from works:

7 "Blessed are those whose
   iniquities are forgiven,
   and whose sins are covered;
8  blessed is the man against
   whom the Lord will
   not reckon his sin."[41]

9 Is this blessing pronounced only upon the circumcised, or also upon the uncircumcised?[42] We say that faith was reckoned to Abraham as righteousness. 10 How then was it reckoned to him? Was it before or after he had been circumcised? It was not after, but before he was circumcised.[43] 11 He received circumcision as a sign or seal of the righteousness which he had by faith while he was still uncircumcised. The purpose was to make him the father of all who believe without being

6 So also David pronounces a blessing upon the man to whom God reckons righteousness apart from works:

7 "Blessed are those whose
   iniquities are forgiven,
   and whose sins are covered;
8  blessed is the man against
   whom the Lord will
   not reckon his sin."

9 Is this blessing pronounced only upon the circumcised, or also upon the uncircumcised? We say that faith was reckoned to Abraham as righteousness. 10 How then was it reckoned to him? Was it before or after he had been circumcised? It was not after, but before he was circumcised. 11 He received circumcision as a sign or seal of the righteousness which he had by faith while he was still uncircumcised. The purpose was to make him the father of all who believe without being circum-

circumcised and who thus have righteousness reckoned to them, 12 and likewise the father of the circumcised who are not merely circumcised but also follow the example of the faith which our father Abraham had before he was circumcised.[44]

13 The promise to Abraham and his descendants, that they should inherit the world, did not come through the law but through the righteousness of faith.[45] 14 If it is the adherents of the law who are to be the heirs, faith is null and the promise is void. 15 For the law brings *retributive justice*, but where there is no law there is no transgression.[46]

16 That is why it depends on the *dynamic power* of faith, in order that the promise may rest on grace and be guaranteed to all his descendants—not only to the adherents of the law but also to those who share the faith of Abraham, for he is the father of us all,[47] 17 as it is written, "I have made you the father of many nations"—in the presence of the God in whom he believed, who gives life to the dead and calls into existence the things that do not exist.[48] 18 In hope he believed against hope, that he should become the father of many nations; as he had been told, "So shall

cised and who thus have righteousness reckoned to them, 12 and likewise the father of the circumcised who are not merely circumcised but also follow the example of the faith which our father Abraham had before he was circumcised.

13 The promise to Abraham and his descendants, that they should inherit the world, did not come through the law but through the righteousness of faith. 14 If it is the adherents of the law who are to be the heirs, faith is null and the promise is void. 15 For the law brings wrath, but where there is no law there is no transgression.

16 That is why it depends on faith, in order that the promise may rest on grace and be guaranteed to all his descendants—not only to the adherents of the law but also to those who share the faith of Abraham, for he is the father of us all, 17 as it is written, "I have made you the father of many nations"—in the presence of the God in whom he believed, who gives life to the dead and calls into existence the things that do not exist. 18 In hope he believed against hope, that he should become the father of many nations; as he had been told, "So shall your descendants be." 19 He

your descendants be." 19 He did not weaken in faith when he considered his own body, which was as good as dead because he was about a hundred years old, or when he considered the barrenness of Sarah's womb. 20 No distrust made him waver concerning the promise of God, but he grew strong in his faith as he gave glory to God, 21 fully convinced that God was able *to counter the natural order as he had promised.* 22 That is why his faith was "reckoned to him as righteousness." 23 But the words, "it was reckoned to him," were written not for his sake alone, 24 but for ours also.[49] *At this time God has chosen to counter the natural order of the cosmos. God who in the past gave life to the dead by allowing them to resurrect has promised that faith would be reckoned to us as righteousness (justification, innocence), in order that we may be freed from the cyclical process of sin and death. This promise, like that made to Abraham, is conditional upon faith in God's ability and willingness to do that which he has promised.* It will be reckoned to us who believe in him that raised from the dead Jesus our Lord,[50] 25 who was put to death for our tres-

did not weaken in faith when he considered his own body, which was as good as dead because he was about a hundred years old, or when he considered the barrenness of Sarah's womb. 20 No distrust made him waver concerning the promise of God, but he grew strong in his faith as he gave glory to God, 21 fully convinced that God was able to do what he had promised. 22 That is why his faith was "reckoned to him as righteousness." 23 But the words "it was reckoned to him," were written not for his sake alone, 24 but for ours also. It will be reckoned to us who believe in him that raised from the dead Jesus our Lord, 25 who was put to death for our trespasses and raised for our justification.

passes and raised for our justification.

5 Therefore, since *our justification rests on the principle of the actualizing spiritual
dynamic of faith and not that of
works/law, through faith in our
Lord Jesus Christ we are no
longer subject to regeneration
unto death.*[51] 2 Through him we
have obtained access to this grace
in which we stand, and we rejoice
in our hope of *unhindered access
after death to the presence of
God.*[52] 3 More than that, we rejoice in our sufferings,[53] knowing that suffering produces endurance, 4 and endurance produces
character, and character produces
hope, 5 and hope does not disap-
point us, because God's love has
been poured into our hearts
through the Holy Spirit which has
been given to us.

6 While *humanity was* still
weak, *unable to keep from sink-
ing further into sin and death*, at
the right time Christ died for the
ungodly. 7 Why, one will hardly
die for a righteous man—though
perhaps for a good man one will
dare even to die. 8 But God shows
his love for us in that while we
were yet sinners Christ died for
us. 9 Since, therefore, we are now
justified by his blood, much more

5 Therefore, since we are justified by faith, we have peace
with God through our Lord Jesus
Christ. 2 Through him we have
obtained access to this grace in
which we stand, and we rejoice
in our hope of sharing the glory
of God. 3 More than that, we rejoice in our sufferings, knowing
that suffering produces endurance, 4 and endurance produces
character, and character produces
hope, 5 and hope does not disap-
point us, because God's love has
been poured into our hearts
through the Holy Spirit which has
been given to us.

6 While we were still weak, at
the right time Christ died for the
ungodly. 7 Why, one will hardly
die for a righteous man—though
perhaps for a good man one will
dare even to die. 8 But God shows
his love for us in that while we
were yet sinners Christ died for
us. 9 Since, therefore, we are now
justified by his blood, much more
shall we be saved by him from
the wrath of God. 10 For if while

shall we be saved by him from the *retributive justice of* the wrath of God.[54] 10 For if while we were enemies we were reconciled to God by the death of his Son, much more, now that we are reconciled, shall we be saved by his life.[55] 11 Not only so, but we also rejoice in God through our Lord Jesus Christ, through whom we have now received our reconciliation.

12 Therefore as *universal sin came into the world through the disobedience of one man* and death through sin,[56] and so death spread to all men because all men sinned—[57] 13 sin indeed was in the world before the law was given, *but the thoughts, words and actions of those who came after Adam to whom the law now applies were not counted because then there was no law.* 14 *Yet because of the particular sin of Adam, men were enslaved to cyclical regeneration and death* from Adam to Moses, even over those whose sins were not like the transgression of Adam, who was a type of the one who was to come.[58]

15 But the free gift *through Christ is different from the trespass through Adam. For if many were subjected to unending rebirth and death through one*

we were enemies we were reconciled to God by the death of his Son, much more, now that we are reconciled, shall we be saved by his life. 11 Not only so, but we also rejoice in God through our Lord Jesus Christ, through whom we have now received our reconciliation.

12 Therefore as sin came into the world through one man and death through sin, and so death spread to all men because all men sinned—13 sin indeed was in the world before the law was given, but sin is not counted where there is no law. 14 Yet death reigned from Adam to Moses, even over those whose sins were not like the transgression of Adam, who was a type of the one who was to come.

15 But the free gift is not like the trespass. For if many died through one man's trespass, much more have the grace of God and the free gift in the grace of

*man's trespass*, much more have the grace of God and the free gift in the grace of that one man Jesus Christ abounded for many. 16 *And the effect of the free gift is opposite the effect of the trespass, quantitatively as well as qualitatively.* For the judgment following one trespass brought *universal rebirth, suffering and death*, but the free gift following many trespasses brings *release from the process*. 17 If, because of one man's trespass, death reigned through that one man, much more will those who receive the abundance of grace and the free gift of righteousness reign in *eternal* life through the one man Jesus Christ.

18 Then as one man's trespass *condemned all men to death/rebirth/death ad infinitum*, so one man's act of righteousness leads to acquittal and *release from the process unto eternal life for all who believe.* 19 For as by one man's disobedience[59] many were made sinners, so by one man's obedience many will be made righteous.[60] 20 Law came in, to increase the trespass; but where sin increased, grace abounded all the more, *and many who were undeserving were sustained and given the opportunity to resurrect* 21 so that, as sin reigned in

that one man Jesus Christ abounded for many. 16 And the free gift is not like the effect of that one man's sin. For the judgment following one trespass brought condemnation, but the free gift following many trespasses brings justification. 17 If, because of one man's trespass, death reigned through that one man, much more will those who receive the abundance of grace and the free gift of righteousness reign in life through the one man Jesus Christ.

18 Then as one man's trespass led to condemnation for all men, so one man's act of righteousness leads to acquittal and life for all men. 19 For as by one man's disobedience many were made sinners, so by one man's obedience many will be made righteous. 20 Law came in, to increase the trespass; but where sin increased, grace abounded all the more, 21 so that, as sin reigned in death, grace also might reign through righteousness to eternal life through Jesus Christ our Lord.

*perpetual* death, grace also might *ultimately* reign through righteousness to eternal life through Jesus Christ our Lord.

**6** What shall we say then? Are we to continue in sin that grace may abound?[61] 2 By no means! How can *we who are free from the regenerating power of* sin still live in it? 3 Do you not know that all of us who have been baptized into Christ Jesus were baptized into his death? 4 We were buried therefore with him by baptism into death, so that as Christ was raised from the dead by the glory of the Father,[62] we too might walk in newness of life.[63]

5 For if *through faith we are* united with him in a death like his *which is final*, we shall certainly be united with him in a resurrection like his *which is also final*.[64] 6 *As Christians we know that our old self was crucified with him so that the sinful body*[65] *which is subject to rebirth and death* might be destroyed and we might no longer be enslaved to sin. 7 For he who has died *to sin* is freed from sin. 8 But if we have died with Christ, we believe that we shall also live with him *in eternal life*. 9 For we know that Christ being raised from the dead

**6** What shall we say then? Are we to continue in sin that grace may abound? 2 By no means! How can we who died to sin still live in it? 3 Do you not know that all of us who have been baptized into Christ Jesus were baptized into his death? 4 We were buried therefore with him by baptism into death, so that as Christ was raised from the dead by the glory of the Father, we too might walk in newness of life.

5 For if we have been united with him in a death like his, we shall certainly be united with him in a resurrection like his. 6 We know that our old self was crucified with him so that the sinful body might be destroyed, and we might no longer be enslaved to sin. 7 For he who has died is freed from sin. 8 But if we have died with Christ, we believe that we shall also live with him. 9 For we know that Christ being raised from the dead will never die again; death no longer has dominion over him. 10 The death he died he died to sin, once for

will never die again; the *futile/vain process of rebirth and death no longer has dominion over him.* 10 The death he died he died to sin, once for all, but the life he lives he lives to God. 11 So you also must consider yourselves dead to sin and alive to God in Christ Jesus.[66]

12 *Therefore, now that we are acquitted from past sin/negative karma through faith in Christ,* let not sin reign in your mortal bodies, to make you obey their passions. 13 Do not yield your members to sin as instruments of wickedness, but yield yourselves to God as men who have been brought from death to life, and your members to God as instruments of righteousness. 14 For sin will have no dominion over you,[67] since you are not under the *recompensatory dynamic of the Immutable Law/God's Law of Justice,* but under grace.[68]

15 What then? Are we to sin because we are not under law but under grace? By no means! 16 Do you not know that if you yield yourselves to any one as obedient slaves, you are slaves of the one whom you obey, either of sin, which leads to *rebirth and death,* or of obedience, which leads to *release from the process?* 17 But thanks be to God, that you who were once slaves of sin have be-

all, but the life he lives he lives to God. 11 So you also must consider yourselves dead to sin and alive to God in Christ Jesus.

12 Let not sin therefore reign in your mortal bodies, to make you obey their passions. 13 Do not yield your members to sin as instruments of wickedness, but yield yourselves to God as men who have been brought from death to life, and your members to God as instruments of righteousness. 14 For sin will have no dominion over you, since you are not under the law but under grace.

15 What then? Are we to sin because we are not under law but under grace? By no means! 16 Do you not know that if you yield yourselves to any one as obedient slaves, you are slaves of the one whom you obey, either of sin, which leads to death, or of obedience, which lead to righteousness? 17 But thanks be to God, that you who were once slaves of sin have become obedient from

come obedient from the heart to the standard of teaching to which you were committed, 18 and, having been set free from sin, have become slaves of righteousness. 19 I am speaking in human terms, because of your natural limitations. For just as you once yielded your members to impurity and to greater and greater iniquity, so now yield your members to righteousness for sanctification.

20 When you were slaves of sin, you were free in regard to righteousness. 21 But then what return did you get from the things of which you are now ashamed? The end of those things is *rebirth and death, the latter of which you have yet to suffer*. 22 But now that you have been set free from sin/*negative karma* and have become slaves of God,[69] the return you get is sanctification, and its end *is not rebirth unto death but* eternal life. 23 For the wages of sin *are rebirth and death*, but the free gift of God is eternal life in Christ Jesus our Lord.[70]

7 Do you not know, brethren —for I am speaking to those who know the law—[71] that the law is binding on a person only during his life? 2 Thus a married woman is bound by law to her husband as long as he lives; but

the heart to the standard of teaching to which you were committed, 18 and, having been set free from sin, have become slaves of righteousness. 19 I am speaking in human terms, because of your natural limitations. For just as you once yielded your members to impurity and to greater and greater iniquity, so now yield your members to righteousness for sanctification.

20 When you were slaves of sin, you were free in regard to righteousness. 21 But then what return did you get from the things of which you are now ashamed? The end of those things is death. 22 But now that you have been set free from sin and have become slaves of God, the return you get is sanctification, and its end, eternal life. 23 For the wages of sin is death, but the free gift of God is eternal life in Christ Jesus our Lord.

7 Do you not know, brethren —for I am speaking to those who know the law—that the law is binding on a person only during his life? 2 Thus a married woman is bound by law to her husband as long as he lives; but

if her husband dies she is discharged from the law concerning the husband. 3 Accordingly, she will be called an adulteress if she lives with another man while her husband is alive. But if her husband dies she is free from that law, and if she marries another man she is not an adulteress.

4 Likewise, my brethren, you have died to the law through the body of Christ,[72] so that you may belong to another, to him who has been raised from the dead *and will not return to die again, in order that we too may do likewise and* bear fruit for God.[73] 5 While we were living in the flesh,[74] our sinful passions, *made conscious and explicit by the law*, were at work in our members to bear fruit for *rebirth, suffering and* death. 6 But now we are discharged from the law/*the Immutable Law*, dead to the *dynamic of retributive justice* which held us captive, so that we serve not *the flesh* under the old written code but in the new life of the Spirit.[75]

7 What then shall we say? That the law is sin? By no means! Yet, if it had not been for the law, I should not have known sin. I should not have known what it is to covet if the law had not said, "You shall not covet."[76] 8 But sin,

---

if her husband dies she is discharged from the law concerning the husband. 3 Accordingly, she will be called an adulteress if she lives with another man while her husband is alive. But if her husband dies she is free from that law, and if she marries another man she is not an adulteress.

4 Likewise, my brethren, you have died to the law through the body of Christ, so that you may belong to another, to him who has been raised from the dead in order that we may bear fruit for God. 5 While we were living in the flesh, our sinful passions, aroused by the law, were at work in our members to bear fruit for death. 6 But now we are discharged from the law, dead to that which held us captive, so that we serve not under the old written code but in the new life of the Spirit.

7 What then shall we say? That the law is sin? By no means! Yet, if it had not been for the law, I should not have known sin. I should not have known what it is to covet if the law had not said, "You shall not covet." 8 But sin,

*rendered conscious and explicit in the commandment,* wrought in me all kinds of covetousness. Apart from the law sin lies dead. 9 I was once alive apart from the law, but when *I was born a Jew* the commandment came, sin revived and I died; 10 the very commandment which promised life proved to be death to me. 11 For sin, finding opportunity in the commandment, deceived me and by it killed me. 12 So the law is holy, and the commandment is holy and just and good.[77]

13 Did that which is good, then, bring death to me? By no means! It was sin, working death in me through what is good, in order that sin might be shown to be sin, and through the commandment might become sinful beyond measure.[78] 14 We know that the law/*Immutable Law* is spiritual;[79] but I am carnal, sold under sin/ *negative karma.* 15 I do not understand my own actions *because I am influenced by a past which, though unknown to me, is one with my mortal being.* For I do not do what I want, but I do the very thing I hate. 16 Now if I do what I do not want, I agree that the law is good. 17 So then it is no longer I that do it, but sin which dwells within me. 18 For I know that nothing good dwells

finding opportunity in the commandment, wrought in me all kinds of covetousness. Apart from the law sin lies dead. 9 I was once alive apart from the law, but when the commandment came, sin revived and I died; 10 the very commandment which promised life proved to be death to me. 11 For sin, finding opportunity in the commandment, deceived me and by it killed me. 12 So the law is holy, and the commandment is holy and just and good.

13 Did that which is good, then, bring death to me? By no means! It was sin, working death in me through what is good, in order that sin might be shown to be sin, and through the commandment might become sinful beyond measure. 14 We know that the law is spiritual; but I am carnal, sold under sin. 15 I do not understand my own action. For I do not do what I want, but I do the very thing I hate. 16 Now if I do what I do not want, I agree that the law is good. 17 So then it is no longer I that do it, but sin which dwells within me. 18 For I know that nothing good dwells within me, that is, in my flesh. I can will what is right, but I cannot do it. 19 For I do not do the good I want, but the evil I do not

within me, that is, in my flesh. I can will what is right, but I cannot do it. 19 For I do not do the good I want, but the evil I do not want is what I do. 20 Now if I do what I do not want, it is no longer I that do it, but sin which *has been stored up* (see 2:5) *and* dwells within me.[80]

21 So I find it to be a law that when I want to do right, evil lies close at hand. 22 For I delight in the law of God, in my inmost self, 23 but I see in my members another *L*aw at war with the *l*aw of my mind and making me captive to the Law of sin/*negative karma* which dwells in my members.[81] 24 Wretched man that I am! Who will deliver me from this *self-perpetrating* body of death? 25 Thanks be to God through Jesus Christ our Lord! So then, I of myself serve the law of God with my mind, but with my *body* I serve the *L*aw of sin.[82]

8 There is therefore now no condemnation for those who are in Christ Jesus.[83] 2 For the *Law* of the Spirit of life in Christ Jesus has set me free from the *L*aw of sin and death.[84] 3 For God has done what the law, weakened by the flesh, could not do: sending his own Son[85] in the likeness of sinful flesh and for sin,

want is what I do. 20 Now if I do what I do not want, it is no longer I that do it, but sin which dwells within me.

21 So I find it to be a law that when I want to do right, evil lies close at hand. 22 For I delight in the law of God, in my inmost self, 23 but I see in my members another law at war with the law of my mind and making me captive to the law of sin which dwells in my members. 24 Wretched man that I am! Who will deliver me from this body of death? 25 Thanks be to God through Jesus Christ our Lord! So then, I of myself serve the law of God with my mind, but with my flesh I serve the law of sin.

8 There is therefore now no condemnation for those who are in Christ Jesus. 2 For the law of the Spirit of life in Christ Jesus has set me free from the law of sin and death. 3 For God has done what the law, weakened by the flesh, could not do: sending his own Son in the likeness of sinful flesh and for sin,

he condemned sin in the flesh, 4 in order that *through faith that Christ died for our sins—known and unknown*—the just requirement of the law/*Immutable L*aw might be fulfilled in us,[86] who walk not according to the flesh but according to the Spirit.[87] 5 For those who live according to the flesh set their minds on the things of the flesh, but those who live according to the Spirit set their minds on the things of the Spirit. 6 To set the mind on the flesh is to be *resurrected unto mortality and death*, but to set the mind on the Spirit is *resurrection unto eternal life* and peace. 7 For the mind that is set on the flesh is hostile to God; it does not submit to God's law, indeed it cannot; 8 and those who are in the flesh cannot please God.

9 But you are not in the flesh, you are in the Spirit,[88] if in fact the Spirit of God dwells in you. Any one who does not have the spirit of Christ does not belong to him. 10 But if Christ is in you, although your bodies are dead because of sin, your spirits are alive because of righteousness.[89] 11 If the Spirit of him who raised Jesus from the dead dwells in you, he who raised Christ Jesus from the dead will give life to your mortal bodies also through his

he condemned sin in the flesh, 4 in order that the just requirement of the law might be fulfilled in us, who walk not according to the flesh but according to the Spirit. 5 For those who live according to the flesh set their minds on the things of the flesh, but those who live according to the Spirit set their minds on the things of the Spirit. 6 To set the mind on the flesh is death, but to set the mind on the Spirit is life and peace. 7 For the mind that is set on the flesh is hostile to God; it does not submit to God's law, indeed it cannot; 8 and those who are in the flesh cannot please God.

9 But you are not in the flesh, you are in the Spirit, if in fact the Spirit of God dwells in you. Any one who does not have the spirit of Christ does not belong to him. 10 But if Christ is in you, although your bodies are dead because of sin, your spirits are alive because of righteousness. 11 If the Spirit of him who raised Jesus from the dead dwells in you, he who raised Christ Jesus from the dead will give life to your mortal bodies also through his Spirit

Spirit which dwells in you.[90]

12 So then, brethren, we are debtors, not to the flesh, to live according to the flesh—[91] 13 for if you live according to the flesh you will *be reborn and* die, but if by the Spirit you put to death the deeds of the body you will live.[92] 14 For all who are led by the Spirit of God are sons of God. 15 For you did not receive the spirit of slavery to fall back into fear, but you have received the spirit of sonship. When we cry, "Abba! Father!"[93] 16 it is the Spirit himself bearing witness with our spirit that we are children of God,[94] 17 and if children, then heirs, heirs of God and fellow heirs with Christ, provided we suffer with him in order that we may also be glorified with him.[95]

18 I consider that the sufferings of this present time are not worth comparing with the glory that is to be revealed to us.[96] 19 For the creation waits with eager longing for the revealing of the sons of God; 20 for the creation was subjected to futility, not of its own will but by the will of him who subjected it in hope;[97] 21 because the creation itself will be set free from its bondage to decay and obtain the glorious lib-

which dwells in you.

12 So then, brethren, we are debtors, not to the flesh, to live according to the flesh—13 for if you live according to the flesh you will die, but if by the Spirit you will put to death the deeds of the body you will live. 14 For all who are led by the Spirit of God are sons of God. 15 For you did not receive the spirit of slavery to fall back into fear, but you have received the spirit of sonship. When we cry, "Abba! Father!" 16 it is the Spirit himself bearing witness with our spirit that we are children of God, 17 and if children, then heirs, heirs of God and fellow heirs with Christ, provided we suffer with him in order that we may also be glorified with him.

18 I consider that the sufferings of this present time are not worth comparing with the glory that is to be revealed to us. 19 For the creation waits with eager longing for the revealing of the sons of God; 20 for the creation was subjected to futility, not of its own will but by the will of him who subjected it in hope; 21 because the creation itself will be set free from its bondage to decay and obtain the glorious lib-

erty of the children of God.[98] 22 We know that the whole creation has been groaning in travail together until now; 23 and not only the creation, but we ourselves, who have the first fruits of the Spirit, groan inwardly as we wait for adoption as sons, the redemption of our bodies.[99] 24 For in this hope we were saved. Now hope that is seen is not hope. For who hopes for what he sees? 25 But if we hope for what we do not see, we wait for it with patience.[100]

26 Likewise the Spirit helps us in our weakness; for we do not know how to pray as we ought, but the Spirit himself intercedes for us with sighs too deep for words. 27 And he who searches the hearts of men knows what is the mind of the Spirit, because the Spirit intercedes for the saints according to the will of God.[101]

28 We know that in everything God works for good with those who love him, who are called according to his purpose. 29 For those whom he foreknew he also predestined to be conformed to the image of his Son, in order that he might be the first-born among many brethren. 30 And those whom he predestined he also called; and those whom he called he also justified; and those whom

erty of the children of God. 22 We know that the whole creation has been groaning in travail together until now; 23 and not only the creation, but we ourselves, who have the first fruits of the Spirit, groan inwardly as we wait for adoption as sons, the redemption of our bodies. 24 For in this hope we were saved. Now hope that is seen is not hope. For who hopes for what he sees? 25 But if we hope for what we do not see, we wait for it with patience.

26 Likewise the Spirit helps us in our weakness; for we do not know how to pray as we ought, but the Spirit himself intercedes for us with sighs too deep for words. 27 And he who searches the hearts of men knows what is the mind of the Spirit, because the Spirit intercedes for the saints according to the will of God.

28 We know that in everything God works for good with those who love him, who are called according to his purpose. 29 For those whom he foreknew he also predestined to be conformed to the image of his Son, in order that he might be the first-born among many brethren. 30 And those whom he predestined he also called; and those whom he called he also justified; and those whom

he justified he also glorified.[102]

31 What then shall we say to this? If God is for us, who is against us? 32 He who did not spare his own Son but gave him up for us all, will he not also give us all things with him? 33 Who shall bring any charge against God's elect? It is God who justifies; 34 who is to condemn? Is it Christ Jesus, who died, yes, who was raised from the dead, who is at the right hand of God, who indeed intercedes for us?[103] 35 Who shall separate us from the love of Christ? Shall tribulation, or distress, or persecution, or famine, or nakedness, or peril, or sword?[104] 36 As it is written,

"For thy sake we are being
    killed all the day long;
we are regarded as sheep to
    be slaughtered."

37 No, in all these things we are more than conquerors through him who loved us. 38 For I am sure that neither death, nor life, nor angels, nor principalities, nor things present, nor things to come, nor powers, 39 nor height, nor depth, nor anything else in all creation,[105] will be able to separate us from the love of God in Christ Jesus our Lord.[106]

9 I am speaking the truth in *the presence of* Christ, I am

he justified he also glorified.

31 What then shall we say to this? If God is for us, who is against us? 32 He who did not spare his own Son but gave him up for us all, will he not also give us all things with him? 33 Who shall bring any charge against God's elect? It is God who justifies; 34 who is to condemn? Is it Christ Jesus, who died, yes, who was raised from the dead, who is at the right hand of God, who indeed intercedes for us? 35 Who shall separate us from the love of Christ? Shall tribulation, or distress, or persecution, or famine, or nakedness, or peril, or sword? 36 As it is written,

"For thy sake we are being
    killed all the day long;
we are regarded as sheep to
    be slaughtered."

37 No, in all these things we are more than conquerors through him who loved us. 38 For I am sure that neither death, nor life, nor angels, nor principalities, nor things present, nor things to come, nor powers, 39 nor height, nor depth, nor anything else in all creation, will be able to separate us from the love of God in Christ Jesus our Lord.

9 I am speaking the truth in Christ, I am not lying; my

not lying; my conscience bears me witness in the Holy Spirit,[107] 2 that I have great sorrow and unceasing anguish in my heart. 3 For I could wish that I myself were accursed and cut off from Christ for the sake of my brethren, my kinsmen by race.[108] 4 They are Israelites, and to them belong the sonship, the glory, the covenants, the giving of the law, the worship, and the promises; 5 to them belong the patriarchs, and of their race, according to the flesh, is the Christ. *The promise of eternal life through belief in Jesus Christ is meant for them as well. But because they refuse to accept that God changed the criteria for salvation from obedience to the particulars of the Jewish law to obedience to its universal precepts, together with belief in the saving power of Jesus Christ, they have relinquished their unique position within salvation history. Yet they retain their advantages in salvation history gained through obedience of the law and made manifest in the world.*[109] God who is over all be blessed for ever. Amen.[110]

6 But it is not as though the word of God had failed. For not all who are descended from Israel belong to Israel, 7 and not

conscience bears me witness in the Holy Spirit, 2 that I have great sorrow and unceasing anguish in my heart. 3 For I could wish that I myself were accursed and cut off from Christ for the sake of my brethren, my kinsmen by race. 4 They are Israelites, and to them belong the sonship, the glory, the covenants, the giving of the law, the worship, and the promises; 5 to them belong the patriarchs, and of their race, according to the flesh, is the Christ. God who is over all be blessed for ever. Amen.

6 But it is not as though the word of God had failed. For not all who are descended from Israel belong to Israel, 7 and not

all are children of Abraham because they are his descendants;[111] but "Through Isaac shall your descendants be named." 8 This means that it is not *necessarily* the children of the flesh who are the children of God, but the children *who receive the promise* are reckoned as descendants.[112] *Their spiritual legitimacy depends on the free will of God.* 9 For this is what the promise said, "About this time I will return and Sarah shall have a son." 10 And not only so, but also when Rebecca had conceived children by one man, our forefather Isaac, 11 though they were not yet born and had done nothing either good or bad, in order that God's purpose of election might continue, not because of works but because of his call, 12 she was told, "The elder will serve the younger." 13 As it is written, "Jacob I loved, but Esau I hated."[113]

14 What shall we say then? Is there injustice on God's part? By no means! 15 For he says to Moses, "I will have mercy on whom I have mercy, and I will have compassion on whom I have compassion." 16 So it depends not upon man's will or exertion, but upon God's mercy. 17 For the scripture says to Pharaoh, "I have *allowed you to appear*[114] for

all are children of Abraham because they are his descendants; but "Through Isaac shall your descendants be named." 8 This means that it is not the children of the flesh who are the children of God, but the children of the promise are reckoned as descendants. 9 For this is what the promise said, "About this time I will return and Sarah shall have a son." 10 And not only so, but also when Rebecca had conceived children by one man, our forefather Isaac, 11 though they were not yet born and had done nothing either good or bad, in order that God's purpose of election might continue, not because of works but because of his call, 12 she was told, "The elder will serve the younger." 13 As it is written, "Jacob I loved, but Esau I hated."

14 What shall we say then? Is there injustice on God's part? By no means! 15 For he says to Moses, "I will have mercy on whom I have mercy, and I will have compassion on whom I have compassion." 16 So it depends not upon man's will or exertion, but upon God's mercy. 17 For the scripture says to Pharaoh, "I have raised you up for the very

the very purpose of showing my power in you, so that my name may be proclaimed in all the earth." 18 So then he has mercy upon whomever he wills, and he hardens the heart[115] of whomever he wills.

19 You will say to me then, "Why does he still find fault? For who can resist his will?" 20 But who are you, a man, to answer back to God? Will what is molded say to its molder, "Why have you made me thus?" 21 Has the potter no right over the clay, to make out of the same lump one vessel for beauty and another for menial use? 22 What if God, desiring to show his wrath and to make known his power, has endured with much patience the vessels of wrath made for destruction,[116] 23 in order to make known the riches of his glory for the vessels of mercy,[117] which he has prepared beforehand for glory,[118] 24 even us whom he has called, not from the Jews only but also from the Gentiles?[119] 25 As indeed he says in Hosea,

"Those who were not my
people
I will call 'my people,' and her
who was not beloved I will
call 'my beloved.'"
26 "And in the very place where it was said to them, 'You are not

purpose of showing my power in you, so that my name may be proclaimed in all the earth." 18 So then he has mercy upon whomever he wills, and he hardens the heart of whomever he wills.

19 You will say to me then, "Why does he still find fault? For who can resist his will?" 20 But who are you, a man, to answer back to God? Will what is molded say to its molder, "Why have you made me thus?" 21 Has the potter no right over the clay, to make out of the same lump one vessel for beauty and another for menial use? 22 What if God, desiring to show his wrath and to make known his power, has endured with much patience the vessels of wrath made for destruction, 23 in order to make known the riches of his glory for the vessels of mercy, which he has prepared beforehand for glory, 24 even us whom he has called, not from the Jews only but also from the Gentiles? 25 As indeed he says in Hosea,

"Those who were not my
people
I will call 'my people,' and her
who was not beloved I will
call 'my beloved.'"
26 "And in the very place where it was said to them, 'You are not

my people,' they will be called 'sons of the living God.'"[120]

27 And Isaiah cried out concerning Israel: "Though the number of the sons of Israel be as the sand of the sea, only a remnant of them will be saved;[121] 28 for the Lord will execute his sentence upon the earth with rigor and dispatch." 29 And as Isaiah predicted,

"If the Lord of hosts had not
left us children,
we would have fared like
Sodom and been made
like Gomorrah."

30 What shall we say, then? That Gentiles who did not pursue righteousness have attained it, that is, righteousness through faith *unto eternal life*; 31 but that Israel who pursued the righteousness which is based on law *attained the lesser goal of the law—a renewed and better worldly existence—yet did not succeed in fulfilling the law—the ultimate end of which is eternal life*.[122] Why? Because *instead of pursuing righteousness through the law on the basis of faith, they pursued it on the basis of achievement*.[123] They have stumbled over the stumbling stone, 33 as it is written,

"Behold, I am laying in Zion
a stone that will make

---

my people,' they will be called 'sons of the living God.'"

27 And Isaiah cried out concerning Israel: "Though the number of the sons of Israel be as the sand of the sea, only a remnant of them will be saved; 28 for the Lord will execute his sentence upon the earth with rigor and dispatch." 29 And as Isaiah predicted,

"If the Lord of hosts had not
left us children,
we would have fared like
Sodom and been made
like Gomorrah."

30 What shall we say, then? That Gentiles who did not pursue righteousness have attained it, that is, righteousness through faith; 31 but that Israel who pursued the righteousness which is based on law did not succeed in fulfilling the law. Why? Because they did not pursue it through faith, but as if it were based on works.

They have stumbled over the stumbling stone, 33 as it is written,

"Behold, I am laying in Zion
a stone that will make

men stumble, a rock that will
will make them fall;[124]
and he who believes in him
will not be put to shame."[125]

**10** Brethren, my heart's desire and prayer to God for them is that they may be saved *from futility and death.* 2 I bear them witness that they have a zeal for God, but *their knowledge is inadequate.*[126] *While obedience to the law served them well with respect to worldly renewal and status, it did not establish justification.* 3 For, being ignorant of the righteousness that comes from God, and seeking to establish their own, they did not submit to God's righteousness *which we preach and which rests on faith.* 4 For Christ is the *fulfillment* of the law/*the Immutable Law and the end of birth unto death,* that every *man* who has faith may be justified.[127]

5 Moses writes that the man who practices the righteousness which is based on the law shall be *given the opportunity to resurrect unto a renewed and better mortal existence in relation to his fulfillment of the law.*[128] 6 But the righteousness based on faith says, do not say in your heart, "Who will ascend into heaven?" (that is, to bring Christ

men stumble, a rock that will
will make them fall;
and he who believes in him
will not be put to shame."

**10** Brethren, my heart's desire and prayer to God for them is that they may be saved. 2 I bear them witness that they have a zeal for God, but it is not enlightened. For, being ignorant of the righteousness that comes from God, and seeking to establish their own, they did not submit to God's righteousness. 4 For Christ is the end of the law, that every one who has faith may be justified.

5 Moses writes that the man who practices the righteousness which is based on the law shall live by it. 6 But the righteousness based on faith says, do not say in your heart, "Who will ascend into heaven?" (that is, to bring Christ down) 7 or "who will descend into the abyss?" (that is, to bring Christ up from the dead). 8 But what does it say? The word

down) 7 or "who will descend into the abyss?" (that is, to bring Christ up from the dead). 8 But what does it say? The word is near you, on your lips and in your heart (that is, the word of faith which we preach); 9 because, if you confess with your lips that Jesus is Lord and believe in your heart[129] that God raised him from the dead, you will be saved *from the necessity of regeneration and imminent destruction.* 10 For man believes with his heart and so is *made innocent,* and he confesses with his lips and so is *reborn unto eternal life.*[130] 11 The scripture says, "No one who believes in him will be put to shame"—*unto rebirth into a lower state nor be subject to incessant suffering and death.* 12 For there is no distinction between Jew and Greek; the same Lord is Lord of all and bestows his riches upon all who call upon him. 13 For, "every one who calls upon the name of the Lord will be saved."[131]

14 But how are men to call upon him in whom they have not believed? And how are they to believe in him of whom they have never heard? And how are they to hear without a preacher? 15 And how can men preach unless they are sent?[132] As it is written,

is near you, on your lips and in your heart (that is, the word of faith which we preach); 9 because, if you confess with your lips that Jesus is Lord and believe in your heart that God raised him from the dead, you will be saved. 10 For man believes with his heart and so is justified, and he confesses with his lips so is saved. 11 The scripture says, "No one who believes in him will be put to shame." 12 For there is no distinction between Jew and Greek; the same Lord is Lord of all and bestows his riches upon all who call upon him. 13 For, "every one who calls upon the name of the Lord will be saved."

14 But how are men to call upon him in whom they have not believed? And how are they to believe in him of whom they have never heard? And how are they to hear without a preacher? 15 And how can men preach unless they are sent? As it is written,

"How beautiful are the feet of those who preach good news!" 16 But they have not all obeyed the gospel; for Isaiah says, "Lord, who has believed what he has heard from us?" 17 So faith comes from what is heard, and what is heard comes by the preaching of Christ.

18 But I ask, have they not heard? Indeed they have; for

"Their voice has gone out to
    all the earth,
and their words to the ends of
    the world."

19 Again I ask, did Israel not understand? First Moses says,

"I will make you jealous of
    those who are not a nation;
with a foolish nation I will
    make you angry."

20 Then Isaiah is so bold as to say, "I have been found by those who did not seek me;

I have shown myself to those
    who did not ask for me."[133]

21 But of Israel he says, "All day long I have held out my hands to a disobedient and contrary people."

11 I ask, then, has God rejected his people? By no means! I myself am an Israelite, a descendant of Abraham, a member of the tribe of Benjamin. 2 God has not rejected his people

whom he foreknew.[134] Do you not know what the scripture says of Elijah, how he pleads with God against Israel? 3 "Lord, they have killed thy prophets, they have demolished thy altars, and I alone am left, and they seek my life." 4 But what is God's reply to him? "I have kept for myself seven thousand men who have not bowed the knee to Baal."[135] 5 So too at the present time there is a remnant, chosen by grace.[136] 6 But if it is by grace, it is no longer on the basis of works; otherwise grace would no longer be grace.

7 What then? Israel failed to obtain what it had sought—*eternal life*—[137]*on the basis of works*. The elect obtained it, but the rest were hardened, 8 as it is written,

"God gave them a spirit of
stupor, eyes that should not
see and ears that should not
hear, down to this very day."
9 And David says,
"Let their table become a snare
and a trap, a pitfall and a
retribution for them;
10 Let their eyes be darkened so
that they cannot see,
and bend their backs for ever."

11 So I ask, have they stumbled so as to fall? By no means![138] But through their tres-

whom he foreknew. Do you not know what the scripture says of Elijah, how he pleads with God against Israel? 3 "Lord, they have killed thy prophets, they have demolished thy altars, and I alone am left, and they seek my life." 4 But what is God's reply to him? "I have kept for myself seven thousand men who have not bowed the knee to Baal." 5 So too at the present time there is a remnant, chosen by grace. 6 But if it is by grace, it is no longer on the basis of works; otherwise grace would no longer be grace.

7 What then? Israel failed to obtain what it sought. The elect obtained it, but the rest were hardened, 8 as it is written,

"God gave them a spirit of
stupor, eyes that should not
see and ears that should not
hear, down to this very day."
9 And David says,
"Let their table become a snare
and a trap, a pitfall and a
retribution for them;
10 Let their eyes be darkened so
that they cannot see,
and bend their backs for ever."

11 So I ask, have they stumbled so as to fall? By no means! But through their trespass

pass salvation has come to the Gentiles, so as to make Israel jealous. 12 Now if their trespass means riches for the world, and if their failure means riches for the Gentiles, how much more will their full inclusion mean!¹³⁹

13 Now I am speaking to you Gentiles. Inasmuch then as I am an apostle to the Gentiles, I magnify my ministry 14 in order to make my fellow Jews jealous, and thus save some of them. 15 For if their rejection means the reconciliation of the world, what will their acceptance mean but *the end of cyclical rebirth and death*? 16 If the dough offered as first fruits is holy, so is the whole lump; and if the root is holy, so are the branches.

17 But if some of the *Jews* were broken off, and you, *a Gentile*, were grafted in their place to share the richness of the *eschatological* olive tree, 18 do not boast over the *Jews who were broken off*. If you do boast, remember it is not you that support the root, but the root that supports you. 19 You will say, "*Jews* were broken off so that I might be grafted in." 20 That is true. They were broken off because of their unbelief, but you stand fast only through faith. So do not become proud, but stand

salvation has come to the Gentiles, so as to make Israel jealous. 12 Now if their trespass means riches for the world, and if their failure means riches for the Gentiles, how much more will their full inclusion mean!

13 Now I am speaking to you Gentiles. Inasmuch then as I am an apostle to the Gentiles, I magnify my ministry 14 in order to make my fellow Jews jealous, and thus save some of them. 15 For if their rejection means the reconciliation of the world, what will their acceptance mean but life from the dead? 16 If the dough offered as first fruits is holy, so is the whole lump; and if the root is holy, so are the branches.

17 But if some of the branches were broken off, and you, a wild olive shoot, were grafted in their place to share the richness of the olive tree, 18 do not boast over the branches. If you do boast, remember it is not you that support the root, but the root that supports you. 19 You will say, "Branches were broken off so that I might be grafted in." 20 That is true. They were broken off because of their unbelief, but you stand fast only through faith. So do not become proud, but stand in awe. 21 For if God did

in awe. 21 For if God did not spare the *Jews*—the natural branches, neither will he spare you. 22 Note then the kindness and the severity of God: severity toward those who have fallen, but God's kindness to you, provided you continue in his kindness; otherwise you too will be cut off. 23 And even the others, if they do not persist in their unbelief, will be grafted in, for God has the power to graft them in again. 24 For if you have been cut from what is by nature a wild, *untended* olive tree, and grafted, contrary to nature *by the power of faith in Christ*, into a cultivated *eschatological* olive tree, how much more will these natural branches be grafted back into .their own olive tree.[140]

25 Lest you be wise in your own conceits, I want you to understand this mystery, brethren: a hardening has come upon part of Israel, until the full number of the Gentiles come in, 26 and so all Israel will be saved; as it is written,

"The Deliverer will come from Zion, he will banish ungodliness from Jacob";

27 "and this will be my covenant with them when I take away their sins."

28 As regards the gospel they are

not spare the natural branches, neither will he spare you. 22 Note then the kindness and the severity of God: severity toward those who have fallen, but God's kindness to you, provided you continue in his kindness; otherwise you too will be cut off. 23 And even the others, if they do not persist in their unbelief, will be grafted in, for God has the power to graft them in again. 24 For if you have been cut from what is by nature a wild olive tree, and grafted, contrary to nature, into a cultivated olive tree, how much more will these natural branches be grafted back into their own olive tree.

25 Lest you be wise in your own conceits, I want you to understand this mystery, brethren: a hardening has come upon part of Israel, until the full number of the Gentiles come in, 26 and so all Israel will be saved; as it is written,

"The Deliverer will come from Zion, he will banish ungodliness from Jacob";

27 "and this will be my covenant with them when I take away their sins."

28 As regards the gospel they are

enemies of God, for your sake; but as regards election they are beloved for the sake of their forefathers. 29 For the gifts and the call of God are irrevocable. *Thus they retain the advantages under the law which guided their spirituality prior to the coming of Christ.* 30 Just as you were once disobedient to God but now have received mercy because of their disobedience, 31 so they have now been disobedient in order that by the mercy shown to you they also may receive mercy. 32 For God has consigned all men to disobedience, that he may have mercy upon all.[141]

33 O the depth of the riches and wisdom and knowledge of God! How unsearchable are his judgments and how inscrutable his ways!
34 "For who has known the
        mind of the Lord, or who
        has been his counselor?"
35 "Or who has given a gift to
        him that he might be repaid?"
36 For from him and through him and to him are all things. To him be glory for ever. Amen.[142]

12 I appeal to you therefore, brethren, by the mercies of God, to present your bodies as a living sacrifice, holy and acceptable to God, which is your

enemies of God, for your sake; but as regards election they are beloved for the sake of their forefathers. 29 For the gifts and the call of God are irrevocable. 30 Just as you were once disobedient to God but now have received mercy because of their disobedience, 31 so they have now been disobedient in order that by the mercy shown to you they also may receive mercy. 32 For God has consigned all men to disobedience, that he may have mercy upon all.

33 O the depth of the riches and wisdom and knowledge of God! How unsearchable are his judgments and how inscrutable his ways!
34 "For who has known the
        mind of the Lord, or who
        has been his counselor?"
35 "Or who has given a gift to
        him that he might be repaid?"
36 For from him and through him and to him are all things. To him be glory for ever. Amen.

12 I appeal to you therefore, brethren, by the mercies of God, to present your bodies as a living sacrifice, holy and acceptable to God, which is your

spiritual worship. 2 Do not be conformed to this world but be transformed by the renewal of your mind, that you may prove what is the will of God, what is good and acceptable and perfect.

3 For by the grace given to me I bid every one among you not to think of himself more highly than he ought to think *due to the possession of the more rare spiritual gifts,* but to think with sober judgment, each according to the measure of faith which God has assigned him. 4 For as in one body we have many members, and all the members do not have the same function, 5 so we, though many, are one body in Christ, and individually members one of another. 6 Having gifts that differ according to the grace given to us, let us use them: if prophecy, in proportion to our faith; 7 if service, in our serving; he who teaches, in his teaching; 8 he who exhorts, in his exhortation; he who contributes, in liberality; he who gives aid, with zeal; he who does acts of mercy, with cheerfulness.[143]

9 Let love be genuine; hate what is evil, hold fast to what is good; 10 love one another with brotherly affection; outdo one another in showing honor. 11 Never flag in zeal, be aglow with

spiritual worship. 2 Do not be conformed to this world but be transformed by the renewal of your mind, that you may prove what is the will of God, what is good and acceptable and perfect.

3 For by the grace given to me I bid every one among you not to think of himself more highly than he ought to think, but to think with sober judgment, each according to the measure of faith which God has assigned him. 4 For as in one body we have many members, and all the members do not have the same function, 5 so we, though many, are one body in Christ, and individually members one of another. 6 Having gifts that differ according to the grace given to us, let us use them: if prophecy, in proportion to our faith; 7 if service, in our serving; he who teaches, in his teaching; 8 he who exhorts, in his exhortation; he who contributes, in liberality; he who gives aid, with zeal; he who does acts of mercy, with cheerfulness.

9 Let love be genuine; hate what is evil, hold fast to what is good; 10 love one another with brotherly affection; outdo one another in showing honor. 11 Never flag in zeal, be aglow with

the Spirit, serve the Lord. 12 Rejoice in your hope, be patient in tribulation, be constant in prayer. 13 Contribute to the needs of the saints, practice hospitality.

14 Bless those who persecute you; bless and do not curse them. 15 Rejoice with those who rejoice, weep with those who weep. 16 Live in harmony with one another; do not be haughty, but associate with the lowly; never be conceited. 17 Repay no one evil for evil, but take thought for what is noble in the sight of all. 18 If possible, so far as it depends upon you, live peaceably with all. 19 Beloved, never avenge yourselves, but leave it to the wrath of God *whose justice transcends time and is inescapable*; for it is written, "Vengeance is mine, I will repay, says the Lord." 20 No, "if your enemy is hungry, feed him; if he is thirsty, give him drink; for by so doing you will heap burning coals upon his head." 21 Do not be overcome by evil, but overcome evil with good.

13 Let every person be subject to the governing authorities. For there is no authority except from God *whose justice metes out all worldly status*. Those that exist have been instituted by God *just as our indi-*

the Spirit, serve the Lord. 12 Rejoice in your hope, be patient in tribulation, be constant in prayer. 13 Contribute to the needs of the saints, practice hospitality.

14 Bless those who persecute you; bless and do not curse them. 15 Rejoice with those who rejoice, weep with those who weep. 16 Live in harmony with one another; do not be haughty, but associate with the lowly; never be conceited. 17 Repay no one evil for evil, but take thought for what is noble in the sight of all. 18 If possible, so far as it depends upon you, live peaceably with all. 19 Beloved, never avenge yourselves, but leave it to the wrath of God; for it is written, "Vengeance is mine, I will repay, says the Lord." 20 No, "if your enemy is hungry, feed him; if he is thirsty, give him drink; for by so doing you will heap burning coals upon his head." 21 Do not be overcome by evil, but overcome evil with good.

13 Let every person be subject to the governing authorities. For there is no authority except from God, and those that exist have been instituted by God. 2 Therefore he who resists the authorities resists what God

*vidual and corporate status is contingent upon his judgment.* 2 Therefore he who resists the authorities resists what God has appointed, *and will incur judgment.* 3 For rulers are not a terror to good conduct, but to bad. Would you have no fear of him who is in authority? Then do what is good, and you will receive his approval, 4 for he is God's servant for your good. But if you do wrong, be afraid, for he does not bear the sword in vain; he is the servant of God to execute *God's* wrath on the wrongdoer. 5 Therefore one must be subject, not only to avoid God's wrath *meted out through his servants in this world,* but also for the sake of conscience *which, if conflicted, will bear bitter fruit in the life to come.* 6 For the same reason you also pay taxes, for the authorities are ministers of God, attending to this very thing. 7 Pay all of them their dues, taxes to whom taxes are due, revenue to whom revenue is due, respect to whom respect is due, honor to whom honor is due.[144]

8 Owe no one anything, except to love one another; for he who loves his neighbor has fulfilled the law/*the Immutable Law.* 9 The commandments, "You shall not commit adultery, You shall

has appointed, and those who resist will incur judgment. 3 For rulers are not a terror to good conduct, but to bad. Would you have no fear of him who is in authority? Then do what is good, and you will receive his approval, 4 for he is God's servant for your good. But if you do wrong, be afraid, for he does not bear the sword in vain; he is the servant of God to execute God's wrath on the wrongdoer. 5 Therefore one must be subject, not only to avoid God's wrath but also for the sake of conscience. 6 For the same reason you also pay taxes, for the authorities are ministers of God, attending to this very thing. 7 Pay all of them their dues, taxes to whom taxes are due, revenue to whom revenue is due, respect to whom respect is due, honor to whom honor is due.

8 Owe no one anything, except to love one another; for he who loves his neighbor has fulfilled the law. 9 The commandments, "You shall not commit adultery, You shall not kill, You

not kill, You shall not steal, You shall not covet," and any other commandment, are summed up in this sentence. "You shall love your neighbor as yourself." 10 Love does no wrong to a neighbor; therefore love is the fulfilling of the law/*the Immutable Law.*

11 Besides this you know what hour it is, how it is full time now for you to wake from sleep. For salvation is nearer to us now than when we first believed; 12 the night is far gone, the day is at hand. Let us then cast off the works of darkness and put on the armor of light;[145] 13 let us conduct ourselves becomingly as in the day, not in reveling and drunkenness, not in debauchery and licentiousness, not in quarreling and jealousy. 14 But put on the Lord Jesus Christ, and make no provision for the flesh, to gratify its desires.

14 As for the man who is weak in faith, welcome him, but not for disputes over opinions. 2 One believes he may eat anything, while the weak man eats only vegetables.[146] 3 Let not him who eats despise him who abstains, and let not him who abstains pass judgment on him who eats; for God has welcomed him.

shall not steal, You shall not covet," and any other commandment, are summed up in this sentence. "You shall love your neighbor as yourself." 10 Love does no wrong to a neighbor; therefore love is the fulfilling of the law.

11 Besides this you know what hour it is, how it is full time now for you to wake from sleep. For salvation is nearer to us now than when we first believed; 12 the night is far gone, the day is at hand. Let us then cast off the works of darkness and put on the armor of light; 13 let us conduct ourselves becomingly as in the day, not in reveling and drunkenness, not in debauchery and licentiousness, not in quarreling and jealousy. 14 But put on the Lord Jesus Christ, and make no provision for the flesh, to gratify its desires.

14 As for the man who is weak in faith, welcome him, but not for disputes over opinions. 2 One believes he may eat anything, while the weak man eats only vegetables. 3 Let not him who eats despise him who abstains, and let not him who abstains pass judgment on him who eats; for God has welcomed him.

4 Who are you to pass judgment on the servant of another? It is before his own master that he stands or falls. And he will be upheld, for the Master is able to make him stand.

5 One man esteems one day as better than another, while another man esteems all days alike. Let every one be fully convinced in his own mind, *thus purity of conscience is maintained.* 6 He who observes the day, observes it in honor of the Lord. He also who eats, eats in honor of the Lord, since he gives thanks to God; while he who abstains, abstains in honor of the Lord and gives thanks to God. 7 None of us lives to himself, and none of us dies to himself. 8 If we live, we live to the Lord, and if we die, we die to the Lord; so then, whether we live or whether we die, we are the Lord's. 9 For to this end Christ died and lived again, that he might be Lord both of the dead and of the living.

10 Why do you pass judgment on your brother? Or you, why do you despise your brother? For we shall all stand before the judgment seat of God; 11 for it is written,

"As I live, says the Lord,
every knee shall bow to
me, and every tongue shall give

4 Who are you to pass judgment on the servant of another? It is before his own master that he stands or falls. And he will be upheld, for the Master is able to make him stand.

5 One man esteems one day as better than another, while another man esteems all days alike. Let every one be fully convinced in his own mind. 6 He who observes the day, observes it in honor of the Lord. He also who eats, eats in honor of the Lord, since he gives thanks to God; while he who abstains, abstains in honor of the Lord and gives thanks to God. 7 None of us lives to himself, and none of us dies to himself. 8 If we live, we live to the Lord, and if we die, we die to the Lord; so then, whether we live or whether we die, we are the Lord's. 9 For to this end Christ died and lived again, that he might be Lord both of the dead and of the living.

10 Why do you pass judgment on your brother? Or you, why do you despise your brother? For we shall all stand before the judgment seat of God; 11 for it is written,

"As I live, says the Lord,
every knee shall bow to
me, and every tongue shall give

praise to God."

12 So each of us shall give account of himself to God.

13 Then let us no more pass judgment on one another, but rather decide never to put a stumbling block or hindrance in the way of a brother *by making him feel guilty.* 14 I know and am persuaded in the Lord Jesus that nothing is unclean in itself; but it is unclean for any one who thinks it unclean. *Thus is the power of faith/belief.* 15 If your brother is being injured by what you eat, you are no longer walking in love. Do not let what you eat cause the ruin of one for whom Christ died.[147] 16 So do not let your good be spoken of as evil. 17 For the kingdom of God is not food and drink but righteousness and peace and joy in the Holy Spirit. 18 He who thus serves Christ is acceptable to God and approved by men. 19 Let us then pursue what makes for peace and for mutual upbuilding. 20 Do not, for the sake of food, destroy the work of God. Everything is indeed clean, but it is wrong for any one to make others fall by what he eats; 21 it is right not to eat meat or drink wine or do anything that makes your brother stumble. 22 The faith that you have, keep between yourself and God; happy

praise to God."

12 So each of us shall give account of himself to God.

13 Then let us no more pass judgment on one another, but rather decide never to put a stumbling block or hindrance in the way of a brother. 14 I know and am persuaded in the Lord Jesus that nothing is unclean in itself; but it is unclean for any one who thinks it unclean.15 If your brother is being injured by what you eat, you are no longer walking in love. Do not let what you eat cause the ruin of one for whom Christ died. 16 So do not let your good be spoken of as evil. 17 For the kingdom of God is not food and drink but righteousness and peace and joy in the Holy Spirit. 18 He who thus serves Christ is acceptable to God and approved by men. 19 Let us then pursue what makes for peace and for mutual upbuilding. 20 Do not, for the sake of food, destroy the work of God. Everything is indeed clean, but it is wrong for any one to make others fall by what he eats; 21 it is right not to eat meat or drink wine or do anything that makes your brother stumble. 22 The faith that you have, keep between yourself and God; happy is he who has no reason to judge himself for what he approves. 23

is he who has no reason to judge himself for what he approves. 23 But he who has doubts is condemned, if he eats, because he does not act from *what he believes to be true*; for whatever does not proceed from faith/*belief* is sin/*negative karma*.[148]

But he who has doubts is condemned, if he eats, because he does not act from faith; for whatever does not proceed from faith is sin.

15 We who are strong ought to bear with the failings of the weak, and not to please ourselves; 2 let each of us please his neighbor for his good, to edify him. 3 For Christ did not please himself; but, as it is written, "the reproaches of those who reproached thee fell on me." 4 For whatever was written *before the coming of Christ* was written for our instruction, that by steadfastness and by the encouragement of the scriptures we might have hope *of a renewed and better worldly existence.* 5 May the God of steadfastness and encouragement grant you to live in such harmony with one another, in accord with Christ Jesus, 6 that together you may with one voice glorify the God and Father of our Lord Jesus Christ.

7 Welcome one another, therefore, as Christ has welcomed you, for the glory of God. 8 For I tell you that Christ became a servant to the circumcised to show God's

15 We who are strong ought to bear with the failings of the weak, and not to please ourselves; 2 let each of us please his neighbor for his good, to edify him. 3 For Christ did not please himself; but, as it is written, "the reproaches of those who reproached thee fell on me." 4 For whatever was written in former days was written for our instruction, that by steadfastness and by the encouragement of the scriptures we might have hope. 5 May the God of steadfastness and encouragement grant you to live in such harmony with one another, in accord with Christ Jesus, 6 that together you may with one voice glorify the God and Father of our Lord Jesus Christ.

7 Welcome one another, therefore, as Christ has welcomed you, for the glory of God. 8 For I tell you that Christ became a servant to the circumcised to show God's

truthfulness, in order to confirm
the promises given to the patriarchs, 9 and in order that the Gentiles might glorify God for his
mercy. As it is written,
"Therefore I will praise thee
among the Gentiles,
and sing to thy name";
10 and again it is said,
"Rejoice, O Gentiles, with
his people";
11 and again,
"Praise the Lord, all Gentiles,
and let all the peoples
praise him";
12 and further Isaiah says,
"The root of Jesse shall come,
he who rises to rule the Gentiles;
in him shall the Gentiles hope."
13 May the God of hope fill you
with all joy and peace in believing, *that you will no longer arise
unto cyclical birth and death, but*
that by the power of the Holy
Spirit you may abound in hope
*for eternal life.*

14 I myself am satisfied about
you, my brethren, that you yourselves are full of goodness, filled
with all knowledge, and able to
instruct one another.[149] 15 But on
some points I have written to you
very boldly by way of reminder,
because of the grace given me by
God 16 to be a minister of Christ
Jesus to the Gentiles in the
priestly service of the gospel of

truthfulness, in order to confirm
the promises given to the patriarchs, 9 and in order that the Gentiles might glorify God for his
mercy. As it is written,
"Therefore I will praise thee
among the Gentiles,
and sing to thy name";
10 and again it is said,
"Rejoice, O Gentiles, with
his people";
11 and again,
"Praise the Lord, all Gentiles,
and let all the peoples
praise him";
12 and further Isaiah says,
"The root of Jesse shall come,
he who rises to rule the Gentiles;
in him shall the Gentiles hope."
13 May the God of hope fill you
with all joy and peace in believing, so that by the power of the
Holy Spirit you may abound in
hope.

14 I myself am satisfied about
you, my brethren, that you yourselves are full of goodness, filled
with all knowledge, and able to
instruct one another. 15 But on
some points I have written to you
very boldly by way of reminder,
because of the grace given me by
God 16 to be a minister of Christ
Jesus to the Gentiles in the
priestly service of the gospel of

God, so that the offering of the Gentiles may be acceptable, sanctified by the Holy Spirit. 17 In Christ Jesus, then, I have reason to be proud of my work for God. 18 For I will not venture to speak of anything except what Christ has wrought through me to win obedience from the Gentiles, by word and deed, 19 by the power of signs and wonders, by the power of the Holy Spirit,[150] so that from Jerusalem and as far round as Illyricum I have fully preached the gospel of Christ, 20 thus making it my ambition to preach the gospel, not where Christ has already been named, lest I build on another man's foundation, 21 but as it is written,

"They shall see who have
never been told of him,
and they shall understand who
have never heard of him."[151]

22 This is the reason why I have so often been hindered from coming to you. 23 But now, since I no longer have any room for work in these regions, and since I have longed for many years to come to you, 24 I hope to see you in passing as I go to Spain, and to be sped on my journey there by you, once I have enjoyed your company for a little. 25 At present, however, I am going to

God, so that the offering of the Gentiles may be acceptable, sanctified by the Holy Spirit. 17 In Christ Jesus, then, I have reason to be proud of my work for God. 18 For I will not venture to speak of anything except what Christ has wrought through me to win obedience from the Gentiles, by word and deed, 19 by the power of signs and wonders, by the power of the Holy Spirit, so that from Jerusalem and as far round as Illyricum I have fully preached the gospel of Christ, 20 thus making it my ambition to preach the gospel, not where Christ has already been named, lest I build on another man's foundation, 21 but as it is written,

"They shall see who have
never been told of him,
and they shall understand who
have never heard of him."

22 This is the reason why I have so often been hindered from coming to you. 23 But now, since I no longer have any room for work in these regions, and since I have longed for many years to come to you, 24 I hope to see you in passing as I go to Spain, and to be sped on my journey there by you, once I have enjoyed your company for a little. 25 At present, however, I am going to

Jerusalem with aid for the saints. 26 For Macedonia and Achaia have been pleased to make some contribution for the poor among the saints at Jerusalem;[152] 27 they were pleased to do it, and indeed they are in debt to them, for if the Gentiles have come to share in their spiritual blessings, they ought also to be of service to them in material blessings. 28 When therefore I have completed this, and have delivered to them what has been raised, I shall go on by way of you to Spain; 29 and I know that when I come to you I shall come in the fullness of the blessing of Christ.

30 I appeal to you, brethren, by our Lord Jesus Christ and by the love of the Spirit, to strive together with me in your prayers to God on my behalf, 31 that I may be delivered from the unbelievers in Judea, and that my service for Jerusalem may be acceptable to the saints, 32 so that by God's will I may come to you with joy and be refreshed in your company. 33 The God of peace be with you all.[153] Amen.

16 I commend to you our sister Phoebe, a deaconess of the church at Cenchreae, 2 that you may receive her in the Lord as befits the saints, and help

Jerusalem with aid for the saints. 26 For Macedonia and Achaia have been pleased to make some contribution for the poor among the saints at Jerusalem; 27 they were pleased to do it, and indeed they are in debt to them, for if the Gentiles have come to share in their spiritual blessings, they ought also to be of service to them in material blessings. 28 When therefore I have completed this, and have delivered to them what has been raised, I shall go on by way of you to Spain; 29 and I know that when I come to you I shall come in the fullness of the blessing of Christ.

30 I appeal to you, brethren, by our Lord Jesus Christ and by the love of the Spirit, to strive together with me in your prayers to God on my behalf, 31 that I may be delivered from the unbelievers in Judea, and that my service for Jerusalem may be acceptable to the saints, 32 so that by God's will I may come to you with joy and be refreshed in your company. 33 The God of peace be with you all. Amen.

16 I commend to you our sister Phoebe, a deaconess of the church at Cenchreae, 2 that you may receive her in the Lord as befits the saints, and help

her in whatever she may require from you, for she has been a helper of many and of myself as well.

3 Greet Prisca and Aquila, my fellow workers in Christ Jesus, 4 who risked their necks for my life, to whom not only I but also all the churches of the Gentiles give thanks; 5 greet also the church in their house. Greet my beloved Epaenetus, who was the first convert in Asia for Christ. 6 Greet Mary, who has worked hard among you. 7 Greet Andronicus and Junias, my kinsmen and my fellow prisoners; they are men of note among the apostles, and they were in Christ before me. 8 Greet Ampliatus, my beloved in the Lord. 9 Greet Urbanus, our fellow worker in Christ, and my beloved Stachys. 10 Greet Apelles, who is approved in Christ. Greet those who belong to the family of Aristobulus. 11 Greet my kinsman Herodion. Greet those in the Lord who belong to the family of Narcissus. 12 Greet those workers in the Lord, Tryphaena and Tryphosa. Greet the beloved Persis, who has worked hard in the Lord. 13 Greet Rufus, eminent in the Lord, also his mother and mine. 14 Greet Asyncritus, Phlegon, Hermes, Patrobas,

Hermas, and the brethren who are with them. 15 Greet Philologus, Julia, Nereus and his sister, and Olympas, and all the saints who are with them. 16 Greet one another with a holy kiss. All the churches of Christ greet you.

17 I appeal to you, brethren, to take note of those who create dissensions and difficulties, in opposition to the doctrine which you have been taught; avoid them. 18 For such persons do not serve our Lord Christ, but their own appetites, and by *their* fair and flattering words they deceive the hearts of the simple-minded.[154] 19 For while your obedience is known to all, so that I rejoice over you, I would have you wise as to what is good and guileless as to what is evil; 20 then the God of peace will soon crush Satan under your feet. The grace of our Lord Jesus Christ be with you.

21 Timothy, my fellow worker, greets you; so do Lucius and Jason and Sosipater, my kinsmen.

22 I Tertius, the writer of this letter, greet you in the Lord

23 Gaius, who is host to me and to the whole church, greets you. Erastus, the city treasurer, and our brother Quartus, greet you.

Hermas, and the brethren who are with them. 15 Greet Philologus, Julia, Nereus and his sister, and Olympas, and all the saints who are with them. 16 Greet one another with a holy kiss. All the churches of Christ greet you.

17 I appeal to you, brethren, to take note of those who create dissensions and difficulties, in opposition to the doctrine which you have been taught; avoid them. 18 For such persons do not serve our Lord Christ, but their own appetites, and by fair and flattering words they deceive the hearts of the simple-minded. 19 For while your obedience is known to all, so that I rejoice over you, I would have you wise as to what is good and guileless as to what is evil; 20 then the God of peace will soon crush Satan under your feet. The grace of our Lord Jesus Christ be with you.

21 Timothy, my fellow worker, greets you; so do Lucius and Jason and Sosipater, my kinsmen.

22 I Tertius, the writer of this letter, greet you in the Lord

23 Gaius, who is host to me and to the whole church, greets you. Erastus, the city treasurer, and our brother Quartus, greet you.

25 Now to him who is able to strengthen you according to my gospel and the preaching of Jesus Christ, according to the revelation of the mystery which was kept secret for long ages 26 but is now disclosed and through the prophetic writings is made known to all nations, according to the command of the eternal God, to bring about the obedience of faith[155]—27 to the only wise God be glory for evermore through Jesus Christ! Amen.

25 Now to him who is able to strengthen you according to my gospel and the preaching of Jesus Christ, according to the revelation of the mystery which was kept secret for long ages 26 but is now disclosed and through the prophetic writings is made known to all nations, according to the command of the eternal God, to bring about the obedience of faith—27 to the only wise God be glory for evermore through Jesus Christ! Amen.

# CONCLUSION

St. Paul, a Pharisaic Jew and a Gnostic, was familiar with the various ideas and beliefs of the people in his audience and addressed them in his letter to the Romans. Romans can finally be understood if read with the knowledge that its audience, while multifarious, shared a cross-cultural belief in reincarnation. In fact, Roman society itself was structured progressively by birthright, reflecting the belief of many of its people in the progressive nature of reincarnation. Simply put, this cross-cultural belief in reincarnation is the "central concern . . . [and] inner logic" that Kasemann noted has been lost to modern Pauline scholarship, and which resulted in academic frustration over the meaning of Paul's words.

While the Romans shared this core spiritual belief, the often overlapping groups (the Jews, Gnostics, Greeks, Gentiles and pagans) in Paul's Roman audience viewed differently the process of reincarnation and its goals, or lack thereof. Paul's audience included both ethnic and converted Jews (gentile Jews) who believed that adherence to the Jewish law would result in progressively better reincarnation on earth. It also included Jews and Gnostics who despaired within the system of endless death and rebirth, seeking a way out of the cycle.

Paul used terminology in his epistles that would have struck chords in his audience. The Jewish law, referred to by Paul in Romans, was familiar to the people of his audience. Paul referred to the various beliefs of the Romans regarding the origination of man on earth and the processes of resurrection. He told all men that the Christ event ended the cycle of reincarnation for all, regardless of adherence to the Jewish law. Through Christ, all men could live eternally with God and be freed from the anguish of mortality. St. Paul therefore speaks to all, and is "all things to all men."

# NOTES

# CHAPTER TWO

## THE ANCIENT WORLDVIEW: BELIEF IN REINCARNATION

1. W. Macneile Dixon, "Introduction," in *Reincarnation in World Thought*. Ed. by Joseph Head and S.L. Cranston (The Julian Press, 1967).

2. W.R. Alger, "A Critical History of the Doctrine of a Future Life," in *Reincarnation in World Thought*.

3. Ibid., 475.

4. Lewis M. Hopfe, *Religions of the World* (New York: Macmillan College Publishing Company, 1994), 76.

5. Wolfgang Wiefel, "The Jewish Community in Ancient Rome and the Origins of Roman Christianity," in *The Roman Debate*, 86.

6. Hopfe, 80.

7. Ibid., 80, 81.

8. Ibid., 78.

9. Ibid., 80.

10. Ibid., 82.

11. Ibid., 83.

12. Ibid., 89.

13. Ibid., 87.

14. Ibid., 88.

15. Ibid., 89n17.

16. Ibid., 89.

17. Ibid., 88.

18. Ibid., 89.

19. Ibid., 89n18.

20. Ibid., 90.

21. Ibid., 90.

22. Ibid., 93.

23. Henri Charles Puech, "Gnosis and Time," in *Man and Time*. Ed. by Joseph Campbell (New York: Princeton University Press, 1957, second printing 1973), 40.

24. Ibid., 39.

25. Ibid., 40, 41.

26. Ibid., 41.

27. Ibid., 43.

28. Plato, "Phaedrus," in *The Dialogues of Plato*. Trans. by B. Jowlett, M.A. (London: Oxford University Press, 1871, 1875, 1892, 1931), 396.

29. Ibid., 396.

30. Ibid., 397.

31. Ibid., 397.
32. Ibid., 397.
33. Ibid., 397.

# CHAPTER THREE

## THE WORLDVIEW HELD BY FIRST-CENTURY PHARISAIC JUDAISM

1. Morton Smith, "Palestinian Judaism in the First Century," in *Israel: Its Role in Civilization*. Ed. by Moshe Davis (New York: Harper Row, Publishers, 1956), 67-81.

2. Jacob Neusner, *From Politics to Piety* (New York: KTAV Publishing House, Inc., 1979), 3.

3. Ibid., 9.

4. Ibid., 9.

5. Smith, 79-80.

6. Smith, 81.

7. Ellis Rivkin, *A Hidden Revolution* (Tennessee: The Parthenon Press, 1978), 125.

8. Ibid., 125-126.

9. Ibid., 127-128.

10. Ibid., 127.

11. Ibid., 128.

12. Ibid., 129.

13. Ibid., 253.

14. Ibid., 125.

15. Ibid., 125.

16. Ibid., 126, 127. Among the tumultuous events with which the *Tannaitic* literature was apparently unconcerned were the Hasmonean Revolt (166 B.C.E.), the collapse of the Zadokite monarchy and priesthood (165-63 B.C.E.), the taking of Jerusalem for Rome by the Roman general Pompey (63 B.C.E.), the rise and fall of the House of Herod (37-4 B.C.E.), the disturbed era of the procurators, the birth of Christianity, the Great Rebellion against Rome (66 C.E.), the destruction of the Second Temple (70 C.E.), the Hadrianic persecutions, and the Bar Kokhba Revolt (132-135 C.E.).

It should be noted that the Pharisees were indifferent only to secular events that did not directly impinge on their teachings of their oral law. Time or history must have had meaning for the Pharisees, inasmuch as they viewed time or life within the world as the setting within which they practiced obedience to their law.

17. Ibid., 127.

18. Campbell, *Man and Time*, 59-60,63.

19. These texts will suffice for analytical purposes. I do not include other textual references to resurrection because they do not differ in substance from the passages that follow.

20. Rivkin, 231.

22. Ibid., 273. Proof-texting (the use of the scriptural proof-texts) was originated by the Pharisees and is not found in Scripture or any apocryphal or pseudepigraphic work. Proof-texting is found in the *Mishnah*, the *Tosefta* and other *Tannaitic* materials and is the form that underlies the Gospels, Acts and the Epistles of Paul.

22. Ibid., 247. The Pharisees found within the prophetic and historical books of the Bible allusions bordering at times on the explicit to the belief in immortality and resurrection. Enoch is taken by God (Gen. 5:24); Samuel is drawn out of the earth by the witch of Endor (I Sam. 28:8-19); a child is resurrected by Elijah (I Kings 17:17-24); Elijah is taken to heaven on chariot wings (II Kings 2:9-12); Ezekiel sees the bones of those long dead coming alive (Ezek. 37:1-14); and Job hints of seeing God when out of the flesh (Job 19:25-27).

These allusions to immortality and resurrection are consistent when considered within the context of the Greek worldview of cyclical time and bodily resurrection found in Plato's *Myth of the Charioteer* and the writings of Josephus discussed in Section B of this chapter. According to Plato, the soul experienced many states of being within the cyclical process, none of which was permanent. One of these states of being was existence within the intelligible or with the gods (God for the Pharisee). Significantly, in the Bible, Enoch is taken by God, Elijah is taken to heaven on a chariot, and Job hints of seeing God out of the flesh. In addition, the mortal or corporeal aspects of resurrection are alluded to when Samuel is drawn out of the earth by the witch of Endor and Ezekiel sees the bones of those long dead coming alive.

23. Rivkin, 230.

24. Ibid., 230.

25. Ibid., 231.

26. Ibid., 231.

27. Neusner, 4.

28. Rivkin, 33-38.

29. Ibid., 34.

30. Ibid., 38-39.

31. Ibid., 36.

32. Ibid., 39.

33. Ibid., 39-40.

34. Ibid., 40-42.

35. Ibid., 72.

36. Ibid., 42, 71, 72, 90, 149, 152, 159, 162, 253-255, 263. For example, in one instance Rivkin writes in the singular, capitalizing the letters U and L—Unwritten Law." In another instance he writes in the plural, capitalizing the letter U and using the lower case l— "Unwritten laws." In yet another instance he writes in the singular, capitalizing the letter U and again writing the letter l in lower case— "Unwritten law." In still another instance he writes in the plural, using the lower case u and the lower case l—"unwritten laws."

It is not my intention to single out Rivkin as having been the only one to have had difficulty with the interpretation of the Unwritten Law/unwritten law with respect to the Pharisees. Rather it is suggested that the initial error in interpretation was made at some point in the past and scholars have simply built upon a wrong premise.

Additional scholarly confusion as to the meaning of the word "law" is evident in *The New Oxford Annotated Bible With the Apocrypha*, 1368. Referring to the word law in Rom. 7:1-2 the editors, though not sure, assume that the reference is to Roman law. From our perspective that Romans was written primarily (but not exclusively) to gentiles who had become Jews (indicating the breakdown of the caste system), the "law" in Rom. 7:1-2 refers to Pharisaic law. Those to whom Paul refers—those who know the law—are those gentile Jews who, in my opinion, made up the majority of the church in Rome.

See also William Barclay, *The Letter to the Romans* (Philadelphia: The Westminster Press, 1975), 26, 27. In his interpretation of the letter to the Romans, Barclay, sensing the affinity between the Greek Immutable Law and the Pharisaic wrath of God, notes that " . . . quite frequently Paul speaks about the wrath, without saying it is the wrath of God, as if it ought to be spelled out in capital letters —The Wrath—and was a kind of impersonal force at work in the world . . . ." Thus Paul combined the idea of the Greek impersonal Immutable Law of the cosmos with the idea of the dynamics of the Law being not an impersonal force, but rather the manifestation of God's wrath. Barclay's observation is consistent with Paul's intention to be "all things to all men." Thus Paul would be understood by gentiles who considered the wrath to be an impersonal Immutable Law as well as believing gentile Jews who considered the wrath to be the retributive law of a personal God.

37. Rivkin, 262-263.

38. Ibid., 265.

39. Ibid., 265-266.

40. Ibid., 259.

41. Ibid., 42,43.

42. Ibid., 43-44.

43. Ibid., 44.

44. Ibid., 45.

45. Ibid., 46, 72, 226-234, 259, 260, 265, 266, 268. In the narrative
Josephus refers to the term "laws" in the plural using the lower case "l."
Yet Rivkin in paraphrasing refers to the singular "Unwritten Law" using
the upper case U and L. Did these terms have the same meaning in
Pharisaism?

Josephus relates that " . . . whatever laws introduced by the Pharisees in
accordance with the tradition of the fathers had been abolished . . . these
she (Alexandra) again restored." The Law for the Pharisees was immutable.
How can Immutable Law be abolished and restored? Rivkin trying to
reconcile this apparent incongruity offers the following solution: "Nevertheless, we are not without recourse if we are careful to distinguish between the principles of Pharisaism, which were permanent, and specific
laws and lore which were continuously undergoing change. The unchanging
were (1) the twofold Law; and (2) the authority of the scholar class to
reaffirm, modify, and alter the Law; . . ." In other words, as Rivkin would
have it, impermanence or change is the overriding principle of the Immutable Law of the Pharisees!

The problem is easily resolved if one considers the various meanings of
"law" within the context of what we have learned from Josephus to have
been the first-century Pharisaic worldview, i.e., belief in the Immutable
Law of cyclical regeneration. Within this context the singular Immutable
"Unwritten Law" refers to the "tradition" of the "Fathers" i.e., knowledge
of the dynamics of the Immutable Law. The terms "law" and "laws" refer
to the changeable oral unwritten law(s) of the Pharisees. Josephus tells us
that the laws were introduced in accordance with the tradition of the fathers. This could mean: (1) it was the tradition of the fathers that laws be
introduced, (2) there were specific unchangeable laws that were inherited
from the fathers and (3) the laws that were introduced were compatible or
harmonious to the tradition of the fathers, i.e., the changeable Immutable
Law (Unwritten Law) of cyclical time and bodily resurrection (reincarnation), the knowledge of which was inherited from the fathers.

The first interpretation is rejected because it is unlikely that impermanence or change is the overriding principle of the unchanging Immutable
Law.

The second interpretation is rejected because the idea that there were specific laws that were inherited from the fathers is inconsistent with the policy of the Pharisees to change not only their own oral unwritten law, but the Law of Moses as well.

The third interpretation is held to be correct since it explains scholarly confusion with respect to the various meanings of the terms used for law and allows for the existence of an unchanging law as well as the promulgation of the changeable (unwritten oral laws) of the Pharisees, which were compatible with the "tradition" of the "Fathers," or knowledge about the Immutable Law, which they attributed to God's justice.

Finally, Barclay notes that in Rom. 4:15 Paul says that the law produces wrath. Though in this case he is referring to the Jewish law, a connection is forged between the Jewish law and the Immutable Law if one assumes, (and I think it has been favorably argued) that the man-made law was promulgated in light of the Immutable Law. Therefore, violation of the man-made law is an indirect violation of the Immutable Law and will produce wrath.

For further insight as to scholarly confusion with respect to the law, see Dunn (especially 301-304).

46. Rivkin, 48-49.

47. Ibid., 48-49.

48. Ibid., 49.

49. Ibid., 47-48.

. 50. The word superstition has been defined: (1) any belief or attitude, based on fear or ignorance, that is inconsistent with the known laws of science or with what is generally considered in the particular society as true and rational; esp., such a belief in charms, omens, the supernatural, etc. (2) any action or practice based on such a belief or attitude (3) such belief or attitudes collectively. Webster's *New World Dictionary*, 2nd edition, ed. by David B. Guralnik (New York: Simon and Schuster, 1982).

51. Rivkin, 50.

52. Ibid., 51.

53. Ibid., 196-199. Belief in an afterlife and the practice of foretelling events are central components of the gnostic tradition (See Chapter Four). There is little doubt that the Pharisees were indeed keepers of the gnostic tradition within Judaism. The Pharisees were referred to variously as "Pharisees-Hakhamin-Soferim," Sofers or scribes. The characteristics of the Gnostic that distinguish him from others are attributed to the Soferim by Ben Sira: "The Soferim of Ben Sira's day were loners who were not sought out to be judges, they did not attain eminence in the public assembly, they did not

use Proverbs (38:33-34). What did they do? They kept the fabric of the world stable by praying (38:34). They sought out the wisdom of the ancients (the 'Fathers'), they were concerned with prophecies, they preserved the discourses of notable men, they served the great, they made supplications for their sins, they prayed to be filled with the spirit of understanding, they poured forth words of wisdom (prophesy) and they meditated on their secrets (39:1-8)."

Rivkin distinguishes between the pre-Hasmonean and post-Hasmonean Pharisees-Hakhamin-Soferim. He notes that the Soferim-scribes about which Ben Sira wrote (pre-Hasmonean) were Pentateuchalists, hierocratic intellectuals, Aaronide supremacists and lovers and seekers of Wisdom. They were the devotees of the onefold law, the written law and of the authoritative spokesmen, the Aaronide priests. The post-Hasmonean Pharisees-Hakhamin-Soferim were none of these things. This is undoubtedly so. Rivkin's distinction touches on political or religious leanings of the Soferim, which were subject to change.

I suggest that the pre-Hasmonean and post-Hasmonean Pharisees-Hakhamin-Soferim were the same in that they both maintained the gnostic tradition within Judaism, but that they differed with respect to attitudes toward the law and to what they considered to be authoritative.

54. Rivkin, 54.
55. Ibid., 57.
56. Ibid., 54,56.
57. Ibid., 54.
58. Ibid., 54.
59. Ibid., 291.
60. Ibid., 292.
61. Ibid., 287.
62. Ibid., 290-291.
63. Ibid., 283.
64. Ibid., 289.
65. Ibid., 289-290.
66. Ibid., 288.
67. Ibid., 287.
68. Ibid., 95. Rivkin, not viewing this Gospel account of Pharisaic belief in resurrection from the perspective of a first-century Pharisee who, like Josephus, must have had bodily resurrection in mind, assumes that the Pharisees and Jesus refer to the same kind of resurrection. "Even more fundamental than the attitude of the Pharisees with respect to state sovereignty was their belief in the resurrection of the dead, since this belief

brought them into conflict with the Sadducees who rejected such a notion out of hand. Ironically, this Pharisaic belief is championed so effectively by Jesus in a confrontation with the Sadducees that he wins the approbation of the Pharisees themselves."

69. Ibid., 96. Rivkin states that "Paul's exclamation that he was being tried because of his belief in the resurrection of the dead provokes a violent clash between the Pharisees and the Sadducees." On the basis of Acts 23:6-8, Matt. 22:25-28 and Matt. 22:29,30 he states: "We are left with no doubt that on this doctrine the Pharisees, Jesus and Paul saw eye to eye." Again, as a Pharisee, Paul, like Josephus, must have believed in bodily resurrection. Moreover, at this time of the Church's development it was not impossible to believe in both concepts of resurrection. The Greek or Jew who converted to Christianity would assume that he lived in the past and would be grateful for his present existence. However, having become a Christian he was no longer subject to cyclical regeneration. It seems reasonable to assume that finding himself in a tight spot, Paul identified with the Pharisees by making a statement that could be construed by them to support their view against the Sadducees. The statement, "I am a Pharisee, a son of Pharisees; with respect to the hope and the resurrection of the dead I am on trial . . ." was true. He merely neglected to tell them that his was a hope for a new resurrection. His scheme worked, as the Pharisees and Sadducees began to argue among themselves.

70. Ibid., 103, 231. This assertion is strengthened by the fact that in *Against Apion* Josephus takes for granted that all Jews believe in eternal life and resurrection and that all Jews followed the Pharisaic system. Here again is the failure to distinguish between the concepts of resurrection—immortality (reincarnation) an eternal life of a sort, and eternal life with God after release from cyclical regeneration.

71. Falk's observation regarding the rivalry between the Pharisaic schools of Shammai and Hillel indicates the possibility that extremely diverse and even diametrically opposing views were encompassed under the auspices of Pharisaism. Harvey Falk, *Jesus the Pharisee* (New York, Mahway: Paulist Press, 1985). (See generally, especially 81.) Support for this view is found in Chapter Four of this work, "Voices of Despair in Pharisaism and Paganism."

72. It might be argued that Herod's statement was a figure of speech. In this view he could have meant that Jesus was of the type of John the Baptist. However, the reference to Elijah militates against this interpretation.

73. Contemporary biblical scholarship, specifically the Jesus Seminar, a

California-based panel of nearly one hundred forty biblical scholars, assume that the word "Christ," derived from the Greek and found in Mark, was interpolated into the book sometime after 70 C.E. This conclusion is based on the scholarly determination that Mark was written sometime prior to 70 C.E., when the Greek word would have been unknown to "Mark." It is also based on the fact that Jesus never set foot out of Jerusalem and his disciples and the masses were provincial Jews.

Caution is advised with respect to the interpretation of Holy Writ by those who do not have firsthand knowledge of and/or belief in the paranormal—including the ability of some to spontaneously "come up with" words, ideas or concepts of which they do not have knowledge in the ordinary sense of the term.

74. It could be argued that the belief in reincarnation applied only to Elijah because he did not die in the usual sense but was taken up. ". . . [Elijah] said, You have asked a hard thing; yet, if you see me as I am being taken from you, it shall be so for you; but if you do not see me, it shall not be so. And as they still went on and talked, behold a chariot of fire and horses of fire separated the two of them. And Elijah went up by the whirlwind into heaven" (II Kings 2:10,11,12). However, Mk. 8:28 supports the view that this was not the case because the disciples also said that some believed Jesus was one of the prophets, and Jesus was not taken up.

Dan. 12:2 is noteworthy because it indicates that some in Judaism might have believed in the concept of an eternal life after death that was a final and unchangeable state: "And many of those who sleep in the dust of the earth shall awake, some to everlasting life, and some to shame and everlasting contempt." However, 2 Mac. 7:9 clearly indicates (as did the writings of Josephus) that some believed in the concept of reincarnation: "You accursed wretch, you dismiss us from this present life, but the King of the universe will raise us to an everlasting renewal of life, because we have died for his laws." It shall be clear that the assertion that some believed in reincarnation does not preclude belief in other forms of afterlife. Moreover, it does not necessarily mean that belief in reincarnation and belief in other forms of afterlife are mutually exclusive.

# CHAPTER FOUR
## Voices of Despair in Pharisaism and Paganism

1. Neusner, 10-11. It has been argued that the Hellenization of Pharisaism explains the similarity of Greek and Pharisaic philosophy, terms and language. I have asserted that the apparent affinity between the Pharisees and the Greeks may be explained by the possibility that each culture independently shared a similar worldview and that the apparent "Hellenization" of Pharisaism is actually a result of the fact that because each group shared a similar worldview, their philosophies, terms and language were applicable and interchangeable across cultural lines. So too, it is argued that the negative attitude toward the Immutable Law (Greek) and God's Law of Justice (Pharisaic) was generated within each group independently.

2. Robert Gordis, *Koheleth the Man and His World: A Study of Ecclesiastes* (New York: Schocken Books, 1951, 1955, 1968), 9,11.

3. Ibid., 9-10.

4. Puech, 45n12, 41n4. Marcus Aurelius, a convinced Stoic, believed in universal determinism and in the circular recurrence of time.

5. Rivkin, 66.

6. Gordis, 59.

7. Ibid., 68. West points to a possible date of writing as late as the early Greek period (fourth or third centuries B.C.E.) on the basis of its language, its numerous Aramaisms and familiarity with popular Greek patterns of thought and spirit of individualism. West holds that its influence upon Ben Sira (c. 180 B.C.E.) and its appearance among the manuscripts from Qumran attests that the work is older than the second century B.C.E. James King West, *Introduction to the Old Testament* (New York: The Macmillan Company, 1971), 405.

8. Ibid., 4-5.

9. Ibid., 58. The unknowability of the world is mentioned in Ecc. 3:11, 3:21-22, 6:12, 7:14, 7:24, 8:17, 10:14, 11:5. The divine imperative of joy is mentioned in Ecc. 2:24, 3:12-13, 5:18-19, 8:15, 9:7, 9:9.

10. Ibid., 71-72.

11. Ibid., 40-41. According to Gordis, it is unlikely that *Koheleth* was trying to pass himself off as Solomon on the grounds that: (1) He used the name *Koheleth* (Preacher) rather than the name "Solomon" and (2) in the opening section where "Solomon" speaks, the fact that a long line of kings had preceded him in Jerusalem is not disguised.

12. Ibid., 69-71.

13. Ibid., 40.

14. Ibid., 52. Gordis states that the scholarly reading of *The Catalogue of Seasons* as teaching the Stoic doctrine that one should live according to nature is farfetched. According to Gordis, *Koheleth* is "emphasizing the predestined character of all events, so that all human activity, including the search for ultimate truth, is useless." I think that Gordis and the scholars to whom he refers are saying the same thing. The Stoics viewed the predetermined character of events within cyclical time to be inherent in Nature—the Natural Law. Thus, to live according to nature means to live with consciousness of the recompensation dynamic inherent in nature. The inclusion of the *Catalogue of Seasons* suggests that *Koheleth's* worldview was similar to that of the Stoics. This assertion is supported by the inclusion of passages that, more than the *Catalogue of Seasons*, indicate that *Koheleth* and the Stoics held a similar worldview. These passages are Ecc. 1:9,10; 3:14, 15; and 2:12.

15. Gordis, 41-42.

16. Neusner, 3.

17. Puech, 45.

18. Ibid., 45-46.

19. Ibid., 45n12.

20. Ibid., 56. Puech notes that according to Harnack, Burkitt, Schaeder and Casey, *gnosis* was the extreme Hellenization of Christianity. On the other hand Bousset, Reitzenstein, Steffes and Lietzmann regard Gnosticism as a consequence of a penetration or invasion of Christianity by oriental influences. See also 57n23, referring to the suggestion by Gilles Quispel that Valentinus Hellenized and Christianized the gnostic anthropology. Puech questions whether Valentinus' doctrine, "contrary to what Harnack believes was not a Christianization and Hellenization of oriental gnosis." In my view Puech's observation, together with the added incorporation of Jewish *gnosis* (which includes Oriental *gnosis*), is the correct interpretation.

21. Kelly states that authorities are divided with respect to whether Gnosticism predated or antedated Christianity. According to Kelly, early theologians such as Irenaeus, Tertullian, and Hyppolytus treat Gnosticism as an aberration brought about by the adulteration of apostolic doctrine with pagan philosophy. However, Kelly notes that there seems to have been a Jewish Gnosticism that antedated Christianity. John Norman Davidson Kelly, *Early Christian Doctrines* (New York: Harper & Row, Publishers, Inc., 1978), 22-23. I concur. It is suggested that Jewish Christianity was at its core Pharisaic-Oriental *gnosis*.

22. Puech, 54.

23. *Webster's New Universal Unabridged Dictionary* (New York: Simon &

Schuster, 1979), 781. In Bultmann's view the fundamental difference between Christian *gnosis* and other mystery religions was that faith in Jesus
Christ was the proclaimed means by which salvation of the soul and eternal
life (as opposed to immortality within cyclical regeneration) was attained.
Rudolf Bultmann, *Primitive Christianity in its Contemporary Setting*. Trans.
by the Reverend R.H. Fuller (The German Democratic Republic,
Interdruck, Leipzig, 1983), 154-155.

The conversion of Saul of Tarsus (St. Paul) by revelation as well as the
gifts of the Spirit that he possessed indicate that he was a Gnostic Jewish/
Christian teacher. Like other mystery religions, Christianity offered deliverance from fate or the tyranny of the stars. See Paul's letter to the Galatians
(Gal. 4:3-10).

24. Dusty Sklar, *The Nazis and the Occult* (New York: Dorset Press,
1989). (See generally). The political agenda of the Nazi Party under Adolph
Hitler and his followers is an example of the influence and power of the
gnostic mind bent on destruction.

25. Books written by and/or about contemporary Gnostics are: Miguel
Serrano, C.G. Jung & Hermann Hesse, *A Record of Two Friendships* (New
York: Schocken Books, 1975), (See generally); Shirley MacLaine, *Out on
a Limb* (New York: Bantam Books, Inc., 1983); Jane Roberts, *Seth Speaks*
(New York: Prentice Hall, 1972 and New York: Bantam Books, Inc.,
1974); Thomas Sugrue, *The Story of Edgar Cayce: There is a River* (New
York: Dell Publishing Co., Inc. 1967); Brian L. Weiss, M.D., *Many Lives,
Many Masters* (New York: Simon and Schuster Inc.); *A Course in Miracles*,
Tiburon, California: Foundation for Inner Peace, 1976); Ruth Montgom-
ery, *A Gift of Prophecy* (New York: William Morrow & Company, 1965).

26. William James, *The Varieties of Religious Experience* (New York: The
Modern Library, 1929). (See generally.) This book is a collection of reported *gnosis* or religious/paranormal experiences.

27. Henry Chadwick, *The Early Church* (London: Cox & Wyman Ltd.,
1967), 125-127. The Emperor Constantine, who was central to the development of the church, had a gnostic mind. In response to a dream he put
the *chi rho* monogram on his shields and standards as a talisman of victory.
The sign, which was a monogram of the name of Christ, also appears on
Constantine's coins from 315. Constantine told Eusebius of Caesarea that
he had seen the cross athwart the midday sun inscribed with the words "By
this conquer." Moreover, his decision to found a new capital for the eastern half of the empire at Byzantium on the Bosphorus was in response to a
divinely granted dream.

28. Benjamin Walker, *Gnosticism: Its History and Influence* (Wellingbor-

ough, Northamptonshire: The Aquarian Press, 1983), 29-32. Most of the information about *gnosis*, Gnostics and Gnosticism contained in this chapter was obtained from Benjamin Walker's book, which in my view does a fine job of explaining gnostic thought and integrating it with the New Testament.

29. Kelly, 26-27, 100. Walker, 21, 100.

30. Ibid., 62-63.

31. Ibid., 63.

32. James King West, *Introduction to the Old Testament*, 216-279.

33. Walker, 104-105, 119, 137, 145, 149, 158, 166-168.

34. Kelly, 61.

35. Walker, 30-37.

36. Ibid., 32-34, 38-39.

37. Ibid., 34.

38. C.G. Jung, *Aion: Researches Into the Phenomenology of the Self* (London: Routledge and Kegan Paul, 1968), 65.

39. Walker, 34-36.

40. Ibid., 36-37.

41. Ibid., 38, 42.

42. Ibid., 38,41-43,48-49,52.

43. Ibid., 39, 50, 58.

44. Ibid., 53-54.

45. Ibid., 55-57, 59.

46. Ibid., 60-65.

47. Ibid., 51.

48. Ibid., 46-48.

49. Puech, 38.

50. *The Confessions of St. Augustine*. Trans. by Rex Warner (New York: The New American Library, Inc., 1963), 96. St. Augustine was a member of the Manichean sect for about nine years. See also John F. Callahan, "Augustine: Time, a Distention of Man's Soul," in *Four Views of Time in Ancient Philosophy* (Cambridge: Harvard University Press, 1948), 149-187.

51. Puech, 67.

52. Ibid., 65. *Samsara*—Hinduism. The continuing cycle in which the same soul is repeatedly born.

53. Ibid., 68-69.

54. Ibid., 68-69n50. Ps. 246, in *A Manichaean Psalm-book, Part II*, 54, li. II-23. Tr. in Torgny Save-Soderbergh, *Studies in the Coptic Manichaean Psalm-book* (Uppsala, 1949), 71-72, and in Gilles Quispel, *Gnosis als Weltreligion* (Zurich, 1951), 67. The third verse of the first strophe is trans-

lated differently by these two authors: "which (was bitter) to me" (Save-Soderbergh); "which (made me) forget" (Quispel).

55. Ibid., 69n51. Turfan Fragment T II D178, in *Abhandlungen der preussischen Akademie der Wissenschaften*, 1926, IV, 112-13. (Puech's version, here translated, is in the French of E. Benveniste, Yggdrasill (Paris), August 25, 1937, 9).

56. Ibid., 70n52. Turfan Fragment M7, in *Sitzungsberichte der preussischen Akademie der Wissenschaften* 1934, 874-75. (From the French tr. of Benveniste, 8.—ED.).

57. Ibid., 67n46. Ginza, V, I, 137-38, German tr. Mark Lidzbarski (Gottingen and Leipzig, 1925), 153, 154.

58. Puech, 67n47. Turfan Fragment T II D173a, r., in A. von Le Coq, "Turkische Manichaica aus Chotscho, I," *Abhandlungen der preussischen Akademie der Wissenschaften*, Phil.-hist., Kl., 1911, Appendix VI, 10.

59. Walker, 113, 120.

60. Kelly, 67, 68. Walker, 12, 127, 137, 139, 143, 144. Puech, 59n26, 61-62.

61. Puech, 61.

62. Walker, 44-45.

63. Puech, 60.

64. Walker, 101.

65. Kelly, 57, 67.

66. Ibid., 64, 69, 57.

67. Walker, 126-127.

68. Ibid., 107-108, 111, 113.

69. Ibid., 126, 128-129.

## CHAPTER FIVE
### THE CULTURAL MATRIX OF THE ROMAN EMPIRE

1. For example, the democratization of Western social institutions is a result of the democratic ideal that all men are created equal.

2. A.H.M. Jones, "The Caste System in the Later Roman Empire" in *Eirene* 8:79-96 (1970).

3. Tony Reekmans, "Juvenal's Views on Social Change" in *Ancient Society* 2:117-161 (1971).

4. Wayne A. Meeks, *The First Urban Christians* (New Haven and London: Yale University Press, 1983), 22.

5. Ibid., 20.

6. Ibid., 22.

7. Ibid., 31.

8. A.H.M. Jones, "The Economic Life of the Towns of the Roman Empire" in *LaVille*. Ed. by Jean Firenne, pt. 1, 171-172 (1955).

9. Meeks, 32.

10. Ibid., 31, 32.

11. Ibid., 23, 58, 59. Peter Lampe, "The Roman Christians of Romans 16" in *The Romans Debate*, 229.

12. Marleen B. Flory, *Family and 'Familia': A Study of Social Relations in Slavery*. Ph.D. dissertation, Yale University (1975), 59-79.

13. Meeks, 63.

14. Weaver, *Familia Caesaris: A Social Study of the Emperor's Freedmen and Slaves*, 112-161, 179-195.

15. Weaver, 193f.

16. Meeks, 21.

17. Ramsay MacMullen, *Roman Social Relations* (New Haven and London: Yale University Press, 1974). See especially 88-120.

18. Meeks, 20.

19. Ernst Kasemann, *Commentary on Romans*. Trans. and ed. by Geoffrey W. Bromily (Grand Rapids, Michigan: William B. Eerdmans Publishing Company, 1980), 187. Meeks, 34.

20. Meeks, 34.

21. Bultmann, 44. It has been argued that societies organized according to the caste system were grounded in belief in reincarnation. In this regard it is noteworthy that the prophets, who were the mainstay of the nation in its bondage to foreign rule, established a hierarchy in accordance with the old aristocratic order of the patriarchs. Prophets/Seers (1 Sam. 9:5-10) are by nature Gnostics and belief in reincar-

nation is fundamental to most gnostic thought systems. Therefore, it is probable that the prophets/seers organized society in accordance with the old hierarchical aristocratic order in light of belief in reincarnation.

22. Ibid., 45.

23. Ibid., 44-45. It is noteworthy that the one function that remained within the domain of the priestly caste when it replaced the old aristocratic order of the patriarchs was that of the administration of justice. This attests to the ancient concept that justice and the divine order were inextricably bound and were considered to be outside the domain of secular law. Yet, we know that during the first century the Sadducees did not believe in an afterlife. How can this be explained? Is it possible that by the first century the priesthood (inherited by birth as were all other castes) had lost the knowledge (*gnosis*) on which their tradition was founded? Were first-century Sadducees operating on automatic pilot? In view of the animosity that existed between the Pharisees and the Sadducees over the issue of belief in an afterlife, is it not unreasonable to assume that this was the case. In our own time we are seeing the same phenomena occur in which much of the *gnosis* on which the church was based is lost, yet the form (*cultus*) that derived from this knowledge lives on.

24. Ibid., 45.

25. Meeks, 36-37.

26. Ibid., 35n161.

27. Ibid., 39. F.F. Bruce, "The Romans Debate—Continued," in *The Romans Debate*. Ed. by Karl Donfried (Peabody, Mass.: Hendrickson Publishers, 1991), 178.

28. Ibid., 36.

29. Mary E. Smallwood, "The Jews Under Roman Rule: From Pompey to Diocletian" in *Studies in Judaism in Late Antiquity*, 20. (Leiden: Brill, 1976), 134.

30. Meeks, 36.

31. Ibid., 36n175.

32. The principle finds its parallel in the Greek city state. According to Bultmann: "The State had an aura of sanctity about it, and the relation of the citizen to it was in effect his religion, with its external expression in the official cultus" (108).

33. Meeks, 36.

34. Ibid., 36. James D.G. Dunn, "The New Perspective on Paul: Paul and the Law," in *The Romans Debate*, 305.

35. Meeks, 21, 34, 35, 38-39. Contrary to popular belief, the Jews of

the cities often regarded Rome as their protector.

36. Erwin Ramsdell Goodenough, *An Introduction to Philo Judaeus*, 2nd ed. (Oxford: Blackwell, 1962), 10.

37. Meeks, 33. Meeks notes, "There has been no dearth of attempts to set Paul against the background of various kinds of Judaism." He further states, "The failure of any of these schemas to win allegiance as the context within which the text of Paul's letters makes sense should alert us to the fact that these categories do not add up to an adequate taxonomy of first-century Judaism." Precisely! It is suggested that the enigma of Paul—now a "rabbi," again as a representative of "Jewish apocalyptic," perhaps a "Jewish mystic" or even a "Jewish Gnostic"—is a clue to the context within which Pauline thought makes sense. The confusion derives from looking backward and trying to fit him into pre-Christian categories in a neat, dare I say it, linear mode. Looking forward (this is derived from reading Romans with an awareness of his worldview, i.e., belief in reincarnation), it is apparent that he—his thought—was the center around which humanity moved from a pre-Christian cyclical worldview to a linear worldview. He was living change and synthesis. He epitomized—in his own person—the integration of various carefully chosen aspects of pre-existing traditions as well as the superimposition and integration of a new tradition—Christianity. At the same time, he was clarifying the "true" gospel for others. It must be remembered that Paul's letters reflect the formative stages of Christianity.

38. According to Acts 16:37;21:39, Paul was a Roman citizen as well as a Jew, revealing the extent of the integration of Jewish and pagan culture during the first century. Though Acts is not considered a primary source for the scholarly study of Paul, there is no reason to doubt that Paul, though a Jew, was indeed a Roman citizen. This view is supported by the status-dissonance that, according to sociological studies, was in process within first-century Rome (Meeks, 22).

39. Meeks, 85-86.

40. Ibid., 89.

41. Ibid., 87.

42. Ibid., 96. The language "children of light" and "children of darkness" was used by some but not all Gnostics. It is found specifically among groups that hold a dualistic worldview. Because this language is found in the New Testament, there has been speculation as to whether Jesus and Paul were acquainted with the Essene sect at Qumran. (See: Harvey Falk, *Jesus the Pharisee*, 31.) This is possible. However, it does not necessarily follow that the Qumran community was the only gnostic group with a presence in first-century Palestine. It is suggested that though Jesus and

Paul may have been acquainted with the sect, they were themselves Gnostics who formed their own distinct groups. Jesus taught and initiated his disciples. Paul, after a quintessential gnostic experience in which he saw "the Christ," organized churches.

43. Meeks, 80, 120-121.

44. Ibid., 92.

45. Ibid., 91.

46. Ibid., 91.

47. According to Keck and Furnish, Paul considered the Christ event decisive for the human condition. Leander E. Keck & Victor Paul Furnish, *The Pauline Letters* (Nashville: Abingdon Press, 1984), 65.

48. The following is representative of scholarly opinion with respect to the makeup of the church in Rome:

"Among the house churches of Rome, then, we should probably envisage a broad and continuous spectrum of varieties in thought and practice between the firm Jewish retention of the ancestral customs and pagan remoteness from these customs, with some Jewish Christians, indeed, found on the liberal side of the halfway mark between the two extremes and some pagan Christians on the 'legalist' side" (Bruce, 186).

Wedderburn states, " . . . it is appropriate to think of Paul addressing himself, . . . if not to two distinct groups of readers, at least to a broad spectrum of different views of the relationship between the Christian gospel and Judaism: at one end of the spectrum were those, both Judaizing pagans and, we may infer, at least a few ethnic Jews who had been converted to Christianity, who attended the gatherings of the synagogue and clung to its ways; at the other were those pagan Christians who had flung off whatever ties to Judaism they had before, if any, and had espoused a law-free gospel . . . or had gone ever further in severing all connections with Judaism." (A.J.M. Wedderburn, "Purpose and Occasion of Romans Again," in *The Romans Debate*, 202).

I would add: There must also have been those pagans who had not been Jewish sympathizers or converts to Judaism, but directly converted (or intended to convert) to Christianity.

In Gaston's view there is no evidence that Paul ever preached to Jews. (Lloyd Gaston, "Israel's Misstep in the Eyes of Paul," in *The Romans Debate*, 309). In my view, the phrase "But if you call yourself a Jew," (Rom. 2:17) indicates the presence of pagan Jews whom Paul was trying to bring to Christianity. This is because under the caste system an ethnic Jew would be considered a Jew regardless of what he called himself. The element of choice suggests that Paul is addressing converts—pagans who became Jews.

This does not mean that ethnic Jews were not present in the church. It does mean that there is no way to determine the matter definitively (though in my view it is likely that Paul assumed the presence of some ethnic Jews). Whether or not they were present, much of what Paul says to the pagan Jews (especially that which had universal significance—the wrath of God— the Jewish law in light of the wrath, and the Christ event in light of both) would apply to ethnic Jews as well. This is a logical conclusion because the pagan Jews presumably held the same worldview and practiced the same traditions (or at least they gave lip service to the traditions) as the ethnic Jews.

49. This view is consistent with that of Ernst Kasemann, who states in the introduction to *Commentary on Romans*, " . . . *a problem arises especially in this epistle (Romans) through the very marked mixture of received tradition*, distinctive deviation from that tradition, and independent development of it. As a founder of a community does not work in a vacuum, so Paul as letter writer has to reckon not merely with the lively reaction of the churches to his teaching. There are rivals and opponents in his sphere of mission, which itself is in different stages of development and is affected by constantly changing currents. The result is a presentation which both demands and permits appeal to the common tradition and simultaneously necessitates theological debate and correction. All of the New Testament writers are concerned to take up and set in order the existing, and sometimes very contradictory, positions in primitive Christianity. Paul, who remained a controversial figure since his conversion, can be understood only when we see him, now offensively and now defensively, under the pressure of this need for theological clarification" (Kasemann, 3). (Italics mine.)

I suggest that the core of the mixture of received tradition was belief in reincarnation.

Wedderburn notes that Paul S. Minear assumes that different viewpoints and groups of readers are addressed at different points in Romans (202n11). This is undoubtedly correct. However, I suggest that the different viewpoints represent differences of approach in light of the received tradition agreed upon by all—belief in cyclical regeneration.

According to Keck and Furnish it has been said that "syncretism was the hallmark of the age" (43).

50. Meeks, 73, 214n10. Malherbe 1977a, 31. Filson 1939, quotation from 111. Compare Eck 1971, 381. According to Meeks, "If one takes account of the whole body of sources relevant to this set of questions, and avoids arbitrary generalizations from a few of them, the inference is unavoidable that the adherents to the Christian religion present a virtually

exact mirror image of the general social stratification in the Roman empire. And that was so from the beginnings depicted in the New Testament documents." Meeks further states that "[I]t is a picture in which people of several social levels are brought together. The extreme top and bottom of the Greco-Roman social scale are missing from the picture."

How can this absence of the extreme top and bottom of the social scale be explained within the context of the pre-Christian belief in reincarnation (that one moved up the social/spiritual ladder by small and painful increments) and the Christian promise of spiritual (and implicitly social) equality? First, the absence of those from the extreme top of the social ladder might be explained by the assumption that many at the top were content with their lot. For them Christianity would have no attraction. Second, the absence of those from the extreme bottom of the social hierarchy could reflect the total powerlessness of the poorest of the poor—in relation to those merchants and artisans which comprised the majority of the early Roman churches. But how can the exceptions be explained—those few of the extreme upper classes who became Christians? The answer appears twofold. First, it is erroneous to assume that he who has all the world has to offer is content. Secondly, there is a lack of understanding of what the Christian promise of eternal life with Christ meant to first-century believers—that Christ died for their sins, thus freeing them from the necessity of cyclical return and/or possible eternal punishment. If one considers the state of moral collapse of the Roman Empire in process during the time of Paul, it is not stretching to surmise that there were those, who like *Koheleth's* "King Solomon," were disillusioned by the idea of reincarnation. They simply wanted out.

51. Meeks, 79.

52. In Bornkamm's view, Romans is thoroughly related to the real historical circumstances from which it arose. Thus Bornkamm recognized the significance of pre-Christian history. However, he states "Yet we must not look to the Christians in Rome, whom the Apostle had before him as he wrote, for the history which lay behind Paul and the churches . . ." (Gunther Bornkamm, "The Letter to the Romans as Paul's Last Will and Testament," in *The Romans Debate*, 21).

This can be misleading. Bornkamm agrees that Romans is thoroughly related to the real historical circumstances from which it has arisen. But what does he mean? Does it refer to concrete facts and/or issues? Or, does it include the pre-Christian worldview and concepts presumed by those to whom Paul wrote which are reflected in the facts and/or issues?

An integrated interpretation of Romans must view the historical situation to include and transcend the apparent facts and/or concrete issues. I did so by analyzing the language and socioeconomic and philosophical makeup of the early church(es) and within the Roman culture at large.

53. In the preface to his *Commentary on Romans*, Ernst Kasemann states that "Until I have proof to the contrary, I proceed on the assumption that the text has a central concern and a remarkable inner logic that may no longer be entirely comprehensible to us."

# CHAPTER SIX
## THE LETTER OF PAUL TO THE ROMANS

### Romans 1:

1. Paul's claim to authority and unique status was based upon an instantaneous revelation of the resurrected Savior reflecting the gnostic view of election/salvation. Indeed, *gnosis* was the basis of Paul's claim to apostolic authority (Gal. 1:11,2,15; 1 Cor. 1; 2 Cor. 12:2-4).

2. Verses 2 and 3 integrate Paul's unique status and that of Jesus Christ with Hebrew Scripture. This deference to Jewish tradition does not appear in the introduction to any of the other letters deemed authentically Pauline (1 Cor. 1-3; 2 Cor. 1,2; Gal. 1:1-5; Phil. 1:1,2; 1 Th. 1; Philem. 1-3). Why? In Kasemann's view the deference to Jewish tradition is an attempt by Paul to win over the Jewish Christians who could influence the Church in Jerusalem with respect to Paul and his apostolate (Kasemann, 405).

3. It is suggested that Paul meant the phrase "resurrection from the dead" (v.4) in the gnostic sense. This is based on what has been learned about gnostic thought and Paul as an individual in Chapters Four and Five. Recall that Gnostics viewed earthly life as a necropolis—a city of the dead. For them all of mankind was categorically dead because of the necessity of cyclical regeneration unto corruptible flesh (Acts 13:34). Thus, Christ's resurrection from the dead meant the first resurrection from the necessity of cyclical rebirth, corruption and death. This throws light on Paul's statement that he was a servant (slave) of Jesus Christ (v.1), as opposed to a slave of sin, which infers freedom from the process.

The Gospel of Matthew indicates that Jesus held the gnostic view toward mortal existence: "But Jesus said to him, 'Follow me, and leave the dead to bury their own dead'" (Matt. 8:22). Further evidence that Jesus held the gnostic view are those Gospel passages in which Jesus indicates belief in reincarnation (Mk. 8:28-30; Matt. 11:13-15; Matt. 17:10-13).

Some current biblical scholars, such as those affiliated with the California-based Jesus Seminar, question much of what is purported to have been said by Jesus in the Gospel accounts. This is irrelevant for the purpose of this work, as the task is to demonstrate the existence of a cross-cultural belief in reincarnation during the first century. This is accomplished by the cited passages.

4. "Grace" (v.5) is a gnostic buzz word and further supports the view that Paul was speaking from a gnostic perspective. Recall that the Gnostics held that salvation came to the individual by the revelation of the Savior.

In order to bring about the obedience of faith among all nations (vv.3-5), Paul deviates from strict gnostic thought based on individual experience of grace and places it within the domain of the Church by stating that grace has been received through Jesus Christ and the apostles.

5. Kasemann states that the reference to all God's beloved in Rome who are called to be saints (v.7) effectively transfers the honor of the Old Testament people of God to Christians. He who is admitted to the place of the divine presence is holy. The reference is to heavenly being (Kasemann, 15, 16).

This is consistent with belief in reincarnation and the significance of the Christ event in light of this belief. "Saint" refers to those who because of faith in Christ will, after death, be free from the necessity of cyclical regeneration.

6. Anders Nygren, *Commentary on Romans* (Philadelphia: Fortress Press, 1949), 44. For Paul and his age, the Christ/Messiah concept was viable independently of Jesus and before him. The coupling of Christ with Jesus meant that the Messiah whom Israel had awaited for centuries had come and ushered in the Messianic age.

The phrase "God our Father" (v.7) recalls the familiar terminology used by some pre-Christian Gnostic schools (probably Jewish) to express the abstract divine aspect Nous, or mind. "Son of God" (v.4) recalls the gnostic term *Logos*, meaning "word" or "reason." The conceptual coupling of Jesus with the pre-Christian gnostic concept of Christ, *Logos* or Son of God (vv.3, 4) is unprecedented and uniquely Christian.

7. How can Paul reap harvest among those who are already Christians (v.13)—those already harvested? He cannot. To whom then is he referring?

It is asserted that Paul's reference to "brethren" (1:13) indicates those gentile Jews who were followers of Christ (gentile Jewish Christians) and were instrumental in the founding of the churches at Rome. They brought into their circles "brethren" who were gentiles who adopted Judaism— gentile Jews—and, therefore, knew the law (7:1). Thus, Paul distinguished between those "brethren," who adopted Judaism (and in some cases Christianity) and those "brethren" who were his kinsmen by race (9:1). The rest of the gentiles (1:13) were those gentiles who were not committed to either Judaism or Christianity.

8. Paul's special apostolic obligation neutralized earthly barriers such as the differences between the civilized and the barbarians, the Jew and the gentile (Kasemann, 20).

This revolutionary aspect of Christianity, which gauged the spiritual status of man not by social position and/or personal attributes but by what was in the heart, is alluded to by Paul's statement: "We are not commending ourselves to you again but giving you cause to be proud of us, so that you may be able to answer those who pride themselves on a man's position and not on his heart" (2 Cor. 5:12).

9. Kasemann notes that Paul's claim to authority is steadily diminished until it is reasserted again at the end of vv.11-15. He argues that to explain this in terms of tact on Paul's part is too simple. Instead he asserts that Paul was insecure in relation to those at Rome whom he had not met. He suggests that the reason is that the authority that Paul asserted did not accord with what was conceded to him in fact. This was particularly true with respect to the Jewish Christians (a minority in Kasemann's view) who, most likely, had connections with the church in Jerusalem and could influence it with respect to Paul's apostolate (Kasemann 18-20, 405).

Robert Jewett suggests that Romans distinctly follows the rhetoric of the "ambassador's speech," the purpose of which was to unify the competing house churches as well as encourage house-church cooperation in organizing his project to extend the circle of mission (15:19) to the "barbarians" (1:14) in Spain. ("Following the Argument of Romans," in *The Romans Debate*, 266n7, 267).

It is asserted that Paul's tentative tone with respect to his authority stemmed from his being tactful with respect to those gentiles who were uncommitted to Judaism and/or Christianity as well as to those gentile Jews whom he was trying to win for Christianity.

10. Paul does not explain the brief Gospel message, nor the statement that the " . . . gospel is the power of God for salvation which is given to everyone who has faith . . . (v.16)." Yet he expects it to be understood by those to whom his letter(s) will be read. This implies broad cross-cultural agreement on the nature of the eternal condition (which is, therefore, unmentioned) and the universal need for salvation from it.

11. What does Paul mean when he says that the gospel is "the power of God for salvation to everyone who has faith, to the Jew first, and also to the Greek"? (v.16). J.C. Beker asks rhetorically how Paul is able to maintain the priority of the Jew (1:16) and the equality of gentile and Jew in Christ (11:32) on the basis of justification by faith alone (3:28-31). ("The Faithfulness of God and the Priority of Israel in Paul's Letter to the Romans," in *The Romans Debate*, 329, 330). Answering, he observes that Paul never loses sight of the fact that Jews and gentiles, though in Christ, are two distinct peoples and that emphasis of equality of Jew and Greek in the body of Christ does not nullify Israel's eschatological priority (11:25-26).

In Kasemann's view, Paul's reference "to the Jew first" gives Judaism precedence for the sake of the continuity of the plan of salvation (23). But neither Beker nor Kasemann is specific as to what the Jewish eschatological advantage might be.

From the perspective of the premise of this book, Paul's apparent contradiction is explained by the suggestion that prior to the Christ event, obedience to the Jewish law was the means by which the Jew was assured of incremental advancement up the socio-economic and spiritual ladder (9:1-5). Conversely, the gentiles were helpless under the Immutable Law. It follows that this advantage would remain constant for Israel as a whole whether or not the Jews as a group accepted Christ. Belief in Christ was superior in Paul's eyes (10:1-4), however, because it eliminated the necessity of a slow, painful, tenuous ascent.

12. Verse 17 is illuminated if viewed within the context of belief in reincarnation and the concomitant belief that sin/negative *karma* is the cause of cyclical regeneration and death.

The word "righteousness" is a characteristic catchword from Jewish apocalyptic. It denotes the condition of being recognized as innocent (Kasemann 22, 24, 27, 30).

God's declaration of salvation to the world is beyond human control, independent even of the church and its ministers. In Romans, "righteousness" and "justification" have the same meaning (Barclay 22).

Accordingly then, Paul's meaning is that faith in the gospel—that Christ died for the sins/negative *karma* of the believer once and for all—has universal application and the power to remove the sin (past/unknown and present/known) which is stored up in the heart of man (2:5), thus releasing him from the necessity of rebirth and death.

13. The concept of God's wrath does not derive from Greek tradition but from Old Testament Jewish apocalyptic (Kasemann 35, 37). The wrath of God, though present before the revelation of Christ, comes to light along with the gospel (Barclay 24, 25). The wrath of God had several meanings, all of which were probably known to Paul (Ex. 24:3-8; Num. 16:46; Jer. 50:13; Is. 9:19; Ezek. 7:19; Zeph 3:8). For the prophets, the terror and destruction of the wrath of God is continually operative. It would reach its peak on the coming day of the Lord. Broadly speaking then, the wrath of God is that aspect of the godhead that is an annihilating reaction against sin.

This needs clarification. Though the phrase for the concept of retributive justice, "wrath of God," is found in Jewish apocalyptic, it should be recognized that Jewish apocalyptic, cross-cultural in scope, is grounded in gnostic thought which was concerned with reincarnation and God's Law of Justice and the Immutable Law in general. Jewish apocalyptic, then, is simply one of many cultural adaptations and manifestations of gnostic thought.

It has been shown that pre-Christians generally viewed God's Law of Justice (Jewish) and the Immutable Law (pagan) in a positive light. The negative view is found in Paul's Christian perspective and in a subculture in existence at the time as discussed in Chapter Four.

The combination of the wrath of God with the single God of the Jews (v.18) indicates that in Paul, the positive Greek concept of an impersonal Natural Law that moves cyclically of necessity and the positive Pharisaic concept of a personal God of righteousness/justice who granted the good soul the opportunity to resurrect and eternally punished the evil soul (v.20) were integrated and subsumed under the personal God of the Jews. They were also interpreted negatively. Thus the pre-Christian gentile belief in the Law of Nature/the Immutable Law as well as the Jewish belief in God's Law of Justice were accommodated, albeit with a negative twist.

14. The reference to heaven is not to God's dwelling but to the un-avoidable and unmediated fate, which contains a hostile element and rules out any exception (Kasemann, 38).

Though Paul speaks of the wrath of God, he does not speak about God being angry. Often he speaks about the wrath without saying it is the wrath of God. This implies that the wrath was a kind of impersonal force at work in the world. Each of these observations supports the view that the wrath of God (Rom 1:18) refers to the dynamic of the Immutable Law (reincarnation) subsumed under the Jewish personal God. This is in keeping with Paul's intention to be all things to all men (Barclay, 25).

15. That "the wrath of God is revealed from heaven against all ungod-liness and wickedness of men who suppress the truth" (v.18) indicates belief in the continuous operation of God's wrath. It could be argued that in this instance Paul allows for the possibility that there are some men who escape God's wrath because they do not suppress the truth. The argument is countered when he states that all men, both Jews and Greeks, are under the power of sin/negative *karma* (3:9).

But how does Paul know that God's wrath is continually operative and cross-cultural in scope? On what grounds does he base the assumption that all are ungodly and wicked? What about infants who die shortly after birth? What sin did they commit? If the good are punished along with the wicked, can it be said that God is just? From the perspective of belief in reincarna-tion, the answers are clear. All who are born have sinned in a past existence as well as in their present existence and will, therefore, be reborn unto death. Those who seem unjustly punished are facing just punishments for sins committed in past incarnations.

For Paul, mortal existence was viewed as both a blessing and a curse. How so? It was a blessing because existence indicated that the individual had not sinned in a past life to the point of being denied the opportunity to resurrect, or worse, of incurring eternal punishment. It was a curse because suffering and ultimately death would necessarily follow birth. This is a deviation from first-century mainline Pharisaism, which, according to Josephus, viewed mortality in a positive light. Conversely, it is in accord with that branch of Pharisaism gleaned from *Koheleth*/Ecclesiastes.

16. This is consistent with the view that the continually operative wrath was cyclical regeneration unto birth/death (incessant perishing), which would come to an abrupt end on the day of the final judgment—The Day of the Lord (2:5).

The presumption that the cyclical process of rebirth, suffering and death was what Paul meant by the wrath of God also throws light on Paul's statement that what can be known about God's invisible nature, namely his eternal power and deity, has been clearly perceived in the things that have been made (v.19-20).

Are we to understand Paul in the ordinary sense here? Barclay sees the failed harvest as a consequence of breaking the laws of agriculture, or a collapsed building as a consequence of breaking the laws of architecture (27). This cannot be what Paul meant because it is not necessarily just. An architect may break the laws of architecture, but those who occupy the faulty building may be the ones to suffer.

God is just. Therefore, Paul (as with King Solomon in *Koheleth*/Ecclesiastes) cannot be deducing God's wrath (justice) simply from looking at the apparent connection between sin and suffering in the world. It follows that he is deducing it from the context of his own worldview—belief in reincarnation and the caste system—as the means by which God's invisible eternal power (before and outside of Christ, Rom. 1:20) brings about inescapable justice.

Further support for this view is revealed in the fact that though Paul is concerned with suffering, his ultimate concern is death (Rom. 1:32). The view that belief in reincarnation (the Immutable Law, God's Law of Justice and the Wrath of God) and its relevance to the caste system is at the core of Paul's worldview is supported by Kasemann's suggestion that Paul is building on a complex tradition that suggests a connection with popular Hellenistic philosophy (39).

17. As a result God gave them up (v.24) (Kasemann, 43). This implies some sort of initial fall, which in turn implies a change in the nature of existence. The precise nature of the fall is unexplained, presumably because of the cross-cultural gnostic belief that individual sparks of light fell into time, which moves with the cosmos in cyclical necessity. The result of the fall was sexual perversion (vv.24, 26-27) as well as other evils, which run the gamut from foolishness to murder (vv.28-31). The insidious nature of sin is seen when the resultant immorality, which was initially the punishment for not recognizing God, is transmuted into a self-perpetuating downward spiral of sin/negative *karma* which plunges humanity into increasingly lower states of existence (vv.26-32).

18. Presumed belief in reincarnation throws light on Paul's reference to those who commit shameless acts with their own sex (vv.26-27) and receive in their own persons the due penalty for their error (v.27) . Here Paul could not mean that those who do such things will necessarily receive penalty in this lifetime, because experience proves this untrue. Nor could he mean that the penalty would be received in a disembodied state after death—they receive due penalty "in their own persons"—not their soul or spirit.

If Paul is to be taken at his word, the manner in which a penalty for sin is necessarily received in the person of the perpetrator must be accounted for. From the perspective of belief in reincarnation (and divine justice), Paul's meaning is clear. The penalty for sin/negative *karma* is necessarily received in one's own person by rebirth into a lower caste, perhaps to suffer the same sin which he/she perpetrated in the past, and death, which categorically presumes mortality and relates to all. Paul does not make sense otherwise.

When Paul states that men know that God's justice is made manifest in the things that are made and, therefore, they are without excuse (v.20), he means that men have no one to blame but themselves for their respective lot in life, including the condition of mortality and ultimate death, due to past sin/negative *karma*. This explains the curious connective link that Paul draws between those to whom he wrote and others who came before ("they," "their" and "them," vv.20-32) who are responsible for man's present low condition due to ignoring God in the distant past. Why should those who live suffer for the actions of individuals who came before and whom they never knew? This calls God's justice into question. But "God is not mocked, for whatever a man sows, that he will also reap" (Gal. 6:7). It appears that Paul viewed the Romans to whom he wrote (and all men) as the re-embodiment of those who provoked God's wrath in a past existence(s) and who were "receiving in their own persons the due penalty for their error" (v.27).

19. All human beings must die. The soul does not die. What then is Paul's meaning here (v.32)? Death cannot occur without birth. Mortal existence or life then is implicit in the statement and is also a consequence of sin/negative *karma* committed in one's past existence. Paul did not have to explain this to believers who, according to Kasemann, had knowledge of God and were well versed in metaphysics (40). This explains how Paul could make broad based blanket statements about mankind despite the presence of a variety of pre-Christian traditions in existence within the church (40).

### Romans 2:

20. It is possible to refer 2:1-16 either to that which precedes, as to the gentiles, or to that which follows, about the Jews. Both positions have been posited by interpreters. But it is pretty certain that Paul here turns to the Jews (Nygren, 113, 114; Barclay, 40).

It is asserted that Paul does not specifically address the "Jews" until v.17, and even here with qualification; it is suggested that here Paul is addressing lax gentile Jews whom he is trying to win for Christ. This view is based on the general reference to "man" that precedes it (vv.1, 3), as well as the reference to "every human being," which follows (vv.9,10). Apparently this is yet another instance where Paul attempts to be all things to all people. Recall too, that Josephus stated that many pagans who tried to adopt the Jewish law failed to obey its precepts.

21. To my knowledge, the term "eternal life" is not found in Josephus, who revered the Jewish law because it was the means by which the good soul was given the opportunity to return unto a renewed and better existence. References to a renewal of what appears to be mortal existence are found in abundance in the Jewish apocryphal Second Book of the Maccabees (2 Mac. 7:9; 7:11; 7:14; 7:22,23; 12:43,44). The Third Book of the Maccabees indicates that heaven was thought unapproachable by man (3 Mac. 2:15). The Fourth Book of the Maccabees contains only one reference to life with God (4 Mac. 9:8,9), though life with "the fathers" is mentioned (4 Mac. 5:37) as well as life through blessed eternity (4 Mac. 17:17).

Paul acknowledges both traditions (belief in immortality and eternal life) and infers distinction between them: "to those who by patience in well-doing seek for glory and honor and immortality [a renewed and better existence], he will give eternal life" (v.7).

22. Verses 6-16 address gentile Jews and gentiles who, as non-Christians, stand outside of Christ. Each will be recompensed in accordance with his thoughts, words and deeds (v.12) in relation to his internalized standards, which are mediated by each individual conscience.

Implicit is the existence of a holy law that lies in the heart of every human being (Kasemann, 60). Though the standards by which Jews and gentiles are judged differ (e.g., dietary laws, circumcision), God is impartial (v.11) in that the dynamic for judgment—conflict of conscience in relation to internal standards—is the same for all.

23. Verse 16 implies that there will come a day when belief or nonbelief in the gospel—that Jesus Christ died for the sinner once and for all—will be the criteria by which the secrets of men are judged.

24. It is generally acknowledged that v.17 refers to ethnic Jews (Barclay, 40, Kasemann, 68, Nygren, 128). However, Gaston asserts that since every one of Paul's letters is addressed explicitly to gentile Christians, it is not known what he would have said to Jews. Gaston also notes that Paul would have had occasion to speak to Jews as he was punished in synagogues five times (2 Cor. 11:24). Gaston assumes that Paul went to synagogues to worship (309, 313).

First, the fact that Paul's letters were officially addressed to the gentile churches does not tell us anything about the historical cultic traditions of the individuals within the church, nor does it allow for the presence of potential converts or the simply curious who were undoubtedly among those who formed the solid core of the early Roman church. Thus, those to whom Paul wrote were a very mixed lot with different levels of involvement and/or commitment to pagan cults and Judaism as well as to Christianity. This explains Paul's hope to reap harvest among them (1:13,14).

From the perspective of this thesis, those who would hear the letter consisted of Greeks, barbarians, gentile Jews, gentile Christians, gentile Jewish Christians, a smattering of ethnic Jewish Christians, and many in between, including gentile Jewish half proselytes. (Wolfgang Wiefel, "The Jewish Community in Ancient Rome and the Origins of Roman Christianity," in *The Romans Debate*, 99n141).

Second, it is unlikely that Jews would punish a fellow Jew for worshipping at a synagogue. A more likely explanation is that Paul was punished for trying to win for Christ those gentiles who (according to Josephus) had come under the influence of Judaism (God-fearers and proselytes). This view is supported in Acts (18:4), which states that the majority of Paul's recruits were won from amongst the gentile adherents of the synagogues that permeated the Graeco-Roman world (Wedderburn, 197).

Third, Paul's reference to those who "call" themselves Jews (2:17) warrants close scrutiny in light of the caste system and the fact that it was well into the process of collapse by the first century. Why didn't Paul say: "If you are a Jew" rather than "if you call yourself a Jew"? When the caste system was intact, a Jew by birth was a Jew for life whether or not he obeyed the law. Finally, Gaston's suggestion that Paul is addressing some (not all) Jewish missionaries (2:17-24) is notable (313).

It is suggested that the "Jews" to whom Paul directs his attack are gentile Jews (contra Gaston, who considers this to be a rhetorical aside to ethnic Jews in the midst of an indictment of the gentile world, 314) whose role prior to the Christ event was to be examples to the non-converted gentiles. Though they professed the law and displayed its outward signs such as circumcision (2:25-29), they blasphemed the name of God because they did not obey the law's universal aspects (vv.22, 23—Exod. 20:1-17; Deut. 5:6-21). Therefore, they were not protected under the law. This explains the distinction that Paul made when he wrote: "We ourselves, who are Jews by birth . . ." (Gal. 2:15). This view is echoed by Josephus's writings regarding those gentiles who adopted the law but were unable to follow its precepts. Of course, Paul's diatribe was applicable to ethnic Jews as well (Gal. 2:15,16).

25. Some commentators have come to view Paul as inconsistent with respect to the law and the gospel because Paul does not say that he wishes the Jews to give up Judaism for belief in Christ—that it seems that for Paul it is possible to have a status of righteousness from either of two sources, from the law or from the faithfulness of Christ (Gaston, 312n17, 313, 310). Another opinion is that Paul's exuberance for the law makes sense if the problem regarding the Jews of Chaps. 9-11 are in view (Kasemann, 78).

First, it is clear that Paul wishes the Jews (gentile or ethnic) to retain the universal aspects of the Jewish law (vv.21, 22) and to devalue, if not disregard, its outward symbols (vv.25-29), which he considers to be at best reflective of an inner spiritual state and at worst misleading and divisive. It is also clear that Paul wishes Christians to adhere to the universal aspects of the law because they reflect the requirements of the Immutable Law (2:14,15). By so doing, Jew or gentile would be given the opportunity to resurrect unto a renewed and better life (immortality) within cyclical regeneration. But adherence to the law cannot ultimately save (eternal life) unless followed to the letter. This is the basis for Paul's anguish (Rom. 9:1-5). If Jews could be ultimately saved without full adherence to the law, why was Paul in favor of Peter's preaching to the Jews (Gal. 2:7,8)?

For references to the Jewish tradition that obedience to the law was the means by which the soul was given the opportunity to resurrect to a renewed mortal existence (immortality) in this world or another world much like this one, see: 2 Mac. 7:9-11; 7:14; 7:22,23; 12:43,44; 4 Mac. 7:3. The Jewish tradition that obedience to the law was the means by which to be with God appears in 4 Mac. 9:8. There is no mention whether life in God is expected to be temporary or permanent.

For support of the belief in the near impossibility of attaining even the goal of immortality (as opposed to eternal life) under the law see: 2 Mac. 6:26-28; 7:9-11; 7:20-23; 4 Mac. 7:15.

By de-emphasizing the symbolic aspects of the law (e.g. circumcision) that were endemic to Judaism, Paul deviates from mainline Pharisaism, which promulgated and maintained the law and held, like the Sadducees, that the Mosaic law alone was binding.

### Romans 3:

26. In 3:1,2 Paul states that the Jews had an advantage because they were entrusted with the oracles of God. He does not explain why this is so; he assumes the church understands his meaning. This supports the assertion that the Pharisaic Jewish law was promulgated as a means by which to control the Jew's destiny within the cycle of regeneration, which the gentile did not have, and that this was common knowledge in Rome during the first century.

27. Implicit is that the Jews retain the advantage within the socioeconomic and spiritual order—a renewed and better existence—an advantage that they enjoyed before the Christ event (vv.3, 4).

28. Verses 3:5-8 are illuminated by vv.1:24-31. Both sections are further illuminated by the presumption of a belief in an initial universal fall followed by the generation of sin/negative *karma* and ultimately death (1:32), which is the means by which God punishes sin. It's a Catch-22. God inflicts present wickedness as punishment for past sin (v.5). Thus, the sinner is not really in control (7:14-24). Does this make God unjust? No, because this is the mechanism by which He judges the world (v.6). If my sin exhibits His glory and justice, why am I still condemned as a sinner? (v.7) and why not do evil that God's might may be honored? (v.6).

29. Jews and Paul are the subject of the question in v.9 (Kasemann, 85). This is self-evident and should put to rest the idea that Paul's gospel was not relevant to ethnic Jews despite the fact that he was not directly addressing them.

Paul preached during an age of degeneracy and immorality almost without parallel in human history (Barclay, 30-32). Judaism itself bewailed its moral collapse (Kasemann, 69).

30. The reference to the throat as an "open grave" (v.13) reflects the belief that words reflect an inner spiritual state and have weight in determining individual destiny. Bad speech, especially words that counter actions (1:29,30), is one of the means by which one sins and is reborn unto sin and inevitable death (1:32). Conversely, good speech can neutralize or cancel out other sin(s) and ensure a renewed, if not better existence (3:4).

31. From v.13 on, Jewish hatred of the gospel seems to come into consideration. Kasemann advises that too much should not be made of the details (87).

It is precisely these and other discounted details that provide clues into the pre-Christian belief system of cyclical regeneration. In view of this belief system, it is suggested that v.13 on must be seen as part of the whole—all men—Jews and Greeks (v.9) are under the power of sin. Verses 13 and 19 do not make sense unless read within the context of belief in reincarnation, God's wrath and the Natural Law, together with the knowledge that for the Pharisee, the purpose of the Jewish law was to avoid the wrath of God. Verse 19 is a case in point. Without knowledge of belief in cyclical regeneration, the phrase: "[n]ow we know that whatever the law says it speaks to those who are under the law" appears to refer only to the Jews because it is only they who are under the Jewish law. Yet the second part of the verse refers to all men: " . . . so that every mouth may be stopped, and the whole world may be held accountable to God."

The question arises: if the first part of the statement refers only to Jews who are under the law, how can all mouths (which must include the mouths of the gentiles) be stopped and the whole world be held accountable to God? What does Paul mean?

In accord with pre-Christian belief, individuals and groups were hierarchically organized according to their corresponding spiritual status. The Jews as a group were at the top. Advancement or descent was attributed to the invisible power of God, which was made manifest in the things that were made (1:20). Theologically, then, it was possible for non-Jews who, though without the law, followed its broad precepts and could thus be reborn as Jews and thereby come under the law. If obedient, such an individual would reap the advantages under the law for further spiritual progress within Judaism.

32. Dunn, citing 14:2,5 suggests that Paul's warning against "the works of the law" (3:20) was not about "good works" in general but rather referred to Jewish obedience to those laws by which the Jews maintained

their status within the covenant with respect to the Sabbath and food. There does not appear to be a conceptual relationship between 14:2,5 and 3:20. The references to "vegetables" (14:2) and "days" (14:5) probably refer literally to the pre-Christian cultic practices of some of the gentile Christians. This is not surprising if one considers that many adherents of Oriental religions (Judaism was considered an Oriental religion) such as Hinduism are/were vegetarians (suggesting a possible worldview connection with the subcontinent of India). Likewise, "days" is probably a reference to the feast days of the various cults (307, 308).

Robert J. Karris holds that "vegetables" is meant to cover all cases of abstinence from food and "days" refers to feast days. ("Romans 14:1-15:13 and the "Occasion of Romans," in *The Romans Debate*, 77).

I think Karris' view is reasonable, but this does not preclude the correctness of Dunn's "umbrella" statement regarding v.20.

The law for Paul was the broad ethical precepts of Jewish tradition (2:21-23; Exod. 20:1-17; Deut. 5:6-21). He did not consider the outward manifestations of Judaism to be inextricably bound to these precepts (2:25-29; 14:2,5; Gal. 2:15,16). But to say that all Paul had in mind when he warned against "the works of the law" were the outward manifestations of the law is an oversimplification. If this were so, why does he say that the law and the commandment killed him (7:8-11), and why is faith in the saving power of Christ necessary?

In keeping with the thesis of this work—that the wrath of God/sin/negative *karma* was the Immutable Law which was cross-culturally understood prior to and during the first century, and that the Pharisees considered the Jewish law to be the means by which to return/resurrect and advance in accordance with Immutable Law through the socioeconomic system, Paul's reference to "the works of the law" refers to works performed in accordance with the dictates of the Jewish caste system. Thus, Paul's warning must mean the following: The broad ethical law of the Jews reflected the will of God and could save unto eternal life if perfectly obeyed—an impossibility due not to the imperfection of the law, but rather to the imperfection of man (7:14-20). Knowing the law and being unable to obey it (unable to fulfill the requirement of the Jewish caste system, which was part and parcel of spiritual fulfillment of the law) creates a conflict of conscience (3:20) that kills (causes regeneration unto birth/life/death). Thus the warning against "the works of the law."

33. This section has been called one of the most difficult and obscure in the whole epistle. One of the reasons is that here as elsewhere Paul does not identify the tradition that he uses and, moreover, he interprets it through

additions (Kasemann, 92, 95).

Much of the obscurity of the passage vanishes if it is presumed that Paul is speaking within the context of the pre-Christian cross-cultural belief in cyclical return manifested by the caste system and the role of the Pharisaic law in relation to this belief. Complicating matters is the fact that Paul superimposes the meaning of the Christ event over that which is presumed.

34. Paul knows all are sinners and have not been justified because they exist as mortals.

35. See Romans 2:5.

36. Kasemann questions whether vv.25 and 26, which are conjoined, are to be interpreted in the sense of an intensification or a restatement (98).

It is asserted that an interpretation favoring a restatement is correct. It is suggested that v.25 refers to the forbearance of God which allowed resurrection unto mortal existence as manifested in the various castes, a kind of distributive justice, before the Christ event. Verse 26 refers to the guilt, past and/or unknown, stored up in the heart of man (2:5) during pre-Christian times and canceled out for those who have faith in Jesus.

37. This point (vv.29,30) could not be logically countered without negating monotheism; if God was merely the God of the Jews, he would cease to be the only God (Kasemann, 104).

Paul asks, " . . . what becomes of our boasting?" (v.27) Presumably his reference is to those who boast on the basis of their spiritual status as reflected by their social status/occupation.

38. For Paul, the demonstration of divine righteousness " . . . is no longer the renewal of the covenant with God's ancient people. It is universally oriented to faith" (Kasemann, 101). It could be argued that the meaning of v.30 is that God will justify the circumcised and the uncircumcised on the basis of their respective faiths. This is a gross misinterpretation of Paul's meaning. For him faith/belief is a potent spiritual dynamic with the power to justify (4:3).

## Romans 4:

39. The reference here can be understood as the pre-Christian Jewish belief in justification by works according to the law as manifested in caste. From the perspective of the believer, this would account for the exalted status of Abraham. This is consistent with the view that Paul's meaning is that Abraham was justified in the eyes of men by works but not by God (Kasemann, 106, 112).

40. Kasemann argues that v.4 consists of a reference to a "generally

accepted rule," which catches up what is said in v.2. But Kasemann does not say what that rule might be (111).

It is suggested that the "generally accepted rule" to which Kasemann refers is the rule or law of cause and effect, which is reflected in principle in the pre-Christian belief in works (the cause) as a means by which to return to a better mortal existence as manifested in caste status (the effect). For the believer in this "generally accepted rule," Abraham's worldly status indicated that Abraham was justified by God through works. Paul states that this is not the case.

Kasemann notes too that the use of the technical formula and commercial language (work/wages) is nontheological. He proposes that the reason is that " . . . the apostle's concern is first with the dimension of the word-event and secondly with the paradoxical character of grace." In contrast, it is suggested that the technical formula and commercial language used by Paul literally reflect the pre-Christian view of the interrelatedness of the social/worldly (work for wages) and spiritual/metaphysical (work for spiritual reward) spheres, supporting the thesis of this work.

41. Forgiveness, in Paul's view, finally happens only to the sinner. As a result a different theological horizon and different set of terms arise. Salvation is not only the setting aside of the guilt of the past, but also freedom from the power of sin (Kasemann, 113).

Kasemann does not explain the meaning of " . . . freedom from the power of sin." From our perspective it can only mean freedom from the power of sin (past and present) to cause regeneration, deepening sin and death (1:26-32).

42. The rabbis since Sir. 44:20 asserted that the beatitude quoted in vv.6, 7 and 8 relate to Israel and is, therefore, valid only in the sphere of the circumcision (Kasemann, 114).

43. The reckoning of righteousness to Abraham on the basis of faith/belief (Gen. 15.6) precedes the covenant of circumcision (Gen. 17:10) by 29 years (Kasemann, 114).

44. The meaning here is that " . . . only the Christian is the true Jew, and Abraham is called the father of the circumcision only as the father of Jewish-Christians" (Kasemann, 116).

45. The view that the law is a means by which the promise is fulfilled is supported in 2 Macc. 2:17, which indicates that the law is itself the bearer of the promise and was already known to Abraham and his generation in unwritten form (Kasemann, 119).

Note that the promise to Abraham and his descendants was that they should inherit the world (v.13). This accords with the idea that the law was viewed by some believers as the means by which to ensure a renewed existence in the world.

46. The intermediate thought that wrath is reached by transgression of the law is omitted in v.15 (Kasemann, 121).

47. The issue here is universalism of the promise of Abraham, which could not be attained through the law (Kasemann, 120).

48. "In vv.13-17 the idea that the promise (v.16) is attached to the law is contested" (Kasemann, 118).

49. Kasemann cites a "contrary view" that sees the text as a general discussion in which the specific content of the promise is not at issue. He states that it is precisely the content of the promise—its universalism—which is at issue (120).

While universalism is obviously the content of the promise in this instance, the underlying issue is the saving/actualizing power of faith/belief.

50. It is noteworthy that in the context of the promise in relation to Abraham, God gives life to the dead (v.17). In the context of the promise of God in Christ, God raised Jesus from the dead (v.24). This supports the view that much of the pre-Christian Jewish hope was that God would sustain them within cyclical regeneration. This is in contrast to the Christian hope that God would release believers from the recycling process. The reference to the raising of the dead reflects gnostic thought.

## Romans 5:

51. Rabbinic Judaism is very strongly marked by uncertainty with respect to salvation (Kasemann, 132).

It is logical to assume that such uncertainty with respect to salvation was an integral part of first-century Judaism and that the promise of certain salvation (10:10) was a key incentive for purposes of winning gentile Jews (and ethnic Jews as well) from Judaism to faith in Christ.

52. Kasemann agrees that the interpretation that access to the glory of God means unhindered access to a physical place such as a church or synagogue is simplistic (133). Kasemann's point rings true, particularly in view of the presumed metaphysics that constitutes the backdrop to Romans.

53. Suffering (v.3) is the end time affliction which the Christian must endure as a follower of the messiah Jesus (Kasemann, 134).

54. Here (v.9) Paul speaks of a relation of divine power, or of the powerful God, the relation being to the creature. In God's righteousness this power creates salvation for rebels, in wrath this power reveals itself to rebels as destruction (Kasemann, 135).

55. Paul's meaning (v.10) is that the " . . . power of the life of the risen

Lord embraces and preserves the community . . . .the Christ who died for us also lives for us" (Kasemann, 139).

56. Gen. 2:16, 17; 3:14-19. See also the discussion of the Hebrew model (Chapter Two, Section B) and the gnostic view of the origin of man (Chapter Four, Section B).

57. Sin and death (v.12) have the character of universal forces that no one escapes (Kasemann, 149).

58. Paul's reference to Adam reflects one of the many versions of gnostic thought concerning primal man. In Kasemann's view this is attributable to the influence on Judaism of the motifs of the myth of the primal man during the Hellenistic period (144-146).

It has been shown that *gnosis*, regardless of how or where it occurs, contains core concepts that, though adaptable to particular cultural circumstances, remain fundamentally the same. Thus, while scholars observing the occurrence of similar cross-cultural ideas and concepts assume chronological and/or topographical connections, they are not necessarily present.

59. The disobedience (v.19) refers to rebellion against the first commandment (Kasemann, 154). However, this disobedience cannot refer to Jewish law, as sin was in the world before the law was given (v.13). In view of the cosmic breadth of Paul's metaphysics, it seems more plausible that the reference is to man's original disobedience and fall from grace (vv.12-14).

60. Recall the discussion in Chapter Four, Section B (the Archons) of the Gnostics' fallen *archons* or *aeons*, including Adam and Satan. Kasemann notes that there is obvious reference to the apocalyptic idea of the two aeons (v.19). But ". . . there is good reason to think that Paul did not adopt the historical schema of the succession of the two aeons, even though in Gal. 1:4 he speaks of the present evil aeon, awaits the heavenly consummation, and contrasts primal time and end-time" (142, 144, 147).

It is suggested that here Paul presumed the historical schema of the succession of the two *aeons*, but did not adopt it for the baptized. Indeed, this is one of the differences between the baptized and the nonbaptized. The nonbaptized person is stuck within cyclical regeneration as an individual as well as corporately, which reflects succession of the aeons. The baptized escapes the fate left mankind by the fallen Adam and Satan. This is consistent with Kasemann's observation that the spheres of Adam and Christ, of death and life, are separate alternatives. It is also consistent with the view of Adam and Christ typology as characterization not of stages in history, but history's beginning and end. The emphasis here is that theologically, history ends only for those who are not thrown back into it.

## Romans 6:

61. Kasemann rightly suggests that in vv.1-11 Paul is trying to correct the tradition of the community (161). Verses 1-11 are particularly pertinent for the gentile Christians and gentile Jewish Christians (as opposed to the gentile Jews) who, though committed as followers of Christ, are misguided. Paul distinguishes between them and the uncommitted gentile Jews (v.3) when he writes, "Do you not know that we who have been baptized . . . ."

62. Kasemann notes that the phrase "by the glory of the father" (v.4) may be pre-Pauline (166). This view is consistent with the idea that expressions such as "the Father" and "the Son" derived from gnostic thought and that Pauline Christianity is a modification and reworking of gnostic concepts—not the reverse.

63. Verse 4 is consistent with the understanding of baptism in pre-Pauline communities as a mystery event that incorporated one into the fate of the cultic God. " . . . [N]ewness of life" implies a new life qualitatively different from mortal existence (Kasemann, 162, 165).

64. The phrases "a death like his" and "a resurrection like his" (v.5) presume death and resurrection ad infinitum due to sin/negative *karma*, which is in Adam. This is in contrast to the final resurrection in Christ which is freedom from the process.

65. Kasemann accepts Bultmann's view that all Paul's anthropological terms mean existence in a specific orientation (176). From Paul's perspective then, the sinful body (v.6) is the mortal body (v.12).

66. The baptized are set wholly free from sin only after death (v.11) (Kasemann, 163).

67. For Paul, sin has the character of a power that determines existence in Adam (Kasemann, 167, 180). This is consistent with the idea that sin has determined initial mortal existence and subsequent cyclical regeneration/ death until (for those who believe) the Christ event.

68. The questions arise as to why Paul formulates basic statements and demands in relation to the new life and why he spends so much time on exhortation (Kasemann, 173, 175). In response, it is suggested that though the Christ event covers the sins of believers (4:7) (those of a past existence(s) and those committed prior to baptism in the present life), sins committed after baptism would indicate backsliding with respect to the lordship of Christ. This is consistent with Kasemann's statement: "Not for nothing the demand is derived from baptism" (175).

69. This is consistent in principle with Kasemann's view that the concept in v.22 primarily denotes deliverance "from the compulsion of the

powers" (Kasemann, 185). Recall the "dark powers" described in the description of gods in the gnostic cosmos in Chapter Four, Part B.

70. The logic of the context of 6:1-23 inextricably binds the themes of freedom from death, sin and law (Kasemann, 158, 159). Death obviously must be preceded by birth.

## Romans 7:

71. Kasemann finds the caution, fussiness and consideration with which Paul opens the section (7:1) surprising, suggesting that Paul was aware that he was treading on dangerous ground as far as important groups within the Roman community were concerned. Kasemann further states that since the Roman community consisted mainly of gentile Christians, the reference to the people who "know the law" (even assuming an active Jewish Christian minority) could hardly mean people who new the Torah (Kasemann, 187).

This is consistent with the suggestion that an important aspect of Paul's missionary work was directed toward gentile Jews. In this instance (v.1), the focus is on gentile Jews (gentile Christians had no reason to know the law) who, as converts to Judaism, are " . . . those who know the law"— more or less. If they knew it well, Paul would not have explained it. In his effort to sway the gentile Jews to accept the righteousness of Christ over the righteousness of the law, Paul identifies with them as "brethren," thus identifying and ingratiating himself with "Jews" who, like himself, should adopt Christianity.

72. Verse 4 refers not to the participation in the dead body of Jesus but rather to baptism, upon which we are released from sin, death and dominion of the law (Kasemann, 188, 189, 191).

73. Verse 4 is consistent with Kasemann's view that freedom from the powers of sin and death takes concrete shape in freedom from Torah (Kasemann, 190, 191).

74. From Paul's perspective, "living in the flesh" (v.5) must have meant living under the necessity of cyclical mortal existence caused by the sinful passions at work. The effect is literally the old life in the flesh. This is in contrast to the new life of the Spirit. This new life is present within the believer but will not be fully realized until after death.

75. For Paul, the antithesis of flesh and Spirit (v.6) is the same as that of letter and Spirit (Kasemann, 191).

76. Though the reference is to himself ("I") (v.7), corporate personality in general is indicated. The question arises as to why Paul refers to himself and not corporate personality as in the story of Adam (Kasemann, 192,

196, 197). It is obvious that vv.9-11 do not refer to immediate reality, since Paul is "alive." What is evident here is the gnostic/mystic belief in cyclical regeneration from the Pharisaic point of view. From this vantage point, Paul can be taken literally. He considers himself an example ("I") of the plight of mankind in general (corporate) as well as the specific plight of the Pharisees (individual and corporate) who, as such, are born under the law.

Thus v.9 could mean either or both of the following:

1. The status into which he was born within the Jewish caste system (Pharisee). Thus the statement "I died" (v.9) refers to his status among the dead in the past as well as his present lifetime in which he was subject to rebirth and death before being in Christ.

2. Paul existed in the past as a non-Jew who was not explicitly conscious of many of the sins about which Jews were concerned, but was born into Judaism in his present lifetime. As such he became conscious of sin through the law and died—meaning that after his physical death he would of necessity be reborn and die again. It is important to remember that non-Jews as well as Pharisees believed themselves to be subject to the recycling process. In this way the law, which was supposed to be a means by which to control and ideally transcend the birth/death process, was perverted by the power of sin, making escape impossible (vv.8-13).

77. From the perspective of belief in reincarnation with a negative twist, the reference to life (v.10) must mean eternal life. The reference to death (v.10) must be the opportunity for a renewed mortal existence (birth/death) given to those who obeyed the law, albeit imperfectly.

78. Gaston notes that it has been generally recognized that Romans 7 is not autobiographical (310nn3,4).

I concur with respect to 7:1-6 but submit that 7:7-13 is autobiographical and can be taken literally. The Jewish law in and of itself could not kill. This is true of the outward manifestations of the law—circumcision, food restrictions and Sabbath, as well as the universal aspects (Exod. 20; Deut. 5).

From the perspective of a cross-cultural pre-Christian belief in cyclical regeneration (birth, death and rebirth), together with the Pharisaic modification that only the good soul is given the opportunity to resurrect while the wicked soul suffers eternal punishment and the Pharisaic/Christian negative twist toward the entire system, 7:7-13 cannot be anything other than autobiographical. What does Paul mean? Knowledge of the law is good in that it lays bare sin, but the act of definition of sin honed the consciences of those who could not obey the law due to sin/negative *karma*, which is part and parcel of mortal existence (7:13-25). As a result more sin is stored up. Thus the law can kill.

79. The law gives testimony to the heavenly origin of the will of God, which pertains to the pre-Christian world and as such is cosmic in breadth. Moreover, v.14 shows that Paul is simply referring to the person of flesh and blood in its weakness (Kasemann, 199).

Kasemann's view allows for the possibility that Paul's meaning is that it is flesh and blood, the mortal incarnation of the soul, in and of itself that is sin and paradoxically the means through which sin is punished.

80. Verses 15-20 differ sharply from both Qumran and Greek tradition. In them there can be no question of merely an ethical conflict. In Kasemann's view they illustrate the superscription in v.14 (Kasemann, 201-201). The illustration (vv.15-20) of the superscription in v.14 supports the view that for Paul, mortal existence and being sold under sin/negative *karma* are one and the same.

Kasemann further states that the meaning of "good" and "evil" in vv.16, 18, 19 and elucidated by other statements is that "A person thinks he knows what he is doing and what he can expect." But Paul is clear. He does things that he does not want to do, and he does not understand why (v.15). Here as elsewhere Paul is misunderstood because he is not interpreted from the perspective of the cultural matrix of the Roman Empire at large, his metaphysical beliefs, and his spirituality, all of which formed the backdrop of his theology. From this perspective, the statement that he " . . . was once alive apart from the law, but when the commandment came, sin revived and I died" (7:9) means precisely that. When he states that "the very commandment which promised life proved death to me" (7:10) and "sin finding opportunity in the commandment, deceived me and by it killed me" (7:11), he means that too.

81. Verses 22 and 23 render "inmost self" and "mind" interchangeable. Verse 23 sets "inmost self" and "mind," which serves the law/Law of God, in antithesis to the flesh, which serves the Immutable Law of sin/negative *karma*. In the illumination, I have distinguished between the Jewish law and the law of the mind by the lower case (l) and the Immutable Law (spiritual) by the upper case (L) (vv.14-25).

Adding another link to the chain connecting Paul's theology to the Greek philosophical schools, Galen the physician (mid-second century C.E.) attacked both Jews and Christians as well as adherents to the Greek philosophical schools for the dogmatic basis of their views—their discussion of undemonstrated laws (David E. Aune, "Romans as a Logos Protreptikos," in *The Romans Debate*, 287).

82. Kasemann cites 6:11-12 as support against the idea of dualism in Paul. He states, "If one does not psychologize, the only possible meaning here is to the death of the body of sin effected in baptism."

First, the assumption that Paul's admonition that Christians consider themselves dead to sin and alive to God in Christ (6:11) effected in baptism in their present existence would not necessarily exclude, but would rather include the concomitant concept of their being dead to sin and alive to God in another way (6:5) after the final resurrection.

Second, here as elsewhere Paul distinctly considers mortal bodies to be something other than the essential Self. If this were not so, why does he refer to mortal bodies and their passions (6:12)? Kasemann notes that Paul's lament and the accompanying cry for redemption (7:24) reflect a pre-Pauline tradition of which Paul may or may not be aware. The tradition is to be found in the Hellenistic-Jewish story of Joseph and Asenath 6:2ff, and the Hermetic tractate *Kore Kosmou* 34-37. This tradition indicates "despair at imprisonment in earthly corporeality and at the related blindness." Does this not suggest the thesis of this work—namely that Romans is to be interpreted within the context of the gnostic belief that rebirth, death, sin and corporeality are inextricably joined, and that the heart of Pauline theology is that life in Christ frees one from the process by releasing one from the necessity of future corporeal existence?

Third, Kasemann notes that the core of Paul's teaching against the law is that though the religious person agrees with the will of God and delights in it, "he becomes entangled in his own desire for life which tries to snatch what can only be given and thus falls subject to the powers of the world" (Kasemann, 207-210, 224).

I concur in principle, with the following clarification. The life that was desired by the Pharisee in Paul's day was a renewed and better corporeal existence, and this desire had, for many, overcome the desire for eternal life on another plane. Thus the religious person was continuously subjected to the powers of the world.

### Romans 8:

83. Romans 8:1 does not maintain deliverance from the body of death but from eschatological judgment (Kasemann, 214).

From the perspective of the cultural matrix of the Roman Empire at large as well as from Paul's personal spirituality and metaphysical point of view, the reference is to deliverance from the body of death, which is one and the same as deliverance from eschatological judgment.

84. For Paul, "in Christ" means standing in a field of force (Kasemann, 220).

This is consistent with the concept of regeneration being a kind of "other" force that operates in cyclical necessity according to its own Immutable Law. Being in the force field of Christ, then, is the only hope of breaking free of this Immutable Law.

85. Verse 3 describes the incarnation of the Son of God, which has been shown to be a gnostic concept. (For a comparison see Gal. 4:4; 1 Jn. 3:16; 1 Jn. 4:9.)

86. The Spiritual Law(s) (L) and the Jewish law (l) are distinguished by upper and lower case, respectively (vv.2, 4).

It is noteworthy that Paul states that God sent his Son that the Law might be fulfilled *in* us (v.4). He did not say through us or for us or by us. This indicates that there is an integral part of us (paradoxically separate yet a part—the heart) that must be set right before the Law of retributive justice can be neutralized. The acceptance of the gospel—faith that Jesus Christ died for one's sin/negative *karma* once and for all—is the means by which the law/Law is fulfilled in us.

87. Kasemann rightly points out that Paul's view of the divine spirit (v.4) reflects many traditions and is very complex. The Hellenistic world related spirit to the power of miracle and ecstasy. The Jewish apocalyptic related it to the end time. Early Christianity connected it with the resurrection of Jesus and the work of the exalted Lord in his community, witness to the dawn of the new aeon (212, 213).

88. In terms of the history of religions, "in the flesh" and "in the spirit" (vv.5-7) can be explained against the background of a non-Jewish metaphysical dualism—an explanation that Kasemann feels is inadequate. Yet special studies have made it clear that the Pauline material is more complex and richer in nuance than is generally accepted (Kasemann, 220).

The brief analysis of Paul in Chapter Five, Section C, "All Things to All Men," reveals him as a complex individual whose person and teaching incorporated various pre-Christian traditions that were grounded in gnostic thought. It has also been theorized that gnostic thought, which was the core principle on which some Jewish traditions were based, existed within both Jewish and non-Jewish tradition, independent of each other. Why then is an explanation of "in the flesh" and "in the spirit" (both gnostic metaphysical terms) against a background of metaphysical dualism inadequate?

It is likely that what is meant by being "in the spirit" in this instance is simply that baptized Christians were no longer subject to the force field of sin/negative *karma*, death and mortality if, in fact, the Spirit of God/Christ (acceptance of the gospel) dwelt within them.

89. It is obvious that though Paul refers to the bodies of Christians as dead because of sin, they are in fact alive. Again this reference refers to the gnostic/mystic ability to transcend time (see 7:7-11). For Paul their bodies are dead because he sees beyond the time that they have yet to live to their inevitable death. Their spirits are alive, however, because after physical death they will continue into a resurrection like that of Christ, no more to return to a renewed worldly existence.

90. The change indicated (v.11) is the change in aeons (Kasemann, 224).

It has been shown that the concept of a change in *aeons* is found in Greek as well as Jewish tradition, albeit with minor variations. Generally, this belief held that upon the revolution of the ages/the new *aeon*/the end time, the very same people (in the case of Pharisaism, the righteous) would reappear on a new earth.

This phrase, then, is a concession to those Christians whose tradition had been belief in the resurrection of the flesh within the new *aeon*. Paul was obliged to redirect a great variety of traditions under Christ. Thus he acknowledges the pre-Christian concept of the revolution of the ages, as well as the Jewish belief in an end time. He also allowed for the first-century Jewish hope for bodily resurrection into a renewed and better existence on earth (immortality as opposed to eternal life—2:7). He is attempting to substitute the function of the law in relation to bodily resurrection (individual and/or corporate) with faith in Christ for the various hoped-for modes of resurrection. In doing so he walks gingerly. He does not refer directly to Jesus Christ, but rather to the "Spirit of him (a reference to God which would be more acceptable to Jewish Christians) who raised Jesus from the dead."

91. The Greek phrase (v.12) means "to be under obligation." To Kasemann, the Christian is obligated to stand in conflict with the power of the flesh if he is not to be doomed to death (225).

From the gnostic perspective, the "debtors" owe debt that is incurred as a result of sin/negative *karma* (in a present and/or past lives that must be repaid). Accordingly, Paul means that the debt for deeds/sins of the flesh which ordinarily link past, present and future existences through retributive justice has been broken by the Christ event. As recipients of this gift of grace, baptized Christians are no longer mechanistically compelled by the power of the flesh/Law of sin. They are free to choose whether to live according to the flesh and die again (v.12) or to put to death the deeds of the body and live eternally after death.

92. " . . . [O]ne must reject an understanding which sets the 'true' I at a distance from its works which the body is presented here as doing" (Kasemann, 226).

The only understanding that is to be rejected in interpreting Paul is that which was not his. (See especially 7:15, 24.) Analysis of Pauline concepts and language indicate that Paul, like other Gnostics, did indeed regard the body as separate and distinct from the Self—the "true" I, but enslaved in flesh it was subject to the power (force field) of the flesh. From this perspective Paul is saying that the new creation, the son(s) of God (v.14), the new "true" I, must stand in conflict with the power of the flesh in the present if it is not to be lured back into the regenerative process after death.

93. Kasemann notes that the influence of the Jesus tradition is reflected in the use of the words "Abba! Father!" (v.15) (228).

It has been demonstrated that the words "Abba" and "Father" were gnostic designations that were used by both Jewish and pagan Gnostics to express in language that which is ineffable. It has also been shown that Jesus as well as his disciples and "the people" held the gnostic view of earthly reincarnation (Mk. 6:14-16; Mk. 8:28-30; Jn. 1:19-21; Matt. 11:13-15; Matt. 17:10-13). Accordingly, the use of the words "Abba" and "Father" by Jesus does not indicate a tradition that originated with him but rather reflects a knowledge of and/or connection between Jesus and gnostic concepts. Likewise, Paul's use of the words "Abba" and "Father" indicates his knowledge of and/or connection with gnostic thought.

94. The terms sons of God (v.14), spirit of slavery, spirit of sonship, the cry "Abba! Father!," (v.15), children of God, (v.16) and heirs of God (v.17) all reflect gnostic concepts and language and the anguish and gratitude of the Gnostic for redemption from the flesh. The motif of sonship and slavery common in Paul also reflects gnostic thought. The reference to slavery (v.15), refers to the slavery under Christ, which will bring eternal life, as opposed to slavery under the Immutable regenerative process (sin/ negative *karma*), which brings rebirth/death.

95. Kasemann interprets v.17 to mean that "only those who resist the flesh with suffering can overcome" (229).

From the gnostic/Christian perspective, to suffer with Christ means to bear the burden of one's destiny with its attendant indignities and sufferings. It also means to resist the grasping of the flesh because it is fleshly gratification that perpetuates mortal renewal and ultimate death. The suffering of Jesus was the carrying out his mission from God, even though it was contrary to the interests of the flesh. Likewise, the suffering of the

Christian is the carrying out his/her mission from God through Christ, although it may be contrary to the interests of the flesh.

As a gnostic Pharisee who believed himself to have been condemned to rebirth, suffering and death, Paul the Christian now stands in hope for the end of the process. Thus he distinguishes between past suffering, in which there was no hope of an end (see *Koheleth*/Ecclesiastes), and the suffering that has become bearable after the Christ event: "I consider that the sufferings of this present time are not worth comparing with the glory that is to be revealed to us" (8:18).

Recall that Jewish tradition predominantly held that those who suffered and, if need be, died for the law would attain a renewed and better mortal existence. Verse 17 transfers this concept in principle from suffering for the law to suffering with Christ.

96. Kasemann agrees that v.18 is not speaking merely of "assurance of salvation in face of the enduring afflictions" that are part and parcel of discipleship to Christ (231). In my view, v.18 is speaking of the suffering endured as a consequence of mortal existence, a state worsened by the added burden of persecution as a result of following Christ. The sentiment, distinctly gnostic in tone, is reinforced in vv.19-27.

97. Kasemann is adamant in his view that Paul does not presuppose gnostic mythology (Kasemann, 233, contra Bultmann, *Theology*, I, 174, 175f) ". . . but rather the tradition of Jewish apocalyptic with its idea of the loss of the divine image in the fall into sin." It would be more accurate to say that though Paul does not presuppose all aspects of gnostic mythology per se, he clearly does presuppose the fall, which is an aspect of gnostic mythological thought.

It has been suggested that *gnosis*/gnostic thought lays at the foundation of all religious traditions. Jewish apocalyptic is no exception. This is not inconsistent with Kasemann's view that Paul is presupposing the tradition of Jewish apocalyptic rather than gnostic mythology. Here, Paul incorporates the gnostic concept of the fall, but deviates from that part of gnostic mythology that viewed the world and its futility as a creation of the Demiurge and replaces it with the Jewish God who created the world and subjected it to futility in hope.

98. Here, Paul presumes the pre-Christian pagan and Jewish hope of a new heaven, new earth and renewed mortal existence en masse, but with a twist that renders it uniquely Christian. The creation that was subjected to futility (v.20) will be set free from the process and obtain the glorious liberty of the children of God (v.21).

99. Kasemann points out that the concept of immortality or the resurrection of the flesh is non-Pauline. He believes the apostle longs for an

existence liberated from temptation and decay in favor of a life in a world that belongs to God alone (237). (See Rom. 8:21; 1 Cor. 15:42-44; 2 Cor. 5:6-10.)

First, Rom. 2:6,7 indicate that the concept of immortality or the resurrection of the flesh, though not Pauline, was indeed known and understood by him as one of many possible modes of new life from which the believer was saved by the Christ event. The question arises: if, as Kasemann correctly states, Paul longed for an existence liberated from temptation and decay related to the flesh, why did he refer to the pre-Christian belief in mortal resurrection (immortality) in his letters? (See also 1 Th. 4:13-18.) It appears that the answer lies in the enormity and complexity of Paul's general goal. To create a new unified tradition under Christ (faith in Christ brings eternal life) from the various belief systems within the Roman Empire, Paul found it necessary to integrate the separate traditions (immortality, resurrection of the flesh, continual and final judgment) in relation to Christ's lordship.

Second, for Paul, the Christian ideal was obedience to the universal aspects of the Jewish law (1 Cor. 7:19) and belief that Christ died for the sins of the world—once and for all. In this way, Pauline Christianity maintained what in his view was the heart of the pre-Christian role of the law—a renewed and better mortal existence in the world (and/or a world very much like our own) for those who obeyed the law imperfectly, and eternal life for those who obeyed it to the letter. The faith that Christ died for the sins of all—once and for all—provides salvation for those who tried but were unable to perfectly obey the law. The tolerance for, indeed the acceptance of more than one tradition of resurrection in Pauline Christianity explains why Paul often appears contradictory. He seeks to appeal to aspects of each tradition represented by members in his audience.

It is agreed that Paul longs for an existence liberated from temptation and decay in favor of a life that belongs to God alone. However, that this existence was to be realized, according to Kasemann, "in a world that belongs to God alone," is contradictory. In Paul's view such an existence could not be had in a world of any sort because the world and all in it are perishable and subject to futility (1 Cor. 15:42-45).

100. Kasemann notes that it is unclear whether the reference to hope (v.24) is to the act of hoping or to what is hoped for (238). From our perspective, on a basic level, faith and hope are interchangeable. Thus the act of hope, like the act of faith, is the dynamic power of salvation—"For in this hope we were saved." (v.24).

101. The references to the help of the Spirit in prayer (vv.26, 27) have

no parallels in the New Testament and are alien even in Pauline texts. Further, the most important statement, that we do not know what we should pray for, is completely unfamiliar for primitive Christianity (Kasemann, 239). It is suggested that v.26 refers to that longing that is unconscious in us. "Sighs" reflect and unconscious, unspeakable longing. This view is supported in 1 Cor. 14:23-25, which alludes to the prophetic/gnostic ability to disclose the secrets of the heart, which may or may not be consciously known.

Paul renders this function uniquely Christian (Jewish/Christian) by ascribing this aspect of *gnosis* to the Spirit, who understands our deepest needs which are not conscious and, therefore, are too deep for words. The ascription of a gnostic function to the Spirit, thus rendering it uniquely Christian, is also reflected in 1 Cor. 2:10-16. Paul distinguishes between Christians, who through the Spirit are concerned with things of God, and non-Christians, who do not have the Spirit and as such are concerned with things of the world (1 Cor. 2:12) by stating that the Spirit intercedes for the saints according to the will of God (v.27).

102. Verses 29-30 infer prophetic (gnostic) thought in two respects. First, the gnostic belief in pre-temporal existence is reflected. Second, the prophetic tendency to transcend time and think in paradox is illustrated. Those who are predestined and called are already justified and glorified.

103. The beginning and end of history is in view from the time of the saving event of the death and resurrection of Christ (Kasemann, 247).

This is consistent with the idea that belief in the death and resurrection of Christ meant freedom from the process of reentry into history, whether into a new world or into the existing one.

104. Verse 35 illustrates the actual suffering of the followers of Jesus, who are stigmatized by the cross (Kasemann, 249). Recall that the cross (*stauros*) symbolized to the Gnostics salvation through suffering.

105. The angelic powers (v.39) belong to the fallen creation and are hostile to Christians (Kasemann, 251). It is possible that the reference is to archons, fallen angels believed by the Gnostics to be evil.

106. For Paul life and death are within the demonic circle. Only the apocalyptic worldview describes reality in this way (Kasemann, 251). It is noteworthy that Paul's language reflects the gnostic attitude toward life and death as well as gnostic terminology for those powers that try to prevent the ascension of the spirit after death—principalities, fate (things present/things to come), powers, height, and depth. Again, this is consistent with the view that gnostic thought lies at the foundation of Jewish apocalyptic tradition.

**Romans 9:**

107. "In Christ" is to be taken in the sense of being in the presence of Christ (Kasemann, 257). Paul considers his statements about the ethnic Jews to be guided and justified by the spirit. Here (v.1) the Greek word for the anointed One, Christ, is used in combination with the Jewish term Holy Spirit.

108. Paul is talking about, not to, the ethnic Jews, his "kinsmen by race." Why did he mention them? The reason is clear if, as it has been suggested, it is assumed that there was a large number of gentile Jews who had come under the influence of the Church and were an expected audience of the letter. Under the circumstances. Paul's social position (caste) as an ethnic Jew who had a special relationship to God due to his obedience to the law (2:17) but nonetheless embraced Christ, was a powerful persuasive tool. This is especially true since the gentile Jews, unlike Paul, were lax with respect to the law (2:17-29).

109. For Paul, the Jews are and remain the people whom God has set apart for his gifts. Implicit is the idea that if the promise to the Jews can lose validity, so can the assurance of the gospel (Kasemann, 258, 259, 261).

110. The basic question (9:1-5) is that of the relation between salvation history and the doctrine of justification. Kasemann considers it remarkable that Paul gives no reason for his sorrow (Kasemann, 255, 256, 258).

From the perspective of Paul and his first-century audience, the call for sorrow is apparent. Prior to the Christ event the Jews on the collective and individual levels held a superior position in salvation history. This superiority was self-evident in the caste system. The advantage was acquired and/or maintained through the covenant, the law, the worship, the promises and the patriarchs (9:4,5). It was rigorously defended—sometimes unto death. Christ was of their race according to the flesh (9:5). Moreover, the promise of eternal life in Christ, which depended on faith, was initially offered to them. The problem was that in response to God's former revelation they were culturally conditioned to seek righteousness through works of the law that were extremely demanding. Thus, they were unable and/or unwilling to accept God's new revelation—righteousness through faith in Jesus Christ, as a free gift. In other words, the inability and/or unwillingness of the Jews to accept God's word concerning his free gift was largely due to their habitual mode of faithfulness to God's word. This inability and/or unwillingness did not eliminate the advantages in salvation history that were so painfully won by their predecessors under the grueling demands of the Old Covenant (recall that within their worldview they were their own predecessors). However, it did prevent them from sure attainment of the ultimate goal of perfect obedience to the law—eternal life. From Paul's perspective, the irony of the situation was indeed cause for sorrow.

111. According to Kasemann, theological and historical continuity with Israel is maintained by the implicit inclusion as spiritual children of God of some who are descendants of Israel and some who are descended from Abraham (if not all are descendants, some are). This effectively anticipates and meets the later challenge of Marcion (for the exclusion of Hebrew Scriptures from the Christian canon) while at the same time it opens the floodgates of Christianity to Jews as well as gentiles (v.8) on the basis of God's word alone (261-263).

The context (vv.6-8) forces us to assume the presence of a true Israel within Judaism. " . . . [P]recisely what meaning does it have that Israel according to the flesh is designated the bearer of the promise and the recipient of sonship? For this asserts continuity in the earthly sphere . . . which is partially contested in vv.6b-7 and radically so in v.8." Kasemann sees this as an insurmountable contradiction (263).

Yet again, an apparent contradiction can be explained within the context of the first-century belief in reincarnation, the inextricable connection between caste and spiritual status and the role of the law. The promise as understood by the Pharisees prior to and during the first century was birth as a Jew into a renewed and better existence as a reward for obedience to the law. Thus, the promise (continuity in the earthly sphere in the flesh) and evidence of sonship was literally made manifest by the existence of each individual Jew. Moreover, the promise was valid as long as the Jew upheld his side of the bargain. Following logically then, the continuity of Israel in the earthly sphere, which is contested in vv.6b-7 and v.8, probably refers to those Jews who existed at the time of Paul and had the opportunity to seize the new promise and the new life—the gospel—but refused. Those who did became the bearers of the new promise and, along with believing gentiles, constituted the true Israel.

112. Paul's statement linking the promise through Isaac is supported in Gen. 21:12. Paul's point is that legitimacy does not guarantee that the promise will be fulfilled. Verse 8 is aimed against a dominant view in Judaism that claimed that divine sonship is linked to the fulfillment of the law (Kasemann, 262).

113. This section treats the freedom and omnipotence of God with respect to God's election or predestination, which is in turn connected with the word of God (Kasemann, 265). Recall that the word of God is a gnostic concept.

114. A closer translation is "set up, allow to appear," or "allow to exist" (Kasemann, 268). That one can be allowed to appear implies his pre-existence.

115. In the New Testament, to "harden the heart" means to resist the divine word (Kasemann, 268).

116. Compare with 2:4 in which God's patience is meant to lead to repentance.

117. Though the statement is general, the reference to the vessels of wrath is to unbelievers. The question arises as to whether the vessels refer to individuals or groups (Kasemann, 270, 272). It appears that Paul's statement regarding vessels was applicable to individuals (9:9-13) as well as groups (9:22, 24-29). This is consistent with the view held with respect to caste, i.e., that particular individuals fulfill criteria that qualify or disqualify them with respect to membership in a particular group and/or caste.

118. For Paul, salvation or perdition depends on the omnipotence of God the creator, against which there is no autonomy or legal appeal (Kasemann, 270). Believers are the vessels of mercy that God has predestined for glory—eternal life.

119. Here Paul is explaining that the divine promise that had been given to Israel is not a human privilege that is calculable, nor is it a process of continuous development. Rather the divine word goes forth afresh and in this way accomplishes election and rejection of men. In Christ people are chosen "not from the Jews only but also from the gentiles." Thus, the church as a new creation, universal in scope, cannot be compared either to a gentile or Jewish society (Kasemann, 273). I concur. Pauline Christianity was a new caste—a new creation—based not on spiritual status conferred by birth and indicated by worldly status, but rather on obedience to the universal precepts of the Jewish law and belief in the resurrection and saving power of Jesus Christ.

120. Here Paul "with great audacity" relates the promises made to Israel to the gentile Christians (Kasemann, 274).

121. In Gaston's view the remnant refers to those Jews who, like Paul, are Jewish missionaries to the gentiles (317). To Kasemann, the promise to the Jews remains valid through the preservation of a remnant of Jews (275).

122. Kasemann implies a qualitative distinction between types or modes of righteousness: "God's righteousness exists only as the righteousness of faith" (Kasemann, 278).

123. "The point is that the will of God which calls for righteousness cannot be reached in the law, this being misunderstood and made a summons to achievement" (Kasemann, 277).

124. The stress here is that by God's plan Israel comes to ruin—must come to ruin—"over the God-given Messiah, and consequently over the fulfillment of the promise" (Kasemann, 279). Paul's augury is fulfilled in the Roman destruction of the temple in Jerusalem in 70 C.E. and the cultural ascendancy of Christianity (the Holy Roman Empire).

125. It is suggested that the careful way in which Paul explains the misunderstanding of Israel's Jews who pursued righteousness based on the law(s) (vv.30-32) indicates that one of Paul's main purposes for writing Romans and the reason he wanted to visit Rome even though it was against his policy to go to a place where, as in Rome, Christ was already being preached, was to win over for Christ large numbers of gentile Jews who had come within the influence of the Church. He would not have to convince committed Christians of what for them was the gospel truth— the efficacy of faith over works.

## Romans 10:

126. At this point Paul turns to the Christian community. Verse 2 does not mean an absence of knowledge, but rather a fatefully inadequate knowledge of God (Kasemann, 280).

127. To Kasemann, the meaning of the "end" or "goal" or "fulfillment" of the law is that with Christ, the Mosaic Torah comes to an end (for the believer) because man now renounces his own right in order to grant God his right (282, 283). From our perspective, the "end" or "goal" or "fulfillment" of the law is the end of cyclical regeneration and/or postmortem mortal existence on planet Earth (or a similar world) and release unto eternal life. Because faith in Christ fulfills this goal, Christ is the end of the law/the Immutable Law.

128. In this section, Paul reconstrues and paraphrases Lev.18:5 and Deut. 30:11-14, respectively (Kasemann, 284). What is the meaning of v.5? First, the literal sense—the man who practices the righteousness that is based on the law will practice the law (live by it)—is rejected on the grounds that it is self-evident that he who practices the law as a way of life is living by it. Second, the literal sense is rejected on the basis of first-century Pharisaic belief. From this perspective, Paul is saying that Moses said the man who practices the righteousness that is based on the law will resurrect in relation to the degree to which he obeyed the law in a former existence (live by it). Verses 6-8 follow logically and reflect the pre-Christian attitude by which people judged the fate of others (heaven/up or hell/down) on the basis of caste fulfillment, which in the case of the Jews as well as the Romans, was regulated by law.

129. The heart as the center of personality (Kasemann, 291). In view of our knowledge of Paul as an individual and the nature of *gnosis*, the view that the heart is the center of personality is accepted with qualification. The heart is nothing less than that part of man, the spirit, which interfaces with the judgment seat of God.

130. According to Kasemann, the theme of the word that is near (v.8) is connected with the Spirit who brings the new covenant and removes the veil between Creator and creature by replacing tradition with the presence of God (285).

While this is undoubtedly so, it appears that here Paul makes a specific point about the Word and faith/belief. The word, which is near, on your lips and in your heart, is the word of faith that is the dynamic role of belief which is active in the heart and by which the believer is justified (vv.8-10).

131. Peter Stuhlmacher observes that the early Christians did not have advanced education and asks whether we have already read too much of the Western European theological tradition of interpretation into the gospel. ("The Theme of Romans," in *The Romans Debate*, 338).

Yes!

Eurocentricity has blinded those with a Western "advanced education" to the Eastern worldview. Thus, Western scholars tend to dismiss the fact that Jewish religious customs originated in the Orient, that the Romans considered Judaism as well as other Oriental cults a *superstitio barbara* and that Tiberius expelled the Jews in C.E. 19 as well as the followers of the Egyptian cult of Isis. (Wiefel, 86-88.) The irony is that Western European theological tradition cannot be adequately explained without reference to the Eastern worldview.

A case in point is Dunn's view that "justification by works"—as the antithesis to "justification by faith"—was understood in terms of a system whereby salvation is earned through the merit of good works (299). Nowhere in Romans has Paul qualified "works" with "good." The attribute has been imposed by scholars.

In view of the first-century cross-cultural belief in reincarnation and the Roman and Jewish caste systems which were still in place (though in the process of disintegration), it is reasonable to assume that "works" refers to caste fulfillment, religious and/or secular. Inadvertently supporting this view, William S. Campbell notes that in light of the Christ event distinctions among men have been rendered obsolete. ("Romans III as a Key to the Structure and Thought of Romans," in *The Romans Debate*, 253). The only valid distinctions remaining are those that God makes on the basis of the gospel.

This is true as far as it goes. But what was the basis on which people were distinguished prior to the Christ event? W. Campbell recognizes that the gospel did not originate in a vacuum, that it has a prehistory that must be unearthed if the gospel is to be understood (254). Again, it is asserted that the cross-cultural pre-existing common thread was belief in cyclical regeneration which was manifested in an individual's placement within the caste system of social organization.

Verse 12 reflects the context against which Paul interpreted the significance of the Christ event: the existence of social and spiritual distinctions between Jews and Greeks made on the basis of worldly status.

132. Verse 14 does not follow naturally from what precedes. Verses 14 and 15 cannot be referring to Israel because Israel could not call, believe, hear or preach because it had not been sent (Kasemann, 293, 294).

133. Moses and the prophets represented by Isaiah are shown to have prophesied the conversion of the gentiles, but Israel failed to recognize the dawn of the eschatological age through the fulfillment of the prophecy (Kasemann, 297).

## Romans 11:

134. It has been maintained that the argument, as well as the formulation in v.1 points to readers who are predominantly gentile Christians (Kasemann, 299).

In light of the argument that the Church was a multifarious and fluid group, the fact that Paul may have been directing this part of his discourse to gentile Christians does not necessarily mean that all of his intended readers were gentile Christians. A case can be made that vv.11:1-10 is an appeal by Paul who, coming from a highly respected Jewish caste (Pharisee, tribe of Benjamin), to gentile Jews to become like himself—a part of the remnant, the elect (v.7).

135. Kasemann notes that the point of comparison between Elijah and Paul is that each seemed to be alone among his people and bewailed Israel's unbelief (Kasemann, 301).

136. Election and rejection is an ongoing process that takes place in the historical sphere. The remnant (Jewish Christianity) stands as an antithesis to the people as a whole, and indicates what remains (Kasemann, 299, 300).

137. Israel could not reach its goal (eternal life) by the pathway of works, but Jewish Christianity was able to by abandoning the traditional way (Kasemann, 301).

138. Verse 11 probably points to a tradition " . . . no longer discernible

to us . . . ." (Kasemann, 305). It is suggested that the tradition is precisely that of belief in cyclical birth and death, within which to stumble and fall is inherent. This status quo was maintained for the Jews by the law.

139. Kasemann (304), in agreement with Beker (330) and Gaston (321), notes that the reversal of earthly relations, inherent in the apocalyptic idea that the first shall be last and the last first, is simply a stage on the divinely planned path with an end which, against all appearances, is bound up with the destiny of Israel.

140. Gaston notes W. D. Davies' suggestion that the image of the olive tree (11:17) was chosen because for Greek gentiles "the olive tree could serve as a symbol as powerful as was the vine among the Jews." Perceiving the connection between the natural and unnatural, Gaston notes that ". . . [V]erse 24 functions primarily to underline the unnatural and miraculous grafting of the wild olive branches" (321n53, 322).

From the perspective of this thesis, the cultivated olive tree signifies Israel, which due to the law had spiritual direction within what was otherwise the Immutable/Natural Law (gentiles) and/or God's Law of Justice (Jews) of cyclical regeneration. In contrast, the gentile world, not protected by the law, was a wild olive tree subject helter skelter to the forces of nature—the cyclical motion of the cosmos within which all were ensnared. But by the power of faith in Christ, the gentiles (uncultivated) have been grafted onto the cultivated tree of Judaism "contrary to nature"—the Natural Law. The phrase "contrary to nature" has another meaning in light of this thesis; prior to the Christ event, one would have to have been born a Jew (according to nature/the Law of Nature/the Immutable Law) in order to take part in the eschatological advantage.

141. Here (11:25-32) for the last time, Paul's doctrine of justification of the ungodly appears linking the destiny of Israel to that of the gentiles (Kasemann, 314).

Gaston argues that Paul's meaning is that Israel will be saved not because of conversion to Christianity but because a nominal Jew would become jealous of a faithful Christian and so become a faithful Jew (11:11) (324). The existence of the Jerusalem church (15:26) whose outreach was to ethnic Jews as well as 9:1-3; 10:1-4, argue against this view.

How then will "all Israel" (11:25, 26) be saved? Paul could mean that salvation would come to the Jews either through conversion (directly) and/or intermarriage (indirectly). But Paul is adamant. He allows no exception. What of the "mystery?"

From the perspective of this thesis, "all Israel" will be saved through rebirth as Christians, which would end the cycle of renewed existence.

Finally, Gaston argues that it appears to be possible to have a status of righteousness from either of two sources, from the law or from the faithfulness of Christ. He goes on to say that Paul considers knowing Jesus Christ as Lord superior (Phil. 3:7), but does not deny at all the validity of life in Torah (Gal. 1:14; Phil. 3:3-8) (310).

Notice that before listing his credentials within Judaism, Paul says that he has "reason for confidence in the flesh" (Phil. 3:4). What does he mean? From our perspective, Paul (like Josephus) means that righteousness under the law (Phil. 3:6) gives him confidence of resurrection unto a better mortal existence: "confidence in the flesh." The righteousness of faith in Christ is superior because it is resurrection from the process of cyclical regeneration—the resurrection from the dead (Phil. 3:7-11).

142. In this Hymn of Praise (11:33-36), Paul uses a technique developed in model form in Ephesians. It consists of pieces of very different origin woven into a whole—Jewish, Hellenistic, and Stoic (Kasemann, 318). Recall that the Stoics identified God with nature/the Natural Law.

### Romans 12:

143. Kasemann notes that in an overview of this section, Paul "falls back surprisingly on Greek ethics." The approach is strange because it is not oriented to baptismal instruction, eschatological expectation or, concretely, the commandment to love. It appears that the entire exhortation of this chapter is directed against enthusiasm (332).

It is suggested that Paul's warning against arrogance and his dissatisfaction with respect to spiritual gifts was rooted in the basic assumption of early Christianity that unlike pre-Christian times, when the level of spirituality was manifest in worldly status, Christians were equal on the basis of belief in the saving power of Jesus Christ. Here, Paul is guarding against the ascribing of status with respect to the church on the basis of unique spiritual gifts, much as status in the world had been determined on the basis of material wealth and social class.

### Romans 13:

144. Bruce considers Paul's reference to the Christians' relation to the state (13:1-7) to be problematic (182). He does not think it to be a universal statement of political principle, arguing that Paul was probably outwardly supportive of the governing authorities because the name of Christianity carried subversive associations in Rome and elsewhere (184-185). Moreover, at least some men knew that the founder of the movement had been sentenced to execution by a Roman judge on a charge of sedition

(Bruce, 185n36).

Bruce is right, but for the wrong reason. Indeed his arguments support the view that the culture to which Paul preached the gospel believed in reincarnation, which was inherent in the caste system. Christians not only kept on "acting against the decrees of Caesar" (Acts 17:6), but, as Bruce notes, they provoked the charge that they were subverting the whole world (184).

In what way could Jesus have been considered a threat to the established order? Since Christians, unlike the culture at large, assembled on the basis of faith in Christ and did not distinguish on the basis of worldly status, they were considered a threat to the caste system, which was the foundation of the ancient world order. The one quality that set Jesus apart from other prophets, healers, etc., of the time is that he mingled with all people regardless of social status—poor fishermen, tax collectors, prostitutes, lepers—thus setting the prototype for Christianity. If emulated by a critical mass (as it turned out), the whole world would indeed be subverted.

It would be fair to say that there was probably a symbiosis between the breakdown of the Roman Empire and the rise of Christianity.

145. " . . . wake from sleep" (13:11) is a reference to the *gnosis* that humanity consists of captured sparks of light who are not conscious of who they are, where they came from or where they are going. " . . . work of darkness . . . armor of light," "night and day," ". . . make no provision for the flesh, to gratify its desires" (13:12-14). All gnostic words and images.

## Romans 14:

146. Bruce suggests that the situation is more complex than simply that Jewish Christians retained Jewish food laws and the Sabbath while gentile Christians practiced complete liberty in both respects (185).

Karris suggests that the discussion of the strong and the weak probably was a generalized position Paul worked out earlier with respect to an actual situation, especially in Corinth (1 Cor. 8-10) (71n36).

I concur with both views.

Karris supports the thesis of this work by citing an almost fifty-year-old monograph by Rauer in which he argues that the practice of abstinence from meat stems from their prior religious background in gnostic, Hellenistic mystery religions (68nn20-22, 69n28). Paul is again referring to the customs of the Gnostics in his audience.

147. The theme of mutual acceptance that dominates 14:1-15:6 suggests that the conflict Paul addresses has something to do with the divisive composition of the Church at Rome (Kasemann, 384). The rabbinic com-

bining of sayings from the Torah, Writings and Prophets might have been used in Jewish-Christian missionary preaching (Kasemann, 386).

148. Here Paul refers to the mind or belief as the determinant of reality (11:14) and conscience as that which condemns if one does not act from faith and conviction (14:22,23).

## Romans 15:

149. Verse 14 recognizes the spiritual independence of the congregation and the presence of knowledge in all its variety in a way seldom repeated in church history. The "knowledge" referred to is " . . . insight into salvation history" (Kasemann, 391).

Such insight into salvation history must have included that which was unwritten: Metaphysical knowledge with respect to spiritual Law (karma/ cyclical regeneration) and the significance of the Jewish law in light of this knowledge. The gospel message that Christ died for the sins of all was also understood within this broader context.

150. Verses 5-19 elevate Paul's *gnosis* above that of the congregation. He makes it clear that his knowledge was given to him by Christ (v.15) for the purpose of preaching the gospel of Christ to the gentiles (v.16).

151. Paul is not thinking of individual churches (vv.19-21), but of peoples and lands (Kasemann, 395). It is reasonable to conclude that all the "peoples and lands" were grounded in a worldview within which the gospel message made sense.

152. This reference (v.26) is to the original congregation (Kasemann, 399).

153. This is the true ending of the epistle. In Kasemann's view, the readers of Rom. 16 were not in Rome (406, 415).

## Romans 16:

154. Verses 17 and 18 warn against false teachers, who are not specifically mentioned but were probably libertinizing "and gnosticizing Jewish-Christians" (Kasemann, 417, 418).

It has been argued that Paul was a Gnostic, albeit an ascetic. Thus, it would be more accurate to say that the false teachers were probably Gnostics who, though in agreement with Paul with respect to metaphysics and belief in Christ, differed with the standards of morality imposed by Judaism, which Paul upheld.

155. The concluding formula is found in Hellenistic Judaism. Eternity is viewed as the course of endless times/*aeons* (Macc. 18:24) (Kasemann, 423, 424).

# BIBLIOGRAPHY

Barclay, William, *The Letter to the Romans* (Philadelphia: The Westminster Press, 1975).

Bultmann, Rudolf, *Primitive Christianity in Its Contemporary Setting*. Trans. by the Reverend R.H. Fuller (Leipzig: Interdruck, 1983).

Calder, Nigel, *Einstein's Universe* (New York: Crown Publishers, Inc., 1979).

Callahan, John F, *Four Views of Time in Ancient Philosophy* (Cambridge: Harvard University Press, 1948).

Campbell, Joseph, ed., *Man and Time* (New York: Princeton University Press, 1957, 1973).

Chadwick, Henry, *The Early Church* (New York: Penguin Books Ltd., 1967).

*The Confessions of St. Augustine*. Trans. by Rex Warner (New York: The New American Library of World Literature, Inc., 1963).

Cronin, Mary; Riley, Michael; and Wyss, Dennis, "New Age Harmonies," in *Time* (Dec., 1987), 62-72.

Donfried, Karl P., ed., *The Romans Debate* (Peabody, Mass.: Hendrickson Publishers, 1991).

Head, Joseph, and Cranston, S.L., eds., *Reincarnation in World Thought* (The Julian Press, 1967).

Hopfe, Lewis M., *Religions of the World* (New York: Macmillan College Publishing Company, 1994).

Flory, Marleen B, *Family and 'Familia': A Study of Social Relations in Slavery*. Ph.D. dissertation, Yale University (1975).

Goodenough, Erwin Ramsdell, *An Introduction to Philo Judaeus*, 2d ed. (Oxford: Blackwell, 1962).

Gordis, Robert, *Koheleth the Man and His World: a Study of Ecclesiastes* (New York: Schocken Books, 1951, 1955, 1968).

James, William, *The Varieties of Religious Experience* (New York: The Modern Library, 1936).

Jones, A.H.M., "The Caste System in the Later Roman Empire," in *Eirene* (1970).

Kasemann, Ernst, *Commentary on Romans*. Trans. and ed. by Geoffrey W. Bromily (Grand Rapids, Mich.: William B. Eerdmans Publishing Company, 1980).

Jung, C.G., *Aion: Researches Into the Phenomenology of the Self* (London: Routledge Kegan Paul, 1968).

Keck, Leander E. and Furnish, Victor Paul, *The Pauline Letters* (Nashville: Abingdon Press, 1984).

Kelly, John Norman Davidson, *Early Christian Doctrines* (New York: Harper & Row, Publishers, Inc., 1978).

Lieberman, Saul, *Greek in Jewish Palestine* (New York: Jewish Theological Seminary of America, 1942).

———— *Hellenism in Jewish Palestine* (New York: Jewish Theological Seminary of America, 1950).

MacLaine, Shirley, *Out on a Limb* (New York: Bantam Books, 1983).

MacMullen, Ramsay, *Roman Social Relations* (New Haven and London: Yale University Press, 1974).

May, Herbert G., and Metzger, Bruce M, *The New Oxford Annotated Bible With Apocrypha* (New York: Oxford University Press, 1977).

Meeks, Wayne A., *The First Urban Christians* (New Haven and London: Yale University Press, 1983).

Montgomery, Ruth, *Strangers Among Us* (New York: Ballantine Books, 1982).

Neusner, Jacob, *From Politics to Piety* (New York: KTAV Publishing House, Inc., 1979).

*The New Encyclopedia Britannica* Vol. 2. (Chicago and London: William Benton, Publisher, 1943-1973. Helen Hemingway Benton, Publisher, 1973-1974).

Nygren, Anders, *Commentary on Romans* (Philadelphia: Fortress Press, 1949).

Puech, Henri-Charles, "Gnosis and Time," in *Man and Time*. Ed. by Joseph Campbell (New York: Princeton University Press, 1957, 1973).

Plato, "Phaedrus," in *The Dialogues of Plato*. Trans. by B. Jowett, M.A. (London: Oxford University Press, 1871, 1875, 1892, 1931).

Quispel, Gilles, "Time and History in Patristic Christianity," in *Man And Time*. Ed. by Joseph Campbell (New York: Princeton University Press, 1957, 1973).

Reekmans, Tony, "Juvenal's Views on Social Change," in *Ancient Society* (1971).

Rivkin, Ellis, *A Hidden Revolution* (Tennessee: The Parthenon Press, 1978).

Roberts, Jane, *Seth Speaks* (New York: Prentice Hall, 1972).

Smallwood, Mary E., "The Jews Under Roman Rule: From Pompey to Diocletian," in *Studies in Judaism in Late Antiquity* (Leiden: Brill, 1976).

Smith, Morton, "Palestinian Judaism in the First Century," in *Israel: Its Role in Civilization*. Ed. by Moshe Davis (New York: Harper Row, Publishers, 1956).

Sugrue, Thomas, *The Story of Edgar Cayce: There is a River* (New York: Dell Publishing Co., Inc., New York, 1977).

Walker, Benjamin, *Gnosticism: Its History and Influence* (Wellingborough, Northamptonshire: The Aquarian Press, 1983).

Weaver, P.R.C., *Familia Caesaris: A Social Study of the Emperor's Freedmen and Slaves* (London: Cambridge University Press, 1972).

Weiss, Brian L., *Many Lives, Many Masters* (New York: Simon & Schuster, Inc., 1988).

West, James King, *Introduction to the Old Testament* (New York: The Macmillan Company, 1971).

Wolfson, Harry A., *Philo* Vol 2. (Cambridge, Mass.: Harvard University Press, 1948).

THIS WORK RELIES EXTENSIVELY ON THE TWENTY-FOUR ESSAYS IN *THE ROMANS DEBATE*, EDITED BY KARL P. DONFRIED. THEY ARE AS FOLLOWS:

Aune, David E., "Romans as a Logos Protreptikos."

Beker, J.C., "The Faithfulness of God and the Priority of Israel in Paul's Letter to the Romans."

Bornkamm, Gunther, "The Letter to the Romans as Paul's Last Will and Testament."

Bruce, F.F., "The Romans Debate: Continued."

Campbell, William S., "Romans III as a Key to the Structure and Thought of Romans."

Donfried, Karl Paul, "A Short Note on Romans 16."

———— "False Presuppositions in the Study of Romans."

Dunn, James D.G., "The Formal and Theological Coherence of Romans."

——————— "The New Perspective on Paul: Paul and the Law."

Gaston, Lloyd, "Israel's Misstep in the Eyes of Paul."

Jerve, Jacob, "The Letter to Jerusalem."

Jewett, Robert, "Following the Argument of Romans."

Karris, Robert J., "Romans 14:1-15:13 and the Occasion of Romans."

——————— "The Occasion of Romans: A Response to Prof. Donfried."

Klein, Gunter, "Paul's Purpose in Writing the Epistle to the Romans."

Lampe, Peter, "The Roman Christians of Romans 16."

Manson, T.W., "St. Paul's Letter to the Romans."

Stirewalt, Martin Luther, "The Form and Function of the Greek Letter-Essay."

Stuhlmacher, Peter, "The Purpose of Romans."

——————— "The Theme of Romans."

Watson, Francis, "The Two Roman Congregations: Romans 14:1-15:13."

Wedderburn, A.J.M., "Purpose and Occasion of Romans Again."

Wiefel, Wolfgang, "The Jewish Community in Ancient Rome and the Origins of Roman Christianity."

Wuellner, Wilhelm, "Paul's Rhetoric of Argumentation in Romans: An Alternative to the Donfried-Karris Debate Over Romans."

# INDEX